MW00723941

# Between Ally and Partner

Jae Ho Chung

# Between Ally and Partner

Korea-China Relations and the United States

Columbia University Press    New York

Columbia University Press
*Publishers Since 1893*
New York    Chichester, West Sussex
Copyright © 2007 Columbia University Press

Publication of this book was supported through funds provided
by the Korea Foundation. Columbia University Press would like
to express its sincere thanks and gratitude.

Library of Congress Cataloging-in-Publication Data
Chong, Chae-ho, 1960–
    Between ally and partner : Korea-China relations and the United States / Jae
Ho Chung.
        p. cm.
    Includes bibliographical references and index.
    ISBN 978-0-231-13906-9 (cloth : alk. paper)—ISBN 978-0-231-51118-6 (e-book)
        1. Korea (South)—Foreign relations—China. 2. China—Foreign relations—
Korea (South). 3. Korea (South)—Foreign relations—United States. 4. United
States—Foreign relations—Korea (South). I. Title.
    DS910.2.C5C527    2006
    327.5195051—dc22          200616022

Columbia University Press books are printed on permanent
    and durable acid-free paper.
Printed in the United States of America
c 10 9 8 7 6 5 4 3 2

To Jerome B. Grieder and Michel C. Oksenberg (1938–2001), who were key sources of inspiration and encouragement during my years at Brown University and the University of Michigan

# Contents

# List of Tables

# Preface

The rise of China has become a topic of interest the world over, and is currently one of the most popular themes in academic and policy research. Nowhere has China's ascendancy been more evident than in the Korean Peninsula, which has once again become the strategic hub of great power politics in Asia, and it seems that the shadow of China's rise has been cast too quickly over South Korea. In a sense, South Korea—and its alliance with the United States—was caught largely unprepared, both strategically and psychologically, by the rising China. The gradual but inevitable bifurcation of security concerns and economic necessity is bound to render South Korea torn between its close ally (the United States) and its cooperative partner (China). The dilemma that South Korea now faces has crucial ramifications for many countries in Asia, where explicit attempts to counterbalance China have been rare.

Working on this book was never easy, not only because the entire process, from data collection to manuscript writing, consumed more than ten years, but also because the book goes beyond chronicling a bilateral relationship and seeks to understand the overall strategic dynamics surrounding the Korean Peninsula. Having been trained initially and primarily as a comparativist and specialist in China's central-local relations, I found it both challenging and rewarding to learn about and become comfortable with different concepts, theories, and jargons of international relations. Returning finally to the question of what would happen to Korea-China relations once the cold war was over, which I had asked myself more than twenty years ago upon going to the United States for graduate study, was also highly comforting.

My research for this book benefited from many individuals and institutions. The Brookings Institution's Center for Northeast Asian Policy Studies (CNAPS) provided a very comfortable year of research and writing during 2002 and 2003, and I thank Bates Gill and Richard C. Bush, its former and current director, respectively, for the excellent support. The East Asian Institute of the National University of Singapore also gave me a Visiting Senior Research Fellow position for the summer of 2004, during which final touches were added to the manuscript before its submission to Columbia University Press. I thank Professor Wang Gungwu for the generous support.

Bruce Dickson, Kenneth Lieberthal, Gilbert Rozman, David Shambaugh, Robert Sutter, Takagi Seiichiro, Wang Gungwu, Zheng Yongnian, David Zweig, and Heeyong Cho read the whole or parts of the manuscript and provided excellent comments and useful suggestions. Thanks are also due to the two reviewers from Columbia University Press. I also benefited greatly from hundreds of hours of interviews with Korean, Chinese, and American officials and scholars over a period of more than fifteen years. Most of them remain anonymous, although my gratitude to them deepens over time. I also thank eighty-nine American and Chinese experts who shared their views and insights with me during both structured and unstructured questionnaires conducted in Washington, D.C., Beijing, and Shanghai, from 2002 to 2004.

With many thanks and fond memories, I dedicate this book to the two individuals who have had the greatest academic and personal impact on me. Jerome B. Grieder, my graduate adviser at Brown University's history department, taught me how to become a serious scholar, writer, and academic. I vividly remember the book-review assignments returned to me every week with so many corrections and stylistic suggestions in red ink. Without those years at Brown, I would never have become what I am today. This book is also dedicated to the late Michel C. Oksenberg, who took me as a member of his student corps at the University of Michigan in 1986. His ideas, insights, and encouragements were indispensable in helping me survive my seven tough years there. It was also Mike who reignited my interests in Korea-China relations by enlisting me for the Stanford project, *America's Changing Alliances with Asia*, in 1995. I warmly remember my last hug with Mike, right before his departure, at the international conference in his honor.

At Columbia University Press, Anne Routon provided meticulous support throughout the editing process. I am sincerely indebted to her efforts and encouragements. My wife, Hye Kyung, and my daughter, Jean, were unsparing in offering support and prayer whenever I was down and out. The traces of their encouragement can be found on every page of this volume. I am glad that Jean has now become aware of the fact that the book is about her future as well.

Seoul, Korea
May 2006

# Between Ally and Partner

# 1

# The Rise of Korea-China Relations
# and the United States

Throughout the summer of 2002, news media in the Republic of Korea (hereafter South Korea) flooded the country with numerous reports and articles on "China fever," commemorating the tenth anniversary of the normalization of relations between South Korea and the People's Republic of China (hereafter China). Seoul's diplomatic circles held lavish receptions, and academic conferences were convened to put this historic event in perspective. At about the same time, South Korea–U.S. relations plummeted to a record low: two schoolgirls were run over by a U.S. army vehicle, which led to candlelight anti-American demonstrations throughout the country. These starkly contrasting themes, that of China fever and of increasing anti-American sentiment, foretold a daunting strategic dilemma that Seoul would soon be facing.

The "rise" of China is already a phenomenon of global interest and import. And the pace at which China has increased its cooperation with Asia at large is beyond anyone's best guess.[1] The enormous amount of bilateral trade, investment, tourism, and educational exchanges highlight—but at the same time understate—the "comprehensive cooperative partnership for the twenty-first century" (*mianxiang ershiyi shiji de quanmian hezuoxing huoban guanxi*) forged between China and South Korea in particular.[2] The relationship between Seoul and Beijing has come a long way in the last few decades, from adversaries to cooperative partners.

When South Korea and China normalized diplomatic relations on August 24, 1992, more than four decades after the outbreak of the Korean War, it was seen by many as the accomplishment of something nearly inconceivable, if not impossible. In retrospect, however, the historic event was the natural culmination of what had been going on between Seoul and Beijing since the late 1970s. In Europe, the end of the cold war was heralded by the reunification of Germany and the demise of state socialism in Eastern Europe; its East Asian counterpart was South Korea's normalizing its diplomatic ties with the Soviet Union and China. The remarkable success of *nordpolitik*, as it was then called, was also projected to lead to a thaw in relations between the Democratic People's Republic of Korea (hereafter, North Korea), on the one hand, and Japan and the United States, on the other.

South Korea's "northern diplomacy" in general and engagement with China in particular were no doubt a great success. But the "rise" of China came so suddenly that South Korea was not quite aware of or fully prepared for what was coming. In fact, Seoul had never thought that the very success of its full engagement with China would come back to haunt it as a strategic dilemma. At that point, neither the United States nor Japan fully comprehended the crucial ramifications of the Sino–South Korean normalization of relations and their postnormalization improvements.

This book tackles three questions related to the rise of China over South Korea. The first concerns *why* South Korea and China came to accommodate each other by ending their adversarial relationship even before the end of the cold war. The second relates to *how* the political economy of Sino–South Korean rapprochement laid the ground for diplomatic normalization and the "comprehensive cooperative partnership" between the two nations. The final question deals with *what* sort of strategic dilemma is posed for South Korea and its alliance with the United States, given South Korea's ever-expanding ties with China.

The book posits the following arguments: While, due to high levels of secrecy, we knew little about the two decades of prenormalization relations between Beijing and Seoul, the actual story reveals more and earlier progress in relations. While both realism (strategic considerations) and liberalism (economic interests) were important, the coincidence of domestic interests, the artificial nature of ninety-seven years of separation, and favorable perceptual undercurrents generated the specific context for Sino–South Korean rapprochement. The lack of attention to noneconomic dimensions of relations since 1992 has left South Korea—and the United States, for that matter—unprepared for the strength of South Korea–China relations and the challenges they pose. Given the premise that it is in Seoul's best interest to be on good terms with both Washington and Beijing, South Korea must walk a tightrope between China and the United States.

## The "Rise" of China and Its Impact on Neighbors

China is indeed rising at a very rapid pace. Although the rise is at least the fourth of its kind—after that of the Han, Tang, and Qing—its effects this time around seem bigger than ever.[3] The rise of China—and the success of its reforms—can be substantiated by several key indicators. With the annual growth rate of over 9 percent for the last quarter century, China's economy became the fourth largest in terms of gross national product in 2005. In 2004, China also became the world's third-largest trading nation, after the United States and Germany. In terms of foreign-currency reserves, in 2005, China ranked first. China is also the world's largest consumer of raw materials and is the top producer of steel, coal, chemical fertilizer, televisions, air conditioners, and telephones.[4]

Economics is not the only realm where China's rapidly growing presence is felt. Correctly or not, China is viewed as a rising challenger to the U.S.-centered international order. If Mearsheimer is correct in saying that "great powers fear each other.... They regard each other with suspicion, and they worry that war might be in the offing," the United States is increasingly concerned about the rise of China and its adverse effects on America's regional posture in Asia.[5] Various policy announcements of the U.S. government are indicative of such perceptions and, in some cases, China is already seen as America's "regional peer competitor" in East Asia.[6]

In the context of Asia, China's diplomacy has been particularly proactive. Since the early 1990s, despite the tenet of "maintaining a low profile while waiting for the right time to surge" (*taoguang yanghui*), China's dealings with Asia changed significantly. Under the new framework of "good neighborly policy" (*mulin youhao zhengce*), Beijing has actively sought cooperation with its Asian neighbors. China has become a strong voice in the ASEAN Plus Three, founded the Shanghai Cooperation Organization, laid the groundwork for the Six-Party Talks, and forged a strategic partnership with India.[7]

The process of China becoming a "great power" in Asia will most likely confront America's desire to retain its hegemonic influence in the region.[8] Given that America's dealings with the region have been predominantly dyadic in nature, Beijing's recent, more direct links with Washington—thanks to the contraction of Moscow's influence—has much potential for friction. China's proactive diplomacy toward Asia could simply be its standard policy of peripheral control. Yet these policies might be interpreted and taken otherwise by the United States.[9] For the countries in the region, most of which wish to sustain good relations with both the United States and China, these potentials for conflict generate a serious strategic dilemma.

Other opinions argue that Sino-American confrontation in Asia is not predestined. Some suggest that China's mode of engaging with Asia is sophisticated enough to dispel the prospect of a confrontation with the United States.[10] Others believe China's rise will not be able to replace the United States in Asia and therefore the "imminent-confrontation thesis" is faulty.[11] Still others contend that Asia will not be reduced to a mere chessboard for the United States, as its nations will never choose to balance against China.[12]

One thing is clear, however. As China's economic prowess grows over time, national security and economic logic in Asia will become increasingly complicated and multivalent, weakening America's predominant position.[13] In the face of such a change in the regional balance of influence, different countries are bound to respond differently. Overall, Asia has thus far seen very few acts of explicit positioning against China.[14] While engagement has been the principal modus operandi, some variations are nevertheless discernible. Japan, Taiwan, India, and Mongolia are certainly on the side of guarded suspicion, if not tacit containment. Australia, Indonesia, the Philippines, Thailand, and Singapore appear to prefer hedging their bets. Myanmar and Malaysia welcome China's rise and seek to capitalize on it.[15] Briefly put, while there is no uniform answer to the question of what to do with China, the emergence of China as a great power undoubtedly poses a serious question to its neighbors.

Such dilemmas are perhaps more acute with regard to the countries that maintain formal security ties with the United States, most notably South Korea and Japan. Unlike Tokyo, which has explicitly chosen to stand by Washington by designating Beijing as a potential security threat, Seoul's stance is still up in the air.[16] South Korea–China rapprochement and their rapidly expanding cooperative partnership on virtually all fronts have not only become another main pillar of Seoul's diplomacy but have also introduced an additional key variable to the "Korean equation." Added to that is America's global strategic reconfiguration after the events of September 11, 2001, which inevitably affects the U.S.–South Korea alliance. Given the complexities involved with Seoul's efforts to strike a balance between Washington and Beijing, South Korea is not alone in needing to ponder the magnitude of the challenges posed by the rise of China.

## From Confrontation to Cooperation: The Case of South Korea–China Relations

The rapprochement and normalization of relations between China and South Korea denotes more than improved bilateral ties between the two countries. The highly clandestine process in which the rapprochement was initiated and matured into diplomatic normalization represents a remarkable model of East-West cooperation—both economic and otherwise—blocked for so long by elements of the cold war regime, such as the Coordinating Committee for Multilateral Export Controls (COCOM).[17] The post–cold war mitigation of ideological frictions and military confrontations paved the way for genuine cooperation between the East and West in general and between China and South Korea in particular.[18] In the long run, understanding the politics of East-West rapprochement may also hold crucial implications for the strategies of cooperative engagement vis-à-vis the so-called rogue states and failed states.[19]

The war on terrorism notwithstanding, the primacy of economics and pragmatism appears to remain intact.[20] The "end of ideology"—and of the cold war—has provided fertile soil for extensive cooperation in various issues and areas, by actors hitherto almost inconceivable.[21] The burgeoning of Seoul-

Beijing bilateralism has effectively demonstrated the powerful nexus of pragmatism that can link two states with mutually incompatible ideologies. For example, domestic reforms of the socialist state China have precipitated fundamental changes in its foreign-policy behavior, especially regarding South Korea, thereby leading to cooperative ties between the two.[22] Equally important was the presence of the capitalist powerhouse of South Korea, willing and eager to capitalize on the window of opportunity created by its socialist neighbor.

South Korea–China ties have also become an important cornerstone of regional cooperation in East Asia. Such institutional frameworks and ideas as the ASEAN Plus Three, the "Greater China," and a free-trade area encompassing China, Japan, and South Korea were no doubt extensions of this newly emerging logic of regional cooperation.[23] Given that the lack of Northeast Asian regionalism or regional identity is attributed in significant part to the prevailing bilateral distrust in the region, the case of Sino–South Korean rapprochement offers an interesting exception.[24]

In a similar vein, Sino–South Korean cooperation holds a key to the so-called Korean problem. By virtue of history, geopolitics, and of having participated in the Korean War and signing the Armistice Agreement, China has been a principal actor and mediator in the politics of inter-Korean relations. While the ultimate key to reunification lies in the hands of the Korean people, China's role is crucial, as it has considerably expanded its diplomatic responsibilities, putting it on a par with the United States, as far as the Korean Peninsula is concerned.[25]

China's role has been further accentuated with the normalization of relations with South Korea, particularly considering that the United States and Japan have yet to improve their relations with North Korea.[26] Both the formal and informal influence that Beijing can wield over Pyongyang—and increasingly over Seoul as well—is a valuable asset. The Sino–South Korean normalization has thus added a crucial edge to China's overall influence on the Korean Peninsula, particularly compared to—if not at the expense of—that of the United States, Russia, or Japan.[27] Of course, China's desire to maintain amicable and beneficial relationships with both Koreas have often presented intricate dilemmas for Beijing as well.[28]

As Sino–South Korean relations are gradually moving beyond the realm of economic cooperation and more toward diplomatic and security coordination, a new variable has been added to Northeast Asia's already complex strategic equation. While South Korea has been more successful than most countries in engaging China since the late 1980s, the very success of Seoul's rapprochement with Beijing is now posing an increasingly intricate dilemma for South Korea and its alliance with the United States.[29] Having no independent control over U.S.-China relations, South Korea wishes to maintain amicable and beneficial relationships with both the United States and China, even to the extent of hedging.[30] From America's perspective, however, Seoul's unprecedented efforts to strike a strategic balance between Washington and Beijing—as in the cases of missile defense in 1999 and strategic flexibility in 2003 through 2006—have become a source of concern and even displeasure.[31]

As the rise of China has caught the full attention of the world, the debates regarding the possible hegemonic competition between the United States and China in East Asia and in the Northeast Asian region continue. If the U.S.-China strategic rivalry should become a zero-sum game played between the maritime and continental forces, South Korea will find itself situated at the very center of such a confrontation.[32] Viewed in this light, South Korea–China relations are also very closely connected to the reconfiguration of the regional balance in Northeast Asia and to South Korea's current strategic "soul-searching."[33] South Korea–China relations thus offer an excellent case of the strategic dilemma that many other countries are also facing in the wake of China's rise.

## The Evolution of Sino–South Korean Cooperation: A Literature Review

During the 1980s, South Korea–China relations had rarely been studied as an independent research theme, since most of the bilateral dynamics were highly secretive and very little of the relationship was known to the public at the time. During this early period, only cursory attention was paid to the bilateral relationship, which was viewed mostly as a derivative of major-power dynamics in Northeast Asia.[34] Beginning in the early 1990s, however, South Korea–China relations became a popular subfield, and one on which the pertinent literature grew increasingly large.[35] This was attributed mostly to the fact that by the early 1990s, the overall scope of rapprochement and cooperation between Seoul and Beijing was too extensive to be concealed or ignored.

From the late 1970s, when economic contact was initiated in places such as Hong Kong and Singapore, up to the normalization of relations in 1992, secrecy was the name of the game in the politics of South Korea–China rapprochement.[36] Since both Beijing and Seoul wished to conceal their dealings with each other in order not to provoke Pyongyang and Taipei, respectively, the permissible and feasible boundaries of scholarly research were significantly constrained during much of the cold war–era 1980s.[37]

The situation improved somewhat during the late 1980s, when the bilateral cooperation became too conspicuous to hide. After the 1988 Olympic Games, held in Seoul, South Korea began to publicize its burgeoning economic ties with China. The Chinese also adopted a more relaxed and open position with regard to acknowledging the growth of quasi-governmental cooperation in nonpolitical realms. The gradual changes in the political atmosphere in Seoul, along with South Koreans' improved physical access to China during the early 1990s, made scholarly research on Sino–South Korean relations more feasible than ever before.

South Korea–China relations as a growing area of scholarly inquiry have generated a voluminous literature, although a majority of it was largely policy oriented. Most of the currently available studies of Sino–South Korean relations focus on providing descriptive, snapshot overviews of the bilateral relationship over short periods.[38] Quite considerable overlap and repetition is found among the studies. Studies focusing specifically on issues other than bilateral economic cooperation[39] or Taiwan[40] are rare. Few studies have touched upon such themes as structural constraints,[41] domestic-external linkages,[42] or on the intricate processes of normalization.[43] Fewer have to date examined the long-term strategic implications of the expanding cooperation between South Korea and China.[44]

Almost all of the studies on Sino–South Korean relations were published either as journal articles or as chapters in edited volumes, and to date, there are only two monographs fully devoted to the theme.[45] Given the strategic weight South Korea carries in the economic and security dynamics of East Asia, this paucity is by no means reasonable. More importantly, a sizable amount of new sources and materials in non-English languages—most notably Chinese and Korean—have become available in recent years. These often contain previously unavailable and unutilized information and data on the decade-long process of rapprochement and the intricate politics of the normalization of relations between Seoul and Beijing.[46]

The research for this book benefited substantially from many of the earlier studies noted above. At the same time, this study also seeks to build on and complement them by presenting more in-depth, systematic, and comprehensive accounts of South Korea's evolving relations with China for the period since 1949, as well as analyses of the strategic implications of these relations for the U.S.-Korean security alliance.

Chae-Jin Lee's monograph noted above provides a superb overview, by contrasting China's relations with both North and South Korea from the Korean War up to the point of diplomatic normalization in 1992. Yet Lee's book splits its focus across both Koreas, and thus specifically Sino–South Korean relations are not covered in as much detail as they deserve. Additionally, no study has to date offered detailed accounts and analysis of the secretive processes of rapprochement and negotiation between Seoul and Beijing.[47] Furthermore, this current volume takes up an issue that has rarely been closely scrutinized: the strategic implications of the expanding Sino–South Korean relationship for the latter's security alliance with the United States.

This volume aims to go beyond offering mere descriptions of South Korea–China relations, of which there are plenty. Instead, the book seeks to conceptualize the factors and processes that facilitated the genesis and sustenance of this "unusual" bilateralism between two former adversaries. It discusses Sino–South Korean relations in the context of Northeast Asian studies and without a specifically U.S.-centered focus. The book also suggests that shared cultural elements act as a strange magnet, one that pulls China and South Korea together. While contextual factors such as China's reform and opening, South Korea's search for export markets, and the demise of the cold war were all instrumental, the pace of expansion in Sino–South Korean relations was also strongly affected by shared perceptions and cultural aspects.[48]

This book relies on a wide range of source materials. First, most of the open sources on the theme were consulted, including Korean, Chinese, and Western media reports; academic and policy journals; and declassified government archives.[49] Second, efforts were made to look into various inside stories and behind-the-scenes accounts newly made available in nonacademic writings, memoirs, journalistic reports, and internal policy briefs. Third, over the last fifteen years, face-to-face interviews were conducted with South Korean, Chinese, and American officials and scholars, to crosscheck the validity of the accounts found in the written sources. Fourth, structured questionnaires were also utilized in surveying the perceptions and recommendations of the American, Chinese, and South Korean policy elites regarding Seoul's strategic options with regard to the rise of China.[50] Fifth, the case of Sino–South Korean rapprochement was also occasionally compared with China's normalization experiences with other countries, most notably Israel, Indonesia, and South Africa.[51]

## The Focus of the Book

Korea and China—and their dynastic variants—have long been close neighbors, and their history goes back at least two millennia.[52] While Korea-China relations have gone through numerous ebbs and flows during this long period, they are generally characterized by strong historical bonds, cultural affinity, and geopolitical interconnectedness. Viewed in this vein, South Korea's rapprochement and eventual normalization of relations with China is not so surprising. Yet at least four aspects of the dramatic change in South Korea's relations with China since the late 1970s merit close scholarly scrutiny.

First, both experts and casual observers alike have been struck by the sweeping pace at which China and South Korea accommodated each other, even before the end of the cold war in East Asia. The magnitude of bilateral cooperation, including the incipient phase of military-to-military ties, is all the more interesting—if not puzzling—given the fact that China and South Korea were military adversaries during the Korean War, a little over fifty years ago. The ideological divide between Beijing and Seoul imposed by the cold war since the early 1950s apparently did not deter either China or South Korea from seeking improved relations with each other since the late 1970s. Considering the immutable animosities South Koreans possess toward Japan to this day, the process of rapprochement between Seoul and Beijing is indeed special, if not extraordinary. If this "specialness" is rooted in cultural affinity rather than economic interests, strategic rationales, or diplomatic motives, a very different prediction of the future of this bilateral relationship is possible.[53]

Second, South Korea's normalization of relations with China is an interesting case, as it represents a rapprochement between two divided nations. While, traditionally, Korea-China relations had been a dyadic relationship between two states (or dynasties), cold war abnormalities fragmented both China and Korea, thereby producing two pairs of relationships—namely the South Korea–Taiwan and North Korea–China dyads. Equally interesting are the ways in which Beijing and Seoul chose to improve relations with each other at the expense of their longtime allies and friends Pyongyang and Taipei, respectively. The politics of Sino–South Korean rapprochement thus demonstrates that the cruel game of diplomacy is full of political maneuvers, ideological differences notwithstanding.

Third, South Korea–China relations had initially been mostly economic, nonpolitical, and nongovernmental during the 1980s. With the diplomatic normalization in 1992, however, the nature of the relationship changed and matured across the board. As it stands currently, the Seoul-Beijing relationship is as much diplomatic and strategic as it is economic and commercial.[54] Given that the focal point of the bilateral relationship has been gradually shifting toward the political-diplomatic-security realm, with its economic importance remaining unchanged, sustaining a positive-sum perspective on the derivatives of the bilateral dynamics has become increasingly difficult for Seoul and Beijing. Whether a rising China will be economically and at the same time strategically compatible with South Korea has become the key issue of concern for Seoul.[55]

Fourth, with the full-blown normalization and "comprehensive cooperative partnership" with China, South Korea has entered an uncharted terrain of strategic uncertainty. To a considerable extent, the contemporary conundrum is reminiscent of the earlier dilemma that the Yi Dynasty of Chosun encountered in the late nineteenth century. Just as He Ruzhang, a Qing diplomat based in Tokyo, described in 1880, Korea's problem may once again boil down to the question of how Seoul is to position itself vis-à-vis Beijing, Tokyo, and Washington.[56] However, the contemporary dilemma differs from the earlier one in that Seoul is now facing a reversed order of preference; that is, the rise of China (rather than the ascendancy of the West as in the nineteenth century) may force South Korea to reassess and reconfigure its strategic posture vis-à-vis its long-time ally, the United States.[57]

## The Structure of the Volume

The remainder of the book consists of eight chapters, which are arranged partly in chronological order and grouped partly by theme. Chapters 2 and 3 take up the intriguing question of *why* South Korea and China came to embrace each other despite the severe constraints imposed by the structures of the cold war. Chapter 2 adopts a historical perspective on Sino-Korean geopolitical relations and posits historical and cultural ties as a crucial glue for the revived ties between South Korea and China. Chapter 3 engages in more concrete discussions as to the reasons for the rapprochement between Beijing and Seoul since the late 1970s. While China's efforts to reduce systemic constraints and join the international trading regime were undoubtedly important, Beijing's eagerness to emulate Seoul's path of late development paved the way for the improved ties between the two.

Chapters 4 through 6 investigate *how* the political economy of detente unfolded between South Korea and China, eventually leading to the normalization of diplomatic relations in 1992. Chapter 4 provides detailed accounts of the bilateral ties from 1953 through 1987, before the Seoul Olympic Games, while chapter 5 covers the expansion phase of 1988 through 1992, from the Olympics to the diplomatic normalization. Chapter 6 focuses on the intricate politics of normalization, by identifying key actors and organizations in both China and South Korea and by analyzing the key points and issues of contention during the negotiations for normalization. In brief, South Korea's most crucial domestic ingredient was President Roh Taewoo, while the accession to the United Nations of both Koreas in 1991 assuaged Chinese concern that the issue of "two Koreas" might be equated with the problem of cross-strait relations.

Chapters 7 through 9 explore the questions of *what* has emerged from these fast-growing Sino–South Korean ties in the postnormalization era (the period after 1992), and of what they mean for post–cold war Northeast Asia. Chapter 7 assesses Sino–South Korean economic relations for the postnormalization phase (1993 through 2004) and examines the crucial question of strategic compatibility between Seoul and Beijing. Chapter 8 describes the key dimensions of China's rise over South Korea in recent years, including the emergence among South Koreans of relatively favorable perceptions of China compared to perceptions of the United States. The chapter continues with a discussion of the reasons for the strained alliance between South Korea and the United States.

Results of surveys and structured interviews conducted in 2002 through 2004 are also presented.

Chapter 9 concentrates on the strategic dilemma that the success of South Korea's engagement with China has brought about. South Korea faces a strategic conundrum concerning how it can maintain amicable relationships with both the United States and China, given that the former has no control whatsoever over the relationship between the latter two and that Sino-American relations possess many sources of serious friction. This last chapter is concluded with an assessment of ten strategic options: preventive war, distancing, neutrality, self-help, bandwagoning, binding, engagement, containment, hedging, and issue-based support. It suggests that South Korea may have to choose a hybrid strategy of engagement, containment, and issue-based support.

# 2

## A Sketch of Sino-Korean Relations

It is a cliché that history offers invaluable insights for social scientific inquiry and, in particular, analyses of international relations.[1] Especially when analyzing the role that feelings, emotions, sentiments, and reputations play in the realm of international affairs, the history of the nations involved must always be taken into account, and this often produces explanations that challenge and vex our rational, analytical perspective.[2] This is not to suggest that, in the realm of foreign affairs, states always and necessarily take into consideration their counterparts' past behavior. It is not the "reputation" imprinted in their minds per se, but rather historically induced inclinations and proclivities handed down over generations that make people favor one country over another largely on cultural and perceptual grounds.

Examples supporting the presence of such historically generated sentiments and emotions between states and nations are abundant. Anti-Americanism in the Third World is certainly one such example; anti-Zionism in the Arab world is another.[3] Indian-Pakistani and Turkish-Kurdish enmities represent bilaterally intense negative feelings. Much of this antagonistic sentiment and emotion is reproduced and reinforced in the younger generations by both family (that is, informal) and formal educational methods, making these feelings virtually impossible to change in any significant way.[4]

Emotions, sentiments, perceptions, and reputations have also played important roles in East Asian interstate relations. The "Japan problem" continues to loom large, unlike the "German question," which has been resolved in Europe, more or less.[5] It is no secret that anti-Japanese sentiments have always run high in South Korea—and in North Korea, for that matter—and they are attributed largely to Japan's thirty-six-year colonial rule, from 1910 to 1945.[6] In South Korea, Japan—even more so than North Korea—is still considered the least-favored nation, and one whose militarism should be prevented at all costs. The "old wounds"—South Korea's bitter feelings regarding Japan—have yet to heal.[7]

If Japan's colonial rule over Korea, which ended in 1945, has not been forgotten and perhaps never will, China's military actions against South Korea during the Korean War (1950–1953) appears to have been almost totally forgiven by the

South Koreans.[8] This raises an intriguing question: Is the recency of a negative incident or the duration of that incident more likely to condition one state's sentiments toward another? If recency were the influential factor, South Koreans, with their more vivid memories of the Korean War than of the colonial era, should hold more negative sentiments toward China than Japan. But this is not the case. If duration were the more crucial factor, then strong anti-Japan sentiments in South Korea would certainly make sense. Yet given that the lion's share of the over 930 foreign invasions that Korea has had to endure throughout its history came from various dynasties and tribal groups of China, to maintain Korea within its "sphere of influence," Koreans' positive—even unconditionally favorable—views of China are both interesting and puzzling.[9]

## A "Special" Relationship in Geopolitical Time

There is no need to elaborate here on China's traditional worldview and its complex system of managing "tributary" (*chaogong*) relations with "barbarian" neighbors.[10] While some Chinese sources suggest that Korea-China relations back as far as five millennia, Korea's tributary relations with China were formally established during the Song Dynasty. In fact, before the rise of the Mongol Yuan, the kingdom of Koryo showed little genuine commitment to abiding by the norms of the China-centered tributary system. The Sino-Korean tributary system was firmly institutionalized during the fourteenth century under the reign of the Ming Dynasty. That is, Korea's "vassalization" began to take its full shape when its dynastic change from the military-based Koryo to the literati-centered Chosun was completed.[11]

From China's perspective, Korea had long been viewed as a model tributary, fervently emulating and internalizing much of China's ruling ideology and statecraft—the adoption of the neo-Confucian teachings on political and social control, the institutionalization of the national civil service examination system, the implementation of the annual tributary missions, and so on.[12] Whereas Vietnam, a major tributary from the rice-producing southern "crescent," had often declared its own emperorship internally—and even externally on a few occasions—Korea had almost always held on to kingship, out of deference to China.[13] In fact, a few Chosun scholars were even regarded by the Chinese as crucial contributors to the institutionalization of China's worldview based on "virtue" (*ren*) and "rites" (*li*). Traditional Korean elites were often wholeheartedly supportive of the Chinese dynasties, as their political fate depended heavily on their Chinese "superiors."[14]

Despite the formal suzerain-vassal relationship, China's interference in Chosun's domestic affairs was rare. On most occasions, Chosun was independent and sovereign except for the payment of tribute to the Ming and later to the Qing. From Chosun's viewpoint, China as the continental power was deemed a reliable protector and a crucial source of high culture (that is, "soft power"). Unlike many tribes and nationalities, which were eventually "Sinicized" and lost their identities, Korea's voluntary Sinification saved it from political and cultural extinction. Furthermore, Korea was never subject to the so-called administrative internal colonization (*xingzheng jianzhi de neidihua*).[15]

In addition to the six hundred years of close interaction with tributary ties, Korea and China have also shared the "curse" of geopolitics. Situated at the crossroads between the continental and maritime powers, Korea is often described as the "dagger" pointed at the neck of the Chinese dragon. Ample historical accounts support the central strategic importance China had assigned to Korea. In 1592, a Ming General, Xue Fan, wrote: "Liaodong [a southern coastal part of Manchuria] is an arm to Beijing whereas Chosun is a fence to Liaodong." Another Ming official, Zhao Congshan, observed that "the protection of Chosun is central to the security of China while securing Kyongsang and Cholla Provinces is the key to the protection of Chosun."[16]

On the basis of such geostrategic calculations, in the late sixteenth century, the Ming Imperial Court dispatched huge armies to aid Chosun from the marauding Japanese. The narrowly rescued Chosun was in turn highly grateful to the Ming, which was then officially designated as the "benefactor that mercifully recreated Chosun" (*zaizhaobang zhi enhuiguo*). The level of Chosun's "cronyism" (*shidazhuyi* in Chinese and *sadaejuyi* in Korean) toward the Ming thereafter significantly increased.[17]

After the two wars against the Late Jin (*houjin*) of the Manchus during the seventeenth century, Chosun's relationship with the Manchus—later the Qing Dynasty—also became hierarchical, eventually severing ties with the Ming, whose days were numbered. Paying tribute to the rising Qing by acknowledging the Manchu claims to inherit the Ming mandate was an inevitable choice for Chosun, although the fall of the Ming can be at least partially attributed to its grandiose rescue of Chosun from Japan's marauding.[18]

Irrespective of the dynasties involved, the geopolitical variable continued to weigh in heavily. Overall, however, compared to China's northern (*beidi*) and western (*xirong*) nomadic neighbors, Korea certainly posed much less—if any—of a threat to China. It was a cultural and normative mechanism of control that characterized China's reign over Korea as a sort of "inner management" (*neifan*) as opposed to "outer control" (*waifan*).[19] Above all, Sinicization or Sinification was in significant part an active expression of loyalty by Korea in return for the civilized control by the "Son of the Heaven." Despite the frequent skirmishes between the two, China was viewed largely as Korea's benign protector with virtuous rule.

During the late nineteenth century, after the Opium War, the waning fortune of the Qing Dynasty became obvious. The Qing lost Vietnam to France and had to fight an unavoidable war against Japan over the suzerainty of Chosun. The Qing lost the war along with its face of the "Middle Kingdom."[20] That loss of suzerainty and Japan's subsequent colonization severed the official ties between Korea and China. But below the surface, a gradual bifurcation was taking shape, linking anti-Japanese Korean nationalist groups separately with the Kuomintang forces and with the Communist revolutionaries in China.[21]

Though Korea's loss of sovereignty ended official ties with China, plenty of actions took place in Manchuria, which at the end of the nineteenth century was inhabited by as many as 37,000 Koreans.[22] While numerous anticolonial communist organizations were operating in Manchuria during the 1920s, there were few direct linkages between the Korean and Chinese ones. During the 1930s and 1940s, however, the level of interethnic cooperation significantly increased, as a counterbalance against Japanese aggression. Despite lingering distrust and skirmishes—manifested most notably by the Minsaengdan (*Minshengtuan* in Chinese) incident—anti-imperial solidarity bound together Korean and Chinese resistance organizations against Japan.[23]

Moving toward the mid-twentieth century, as the polarized geopolitical structure of the cold war was forming in Asia and elsewhere, the continental alliance (the People's Republic of China and the Soviet Union) was once again poised against the maritime allies (Japan and the United States) over the Korean Peninsula, where its own polarization was occurring. While ideology was undoubtedly a crucial issue of contention between these two camps, geopolitical necessity was at the very heart of the confrontation.

The Korean War clearly demonstrated the special importance the Korean Peninsula had for China. Considering the kind of political situation China was in when it was sending its troops to Korea, Beijing's willingness to sacrifice its own interests to save Pyongyang offers the best example of the special attention China paid to Korea.[24] With the civil war continuing in Sichuan, Guizhou, and Tibet; Taiwan pledging immediate reunification by force; and unbearable levels of inflation, everything seemed against Beijing's participation in the Korean War.[25] Being a historian himself, Mao must have been aware of the devastating effect that sending armies to save Chosun had on the fate of the Ming Dynasty, some three hundred and fifty years ago. China nevertheless chose to oppose the United States, the U.N.-backed nuclear superpower. There was much more to its decision of supporting North Korea than mere ideological solidarity, certainly, although ideology was no doubt a key factor.[26]

The geopolitical and strategic rationale that China has often utilized when it comes to the issue of Korea is dubbed the "teeth-to-lips" relationship (*chunchi xiangyi* or *chunwang chihan*). Without lips (the Korean Peninsula, or North

Korea in a more contemporary sense), the teeth (China) will be adversely affected.[27] This interdependent rationale in turn inspired such concepts as the "allies sealed in blood" (*xiemeng*) or "brotherhood" (*xiongdi zhi bang*) forged between China and North Korea since the Korean War.[28] While Pyongyang often relied on anticronyistic slogans in dealing with China, especially during the late 1960s, mutual amity, accommodation, and assistance has generally characterized North Korea–China relations for the most part.[29]

Even when Pyongyang was forced into the intriguing position of having to choose between Beijing and Moscow at the height of the Sino-Soviet schism in the 1960s, North Korea's special relationship with China went largely unabated, except for a highly xenophobic period during the Cultural Revolution. Whereas Pyongyang sought to maximize economic and military assistance from Moscow, its overall sentiments were certainly more in line with Beijing.[30] Regardless of the ebbs and flows of the bilateral dynamics, the specialness of North Korea–China relations remained largely intact until Beijing's historic decision to normalize its relations with South Korea in 1992. Yet the level of care Beijing has demonstrated in mitigating Pyongyang's concerns over the South Korea–China rapprochement underscores the very special relationship between the two.[31]

In the final analysis, historical ties, strategic calculations, cultural affinity, and ideological solidarity all came into play to forge the special relationship China has maintained with Korea generally and with, in the contemporary era, specifically North Korea. While there are some indications that, in the wake of the second nuclear crisis of late 2002, China has been reviewing its North Korea policy, whether or not the fundamental quality of the special relationship between Beijing and Pyongyang will be altered remains to be tested.[32]

*The Cheonon incident proves China's continued loyalty*

## South Korea and China: A Contemporary Puzzle

Whereas North Korea's special relationship with China is readily understandable from conventional ideological and strategic viewpoints, the same cannot be said for South Korea's favorable views of and relations with China. Puzzling is the fact that South Korea had already begun to harbor a vision of forging a special relationship with China even before the groundbreaking diplomatic normalization of August 1992.[33] Given that South Korea and China were military foes during the Korean War, the pace at which they became cooperative partners since the late 1970s warrants explanation. *China never came South.*

Seoul's proactive search for improved ties with Beijing can be understood in part within the realist paradigm of South Korea utilizing China's influence to deter North Korean aggression and create some breathing space for its own diplomacy. South Korea's ever-expanding trade with and investment in China can also be understood within the liberalist perspective that profit maximization is in the best interests of both Seoul and Beijing and worked quite well to alleviate tension between the two. On the Chinese side, it may also be argued that Beijing's desire to become a great power must have produced significant changes in its foreign policy, even regarding its former adversaries. Whether prompted by an interest in experimentation or by the fervent desire to emulate successful models, China's reformist zeal produced visible changes in its policy toward South Korea, with which it had hitherto maintained antagonistic relations.

All of these perspectives make good sense and offer persuasive accounts for the genesis of the Sino–South Korean rapprochement.[34] Yet it somehow seems that something important is still missing in accounting for the spectacular pace and manner in which the "comprehensive cooperative partnership" was forged between Seoul and Beijing. While the aforementioned perspectives do offer sensible explanations more conducive to empirical analyses, they at the same time exclude the less tangible factors of emotions, sentiments, and perceptions.[35]

The questions we must ask are these: What accounts for the explosive growth of the trade between South Korea and China by 4,176 times in just twenty-five years, with China replacing the United States as South Korea's number-one trading partner in 2004? How are we to explain the rapidly growing number of South Korean students studying in China, who account for 55 percent of all foreign students at the college level and above in China? How should we discuss the fact that since 2001, the number of citizens traveling between South Korea and China has far surpassed the number of citizens traveling between South Korea and the United States?[36] The rise of China has already been felt in almost every context in South Korea, including that of expanding military-to-military ties with China.[37] Even some premature debates have begun on whether China could possibly constitute a "strategic supplement" to South Korea's alliance with the United States.[38]

What then is the missing ingredient—the strange magnet pulling the two former foes together at such a sweeping pace? It may be speculated that at least two possibilities can be thought of, neither of which are easy to substantiate in empirical terms. On the one hand, it may denote certain historically induced positive sentiments and shared perceptions that Koreans, both South and North, tend to possess regarding China.[39] On the other hand, we may also conceive of South Koreans' favorable views of China as wishful expectations, ones due mainly to the paucity of contact with the "real China." That is, South Koreans' high hopes for China may originate from their disenchantment with the United States—although they may end up similarly disappointed with China.[40]

In twenty years from today, say, if South Koreans still hold the same positive view of China as a global player, we may then conclude that the former possibility perhaps is a better explanation than the latter.

With all that said, the Sino–South Korean rapprochement and normalization needs to be placed in a long-term analytical perspective. Viewed in that manner, the ninety-seven year (1895–1992) separation between (South) Korea and China appears not only very brief in duration but also highly artificial in nature.[41] That is to say, the rapid expansion—if not restoration—of cooperative relations between South Korea and China is only natural, although the specifics of their processes and implications have been and continue to be contingent upon a wide range of factors, most notably Beijing's relations with Pyongyang and Seoul's ties to Washington, as well as the increasingly volatile Sino-American dynamics.

# 3

## Perspectives on the Origins
## of the South Korea–China Rapprochement

One of the most dramatic developments in East Asia during the decade of 1980s was China's embarkation on a reformist path. One of its effects was the gradual yet clear shift in Beijing's policy toward the outside world in general and Seoul in particular. This dramatic shift in China's policy toward South Korea from no policy at all to de facto trade diplomacy was politically, economically, and symbolically noteworthy, as it quietly heralded an end to the remnants of cold war antagonism, underscored the importance of East Asian economic dynamism, and highlighted the newly emerging structure of interstate relations in the region.

Bilateralism between China and South Korea was new in the sense that, for the more than two decades between the Korean War and the mid-1970s, neither country had held any specific policy toward the other besides negative attitudes ranging from indifference to enmity. Therefore, the Seoul-Beijing rapprochement was initially geared more to the construction of a new relationship than to the restoration of traditional ties, which had been severed in 1895. It was no surprise that the improvement of Sino–South Korean relations fundamentally altered the trilateral dynamics among China, North Korea, and South Korea from a stable marriage to a romantic triangle, although the prospect of its eventual transition to a *ménage à trois* remained uncertain.[1]

Despite its great importance, the origin of this new relationship between South Korea and China has yet to be explored in a systematic manner.[2] Understanding the origin of Sino–South Korean rapprochement is not only theoretically attractive in terms of identifying the conditions under which cooperative ties are created between former adversaries, but it may also provide an important clue for projecting their future viability.[3] In this chapter, three perspectives are presented to account for why two antagonistic actors came to seek close cooperation with each other. These perspectives—which are not mutually exclusive—are: (1) a realist view of strategic accommodation; (2) a liberalist explanation of complex interdependence; and (3) domestic-external linkage perspectives of learning, nationalism, and emulation.

## Strategic Accommodation by Minimizing Systemic Constraints

According to the realist paradigm, a state's foreign policy is derived from its conscious perceptions and evaluations of the international environment surrounding it. Such environments, however, are inherently anarchic and therefore potentially hostile. The resulting security dilemma makes national security the top priority for all countries. Consequently, military-strategic issues come to dominate the national agenda, as the dictum "conquer thy neighbor or be conquered by it" aptly puts it. So long as survival is the primary concern of the Leviathan state, strategic considerations weigh most heavily in any country's foreign-policy formulations.[4]

Survival as a sovereign state has always been the paramount concern for China, especially after enduring the painful wounds inflicted by foreign imperialism during the century after the Opium War. The Sino-Soviet schism in the late 1950s and the subsequent friction between the two were due in significant part to China's unwillingness to swallow Soviet direction. China's typical contempt for various forms of multilateral exchanges and international organizations were also rooted in its deep sense of past humiliations.[5] China's anti-imperial and antihegemonic policy, which antagonized both the United States and the Soviet Union, as well as its policy toward the Third World up to the late 1970s, epitomized its hypersensitivity to issues pertaining to sovereignty.[6]

China's perennial concern with survival had necessitated its initial strategic alignment with the Soviet Union (*yi bian dao*) and then later with the United States (*yi tiao xian*). However, China was always keenly aware of the systemic constraints imposed by the strategic reliance on any single superpower. In 1982, China finally opted for a "confident independent" (*duli zizhu*) route of diplomacy. This new line of reasoning, as one analyst has aptly noted, "represents a retreat from its single-minded efforts of the late 1970s to build [a] matrix of strategic relations focused on confrontation with the Soviet Union...and a determination to deal with each country on its own merits and not to allow either to use China as a pawn in some geopolitical game."[7]

Once freed from the constant preoccupation with Soviet hegemonism and American imperialism, China was able to find more diplomatic elbow room.[8] In other words, in formulating its foreign policy, Beijing made a crucial shift from emphasizing vulnerability, contention, and ideological rigidity to highlighting confidence, reconciliation, and flexible diplomacy.[9] Explicit manifestations of this shift were clearly visible in China's new relations with the Soviet Union under Gorbachev and in its dealing with the countries with which it had hitherto maintained highly antagonistic relationships, most notably South Korea, Israel, Saudi Arabia, Indonesia, Malaysia, and South Africa. By successfully minimizing the systemic constraints imposed by the superpower triangle, China became ready to maximize practical benefits with the world at large.[10]

China's confident diplomacy, based on a recalculation of the strategic matrix, was clearly manifested in its new position regarding the Korean Peninsula. As one Chinese analyst has pointed out, "China no longer views the United States as wanting to use Korea as a springboard to attack her ... [and] the Korean contradiction is now less one between the East and the West than one between rival political forces in Korea."[11] To China, the Korean question thus became more malleable and maneuverable than it had been when the issues had been directly linked to superpower rivalry.

This perspective on strategic accommodation offers at best an incomplete explanation for Beijing's unexpected decision to initiate and sustain burgeoning economic relations with Seoul. It does, however, shed light on the systemic conditions under which China freed itself from the inevitable coalition with North Korea as an ideological ally and buffer state against the alliance between the United States and South Korea. The fact that a series of diplomatic overtures by Seoul during the early 1970s were explicitly turned down by Beijing clearly underscores the centrality of changing strategic factors in facilitating South Korea–China rapprochement.[12] That is, opportunities had been there for quite a while, but China could actually put them to use in the early 1980s only after Beijing had successfully minimized the systemic constraints embedded in the strategic environments surrounding it.[13]

## Envisioning an Interdependent Trading State

If the realist-systemic perspective offers only a partial explanation for the genesis of the Sino–South Korean rapprochement, a liberalist-economic thesis may provide a supplementary rationale. As a matter of fact, having adjusted its strategic posture by minimizing systemic constraints, China could still have insisted upon its long-held principle of self-reliance. Yet China instead chose to reach out to the outside world, South Korea in particular, even at the expense of putting its longstanding relationship with North Korea at risk. Why? A liberalist-economic perspective would suggest that China was positively and proactively responding to the changing paradigm of world affairs at the time when the seed of a grand thaw was planted. As a scholar aptly notes:

A new "trading world" of international relations offers the possibility of escaping such a vicious circle [of military conflicts] and finding new patterns of cooperation among nation states. Indeed, it suggests that the benefit of trade and cooperation today greatly exceeds that of military competition and territorial aggrandizement....

Nations [such as the United States and the Soviet Union] which focused primarily upon international and territorial competition often were unable to design a trading strategy of advancement and economic rejuvenation.[14]

A close examination of China's foreign policy since the early 1980s indicates that Beijing has increasingly put more of emphasis on a trading strategy than a military one. This, of course, is not to argue that China completely abandoned its military political strategy: national security and territorial sovereignty remain its top priorities. It is only suggested here that, given the failures of the Soviet Union and to a lesser extent the United States to cope with their domestic economic problems during the 1970s, and considering the remarkable successes of its East Asian neighbors, China did not find it difficult to realize that it was imperative to assign more weight to a trading strategy in managing international affairs.[15]

At the core of this trading strategy lies a genuine desire for cooperation, which is generated only "when actors adjust their behavior to the actual or anticipated preferences of others, through a process of policy coordination."[16] As noted earlier, South Korea had been eager to cooperate with China since the early 1970s for its own security and economic reasons. It was China that eventually reciprocated, by adjusting its behavior during the 1980s, in order to bring about bilateral cooperation. Unlike military and security issues, interstate cooperation in the economic realm is generally much less risky and potentially more beneficial, due to a heightened willingness to reciprocate and the relatively low costs involved in the case of betrayal.[17] Yet in consideration of its longtime ally North Korea, China opted for the very tacit process of permitting indirect trade and nongovernmental exchanges with South Korea.

The genesis of bilateral cooperation between South Korea and China was in fact rooted in the convergence of interests of the two "egoists." First, the search for profitable markets that had been heavily export-dependent coincided with China's desire to join the international trading community, under the new policy framework of "opening" (kaifang).[18] Second, Seoul's positive assessment of Beijing's potential role in the politics of Northeast Asia and in wielding "constructive" influence over Pyongyang in particular was matched by China's confidence that Pyongyang would never tilt too heavily toward the Soviet Union.[19] Third, China also hoped that its desperate search for foreign capital and technology could be realized in significant part by South Korea, which, unlike the United States and Japan, was more forthcoming to provide both—especially intermediate-level technology—with few political strings attached.[20]

Once bilateral exchanges gained a foothold, both China and South Korea immediately recognized the value of cooperation in indirect trade, which was followed by limited athletic and postal exchanges. Consequently, in the minds of the decision makers in both Beijing and Seoul, the weight of future coopera-tive exchanges was considerably enhanced. The mutually beneficial nature of the initial cooperation made both countries greatly appreciate the prospect of continued and expanded interaction in the future.[21]

## Reform and Opening: Linking the Changes from Within

Foreign policy is not simply a strategic response to an external stimulus. It is also a manifestation of complex domestic, political, and economic dynam-ics. The direction of a country's foreign policy is inevitably due to a combina-tion of factors, which may include the effects of both systemic attributes and domestic characteristics. Any foreign-policy analysis without due consider-ation to both will end up telling only one side of the story at best.[22] It is in this context that the genesis of the South Korea–China rapprochement needs to be explored from domestic-external linkage perspectives.[23]

Three conceptual models, which are by no means mutually exclusive, are presented below, in efforts to comprehend China's crucial decision to initiate and sustain a cooperative relationship with South Korea, its former adversary. They are: (1) a "learning model," which focuses on China's reflective determina-tion to correct its past mistakes of putting politics in command and pursuing a strategy of self-reliance; (2) a "nationalism model," which characterizes China's nationalistic zeal to regain its world-class status as its main locomotive of eco-nomic modernization; and (3) an "emulation model," which concentrates on China's willingness to replicate the successes of East Asian newly industrial-izing countries and economies (NICs and NIEs)—above all, South Korea's suc-cesses.

### The Learning Model

Socialist regimes were, at least initially, designed to bring about social transformations. One fundamental goal of such transformations was to cre-ate a system of production and distribution for meeting the basic needs of the majority of the populace.[24] Superficial and latent as they might seem, as one scholar has noted, human needs were a powerful propellant of social change:

> Over time all societies experience conflicts between the institutional values and structures of society on the one hand, and human needs at the level of the individual on the other hand. This dynamic "historic process" by which societies evolve dialecti-cally is driven by the tension between the existence of individual human needs, on the one hand, and the degree to which societies and social institutions are responsive

to these needs on the other hand.... Societies that fail to meet the needs of their members become unstable over time. If they are to survive and be seen as legitimate by the vast majority they will ultimately be forced to undergo change.[25]

In all socialist countries, including China, crucial human needs were cruelly suppressed by the dictatorship of the Communist Party, through its command economy and autarchic system of economic management. The dire consequences of such a dictatorship over human needs were the ubiquity of a shortage economy, popular discontent, social instability, and, ultimately, the legitimacy crisis of the communist regime.[26] China fared no better—if not worse—than most socialist states. The situation in China was further exacerbated by the fiascoes of successive political movements and ideological campaigns, which led to a nationwide economic crisis by the mid-1970s.[27]

The only conceivable way out of this regime-threatening crisis was to limit the mechanisms of the command economy, reduce the omnipresence and omnipotence of ideological control, and utilize the benefits of opening to the outside world.[28] The new leadership that emerged in the aftermath of the death of Mao Zedong and the arrest of the Gang of Four became keenly aware of the magnitude of the crisis it was facing. It immediately came up with two crucial remedies: restructuring the entire economy through reform (*gaige*) and pursuing foreign capital, technology, and management know-how by opening (*kaifang*) China to the outside world.[29]

A wide range of previously inconceivable measures were implemented to reduce the scope of mandatory state plans, promote local initiatives and incentives in various economic projects, and to expand the autonomy of enterprises and individual entrepreneurs in both rural and urban areas.[30] More importantly for this study, China also became increasingly more receptive to various patterns of international exchanges, most effectively demonstrated by its rapidly growing volume of foreign trade and the ever-expanding amount of foreign direct investment.[31]

In brief, China's opening to the outside world since the late 1970s was in significant part a consequence of the conscious yet painful realization by the new leadership under Deng Xiaoping of the crucial limitations of the Maoist model, which had stressed "politics in command" and self-reliance. Once the Chinese leadership was liberated from the omnipresent grips of the "flawless" Maoism, China was willing and ready to expand its contact with the outside world.[32] It became soon apparent that there was no turning back to the old system of autarky.

The most important outcome of opening was that China began to reap tangible benefits from foreign trade and investment, which significantly alleviated its chronic problems of capital shortage and technological retardation. Initial successes reinforced the post-Mao leadership's confidence in the reformist path it had chosen.[33] Consequently, China further adjusted its foreign economic policy on the basis of reciprocity. One additional characteristic worth noting was China's increased interest in omnidirectional diplomacy (*quanfangwei waijiao*) targeted to almost every country on the globe. Whether Israel, South Africa, Indonesia, or South Korea, as long as it was considered beneficial to do business, China was more than willing to let trade precede the flag. It was within this context of deideologization that the genesis of the South Korea–China rapprochement was facilitated.

### The Nationalism Model

Nationalism is a cultural phenomenon, a state of mind, and a "group consciousness that serves to hold together the largest groupings of people that have ever formed."[34] Such feelings of group identification and loyalty are considered crucial to political integration and nation building. In addition, the "us-against-them" sentiments of nationalism are crucially motivated by a notion of national self-esteem. The low self-esteem of a nation gives it a great incentive to change the status quo. In short, as the gauge of a nation's self-esteem, nationalism constitutes an important instrument in facilitating changes in its foreign-policy orientations.[35]

China has long been known for its obstinate insistence on its place as the "Middle Kingdom" or "center of the world" (*zhongguo*). China's Sinocentric view of the world was not simply a symbolic image of its own, but it was also consistently reflected in its actual foreign policy.[36] When the "Middle Kingdom" was constantly harassed by Western imperial powers and eventually degraded into a semicolonial state in the first half of the twentieth century, China's self-esteem hit its nadir. The painful humiliations imposed on China by the imperial powers help explain why the foreign policy of the People's Republic of China has by and large been more driven by nationalistic reactions to such memories than by a manifestation of ideological, communist commitments.[37]

It was only after the post-Mao leadership articulated the nationalistic goal of economic advancement by way of promoting cooperation with the outside world that the intricate dilemma between autonomy and dependence was resolved, at least for the time being. Post-Mao China's concrete plans to regain its world-class status have so far been working quite effectively. The advantage of backwardness has been superbly utilized by China, and its nationalistic zeal for wealth and prestige has to a certain extent replaced the ideological pillars of the communist regime.[38] Without such nationalistic goals and appeals, post-Mao reform and opening would not have persisted, let alone succeeded, in normalizing relations with so many countries during the post-Mao era.[39]

## The Emulation Model

If the learning and nationalism models account for how China came to appreciate a wide range of international exchanges as crucial means to reform its economy and enhance national self-esteem, the emulation model can explain how South Korea was chosen as one of China's most important economic partners. It is suggested here that China's positive assessment of and willingness to emulate South Korea's developmental experiences were the most crucial factor leading to the Sino–South Korean rapprochement.

The will of one actor to emulate the behavior of the other is generally preceded by the former's knowledge of the positive results produced by the latter's behavior. In other words, "diffusion" comes before emulation. Diffusion, defined here as the spread of behaviors, attitudes, and information within and between societies, is an increasingly crucial factor of the present world, which gets smaller every day due to advances in transportation and communication technology.[40] Once the diffusion of specific information occurs, it is up to the individual, the group, or even the nation-state to decide whether and how to emulate the successful (or useful) behavior of others.

While this concept of emulation has been underutilized in the field of international relations, probably because of the practical difficulties associated with acquiring definitive evidence of the process itself, it may shed some light on crucial issues that cannot be easily understood otherwise. For instance, the explanatory utility of the emulation model can be found in accounting for why North Korea's Flying Horse (*Chollima*) movement, Three Great Revolutionary Small Group (*Samdae Hyokmyong Sojo*) movement, and Joint Management Laws (*Hapyongbop*) shared so many similarities with China's Great Leap Forward, Red Guard Movement, and Joint Venture Laws.[41] Another example would be the almost synchronized diffusion of democracy movements in the Philippines (1986), Taiwan (1987), South Korea (1987), and China (1989).

In a similar vein, China's decision to cooperate with South Korea can also be explained by the emulation model. The stellar success of the East Asian NICs and NIEs in their pursuit of economic development was remarkable enough to attract the full attention of China's post-Mao leadership. As one analyst notes, "The economic success of East Asia derived from its open economic policy has influenced many nations to rethink how they ought to go about achieving economic development.... Nowhere is the resulting change in thinking more apparent than in China."[42] Among the East Asian NICs and NIEs, Hong Kong and Singapore early on must have been taken off the list of prospective models for China to emulate, due to their exceptionally small size and unique nature. Taiwan must also have been excluded because of the potential political ramifications of China's adopting a Taiwanese model of development. South Korea, therefore, must have provided a very useful model, one China considered worth emulating.[43]

Despite, out of its concern for North Korea, China's calculated silence on the remarkable economic success of South Korea, China was determined to emulate its developmental experiences. Several indicators clearly suggest that China was very much interested in the South Korean recipe for economic success. This author's counting of the articles that appeared in *Shijie zhishi* (*World Knowledge*), published by the Ministry of Foreign Affairs, between 1979 and 1991 (that is, prior to the diplomatic normalization) is indeed supportive of China's increased interest in South Korea. Of the total of thirty-seven articles concerning the Korean peninsula, nine were on the unification issue, twenty (seven for 1979 through 1985 and thirteen for 1986 through 1991) were on South Korea, while only eight (seven in 1979 through 1985 and only one from 1986 through 1991) were devoted to China's longtime ally North Korea.

On September 7, 1978, the Xinhua News Agency commented that the remarkable economic success of South Korea was worthy of attention. On December 18, 1978, China's foreign trade minister, Li Qiang, mentioned in an interview in Hong Kong that China might consider trading with South Korea. In late 1978, the Chinese Academy of Social Sciences (CASS) allegedly established a small research group—called *Chaoxian jingji yanjiuhui* (Study Group on the Korean Economy)—under its Institute of World Economy and Politics, to study the developmental model of South Korea's economy.[44]

On December 14, 1980, Hu Yaobang, general secretary of the Chinese Communist Party (CCP), commented in an interview with the official newspaper of the Greek Communist Party that China's open policy was in fact based on the developmental experiences of South Korea, Yugoslavia, and Romania. Given the qualitative differences between South Korea's economic performance and the other two, Hu was in effect referring to the experiences of South Korea. In the same month, China's premier, Zhao Ziyang, remarked in an interview with Yugoslavian reporters that China was indeed studying the experiences of South Korea's economic development.[45]

China's initial goal was then directed at becoming another NIC by closely following the developmental path of South Korea. China was particularly interested in emulating the export-oriented strategy of East Asian NICs and NIEs in general and South Korea in particular.[46] China even copied some of South Korea's targets of economic development: Deng Xiaoping's famous projection of reaching a per capita GNP of one thousand dollars by the year 2000 was allegedly molded after Park Chung Hee's 1980 figure.[47] In fact, Deng Pufang, eldest son of Deng Xiaoping, is reported to have confirmed to South Korea's ambassador to China that his father had indeed paid special attention to President Park's development strategies.[48]

As the emulation model prescribes, to exchange information and share experiences, proper emulation requires close contact and extensive communication. Once China decided on emulating South Korea, bilateral contact had to grow and the ground for mutual cooperation opened. While Beijing's perennial concerns led it to avoid visible and direct contact with Seoul, many crucial breakthroughs were nevertheless on their way. Beginning in 1978, the Chinese government permitted Korean Chinese to visit or return to Korea permanently; later on, many became go-betweens for South Korean–Chinese economic cooperation. More importantly, indirect trade was first allowed in 1979, if not earlier.[49]

In sum, each of these five perspectives accounts for different dimensions of the specific circumstances in which Beijing and Seoul were to initiate secret overtures for economic rapprochement, eventually leading to diplomatic normalization in 1992. Of course, perceptions and willingness to learn and emulate alone do not guarantee close bilateralism. Concrete actions and policies were necessary and sufficient for the rapprochement as it was implemented by China and South Korea (see chapters 4 through 6). There is no doubt, however, that the incipient interdependence forged between the two paved the way for a significant mitigation of antagonism, which again helped provide for further rapprochement.

# 4

# South Korea–China Relations Before 1988

While the bilateral relationship between South Korea and China has only been in existence for twenty-some years, it has nevertheless gone through several distinct phases of development. The particular periodization employed here highlights the evolutionary process by which the transformation of South Korea–China relations from mutual antipathy to a comprehensive, cooperative partnership has been conditioned, precipitated, cultivated, and matured over the course of the last quarter century.

South Korea–China relations of the last twenty-five years can be divided into six phases: (1) the prerapprochement period prior to 1979; (2) the initiation phase, 1979 through 1983; (3) the expansion phase, 1984 through 1987; (4) the take-off phase, 1988 through 1990; (5) the normalization process, 1991 through 1992; and (6) the period of maturation, from 1993 onward. The first three phases are discussed in this chapter, while the fourth and fifth are examined separately in chapters 5 and 6.[1] The postnormalization phase is covered in three other chapters—chapters 7 through 9—focusing on the trade and strategic dimensions of Sino–South Korean relations, South Korean perceptions of the United States and China, and the impact of the South Korea–China partnership on the Korean-American alliance, respectively.

## Sino–South Korean Relations Before 1979

Until the early 1970s, Sino–South Korean relations had been deeply antagonistic, due largely to the enmity engendered during the Korean War and reinforced by the cold war.[2] China maintained a special amicable relationship with North Korea (except during the unusually xenophobic phase of the Cultural Revolution), one that was often dubbed as an "alliance sealed in blood." On the other hand, South Korea sustained a very close relationship with Taiwan (Republic of China).[3] During the cold war, in the absence of official ties severed during the Japanese colonial rule, the traditional China-Korea dyadic relations were reformulated as two parallel relationships—namely, ROK-ROC and DPRK-PRC relations.[4]

The highly antagonistic relationship between China and South Korea continued throughout the 1960s, with the occasional armistice meetings at Panmunjom being the only close encounters between Seoul and Beijing. A few fortuitous incidents could have served as convenient pretexts for initiating official contact between China and South Korea. For instance, in September 1961, when two Chinese military pilots defected to South Korea with their AN-2 reconnaissance plane, Seoul simply chose not to communicate with Beijing and immediately sent the pilots and even the plane to Taiwan, which Seoul then recognized as the sole legitimate government of China.[5] On the other hand, China had often detained South Korean vessels and their crews for periods of up to twelve years, charging that the boats had intruded into Chinese territorial waters—and South Korea had no diplomatic channel or means to negotiate with China for their return.[6]

International strategic environments changed rather dramatically during the early 1970s, manifested most clearly by the rapprochement between China and the United States, and Japan.[7] Keenly aware of China's potential influence over North Korea, Seoul concluded that improving its relations with Beijing would certainly help reduce tension and maintain peace and stability on the peninsula. In 1971, Kim Yong-Sik, South Korea's foreign minister, commented that "it is the policy of my government to approach the question of normalizing diplomatic relations with the Soviet Union and the People's Republic of China with flexibility and seriousness."[8] According to Seoul's internal position as of 1972, South Korea would not take an antagonistic position vis-à-vis China unless Beijing chose to take such a position toward South Korea first.[9]

As China adopted a policy of discriminating against Japanese and American corporations with close commercial ties in South Korea and Taiwan, concerns were voiced with regard to the long-term implications for South Korea's economy of "China fever" in the United States and Japan.[10] Seoul's strategy was to face the challenge directly. In 1972, South Korea amended Article 2 of its foreign-trade laws to permit trade with communist countries other than North Korea and Cuba.[11] The South Korean media also promoted the argument that Seoul should remain alert in security terms but at the same time, as far as China was concerned, keep its diplomatic options open.[12]

Under the surface, South Korea's foreign ministry sought to open windows of contact with China by allowing its diplomats to meet and talk with their Chinese counterparts. Ideas such as expanding indirect trade and permitting sports exchanges were also seriously considered. Seoul even secretly designated five of its embassies, in Washington, London, Ottawa, Paris, and Tokyo, and the consulate general in Hong Kong as key points of contact with China. Most importantly, expanding Seoul's political relations with Taipei beyond what it had already maintained was tacitly discouraged.[13]

In 1973, Seoul issued the June 23 Announcement, which radically altered South Korea's foreign-policy posture by abandoning the long-held Hallstein Principles and opening its doors to all countries, including China and the Soviet Union. In March 1973, South Korea suggested that China should participate in the negotiations for delineating the boundaries of the continental shelf in the Yellow Sea and for the first time referred to Beijing as the People's Republic of China.[14] China quietly turned down the proposal but expressed interest in another made several months later, that Beijing might cooperate with Seoul on joint petroleum exploration in the Yellow Sea. Seoul also allowed the Canadian Pacific Airline and Japan Air to use its flight information region (FIR) on their newly opened routes to China.[15]

In September 1974, South Korea lifted the ban on postal exchanges with communist countries, and China promptly responded by allowing Korean Chinese to exchange letters with their relatives in South Korea via the International Red Cross. The Institute for Asiatic Studies at Korea University also sent Korea-related books to China and received in return copies of the selected poems of Mao Zedong, as well as information on the kinds of books that could be exchanged in the future. At the United Nations General Assembly, China began to refer to South Korea as the Republic of Korea.[16] The same year also witnessed the first transit visit by a Chinese citizen from the mainland, Zhang Liqun, who stayed overnight in Seoul on his way from Honolulu to Hong Kong.[17]

Due to a combination of factors, little overt development took place in Sino–South Korean relations from 1975 through 1977. Above all, this was a period of extreme political uncertainty in China, given the death of Mao, the fall of the Gang of Four, and the ensuing struggle for succession at the Zhongnanhai. Furthermore, regional strategic environments were also in flux, with a major communist victory in Indochina, the fall of Saigon. In 1975, according to an unconfirmed source, Kim Il Sung allegedly proposed in vain to Mao Zedong that North Korea and China undertake a joint military action to regain South Korea and Taiwan.[18] Although some sources suggest that the indirect trade between South Korea and China had started as early as 1976, given the high political uncertainties at that time, it might as well have been toward the end of the 1970s that considerable trade between China and South Korea began.[19]

After the dust of succession politics had settled in Beijing, the two sides resumed the minuet that typified the relationship of 1972 through 1974. On September 7, 1978, an official of the New China News Agency commented that South Korea's economic success was worthy of China's attention. On November 1, 1978, Kim Kyung-Won, then the special assistant for international security affairs to President Park Chung Hee, made remarks at the Hong Kong Press Club that South Korea hoped to improve its relations with China. On November 17, Foreign Minister Park Dong-Jin made it clear that "the government will not prohibit any commercial activities with Communist countries, with which it does not have diplomatic relations."[20] While this merely reiterated the 1972 amendment of the foreign-trade regulations, the statement was synchronized with China's much publicized "opening" to the outside world. One month later on December 18, 1978, China's minister of foreign trade, Li Qiang, mentioned in an interview in Hong Kong that China might consider having trade with South Korea and Israel.[21]

Although sizable indirect trade between Seoul and Beijing started in 1979, neither Chinese nor Korean officials publicly referred to it at the time. Despite the initiation of indirect economic contact, official exchanges were strictly prohibited, even in third countries. For instance, Beijing chose not to host the Asian Youth Soccer Tournament, originally scheduled to convene in Shanghai in October 1979, lest South Korea should claim the right to participate as the previous tournament's champion. Yet significant changes were underway, though they were not visible at the time. Beginning in December 1978, China quietly allowed Korean Chinese to visit and meet with their relatives in South Korea and even return home permanently.[22] Furthermore, as noted earlier, crucial remarks continued to be made by high-level officials such as Hu Yaobang and Zhao Ziyang about the positive aspects of South Korea's developmental experiences.

## The Initiation Phase, 1979–1983

The year 1979 is generally seen as the starting point of South Korea–China economic exchange, since the available data on any significant trade between the two countries date only as far back as this year. In the initiation phase (1979 to 1983), trade was the only meaningful area of bilateral cooperation. Yet the trade was conducted totally indirectly, in the form of re-exports from Hong Kong, Singapore, and Japan.[23] A wide variety of intermediaries were employed in order to accommodate China's wish to keep its business dealings with South Korea totally secret. American, Japanese, Hong Kong, and overseas Chinese general trading firms, as well as trading firms owned by overseas Koreans with other than South Korean citizenship, were utilized for this purpose.[24]

In this initiation phase, Beijing was extremely cautious and highly sensitive to any slight sign of discontent on the part of Pyongyang. Due to fierce complaints filed by North Korea on China's indirect trade with South Korea, for instance, Chinese port authorities went so far as to detain fourteen merchant ships carrying South Korean goods in Qingdao in April 1982.[25] The bilateral economic relationship at this point was thus extremely volatile, as China and South Korea were both testing the waters and highly sensitive to the reactions they might get from North Korea and, to a lesser extent, Taiwan, respectively. Despite all this, the indirect trade between the two expanded more than seven times, from US$19 million in 1979 to US$134 million in 1983.

On January 27, 1979, China's official mouthpiece, *People's Daily* (*Renmin ribao*), referred to South Korea as the "Park Chung Hee authorities [*Piao Zhengxi dangju*]" instead of the usual reference to the "puppet regime." On May 5, 1980, an editorial in the *Beijing Review* for the first time designated South Korea as a "diehard" rather than using familiar terms such as "reactionary" or "running-dog of American imperialism" (*meiguo fuyong zougou*). It was also notable that China was far less active than the Soviet Union in criticizing the South Korean government for the tragic event in Kwangju in May 1980.[26] Huang Hua, China's foreign minister, also reportedly characterized the situation at the time as China's "gate [to South Korea] remaining closed but not locked [*guanmen bu suoshang*]."[27]

During his state visit to Washington in 1981, President Chun Doo Hwan commented, "if the PRC is a friend of the United States, I think I can extend the logic and say a friend of a friend is less of a threat to us."[28] In retrospect, these various tacit signals and developments pointed to the possibility of a more extensive thaw in Sino–South Korean relations. China's weighted emphasis on expanding economic cooperation with the outside world coincided with South Korea's search for more export markets and peace on the peninsula. Seoul was more than prepared to respond with alacrity to any overtures Beijing might make.

One notable incident took place on May 5, 1983. A Chinese civilian airplane was hijacked and forced to make an emergency landing in an air base in Chunchon, South Korea. China immediately requested that South Korea agree to receive a delegation from Beijing to discuss the terms of resolving this urgent matter. In doing so, Beijing for the first time referred to Seoul as the Republic of Korea in their bilateral correspondence, outside of the context of international organizations. A red-carpet reception was provided for Shen Tu, director of the Civil Aviation Administration of China (CAAC), who headed the Chinese delegation. After a series of negotiations, it was agreed that the passengers, crew, and the plane were to be returned to China; however, the hijackers were to be tried first in a South Korean court.[29] While the incident certainly had historic significance in that it was the first direct official contact and diplomatic negotiation between the two countries, equally important was an infrastructural side effect of that contact: Seoul and Beijing managed to open telex communication and a temporary hotline, via Tokyo.[30]

In the immediate aftermath of the incident, China dispatched Foreign Minister Wu Xueqian to brief the concerned leadership in Pyongyang.[31] Yet several signs after the hijacking incident pointed to China's changing position on South

Korea. Beijing began to allow South Korean officials to attend conferences convened in China if they were sponsored by international organizations. In 1983 alone, three South Korean officials entered China to participate in conferences organized by the Food and Agriculture Organization (FAO), the International Postal Union (IPU), and the International Maritime Organization (IMO).[32] Lee Beom-Seok, South Korea's foreign minister, commented on May 16, 1983, that the normalization of relations with China should take place as fast as possible. On May 20, two weeks after the hijacking incident, Chen Xian, deputy chairman of China's National Commission on Sports, announced that China would attend the Seoul Olympic Games in 1988.[33]

## The Expansion Phase, 1984–1987

Three factors appear to have been crucial in boosting South Korea–China relations from initiation to expansion. First, more direct contact, including some unexpected encounters like the 1983 hijacking incident and the 1985 Kunsan torpedo boat incident, considerably enhanced the level of mutual understanding and confidence between the two former adversaries.[34] Second, as Pyongyang's relationship with Moscow visibly improved in the mid-1980s, Beijing might have become more willing than before to play the "South Korean card." Third, owing to its acute need for foreign-currency earnings, developmental capital, and advanced technology, China became more receptive to expanding economic exchanges with South Korea.[35] These exchanges could have developed beyond economic ties had it not been for the two tragic events— the Soviet downing of a Korean airliner in September 1983 and North Korea's Rangoon bombing in October 1984—both of which threw cold water on Seoul's efforts for rapprochement with its communist neighbors.[36]

In this expansion phase, bilateral trade rose sharply from US$462 million in 1984 to US$1,679 million in 1987, making South Korea China's seventh-largest trading partner. It was also during this phase that China began to loosen its ban on South Korean investment in China. In 1984, for the first time, South Korean executives from the Korean Shipbuilding and Construction Corporation entered China to negotiate a project for harbor construction in Shandong.[37] In 1985, a South Korean toy manufacturer (Hansu Industry) for the first time made investments in Guangdong Province, though utilizing a Hong Kong front company. While South Korea's investment in China during this period was minimal and completely indirect in nature, the success of a few early comers paved the way for many other joint ventures.

South Korea–China relations during this period were constantly affected as much by political considerations as by economic aspirations. Yet it seemed that

China became increasingly accustomed to the complaints filed by North Korea regarding economic exchanges with South Korea. The number of Korean-Chinese visits to their native places in South Korea jumped from twenty-five in 1981 to eight hundred in 1987.[38] Furthermore, sports diplomacy was a crucial catalyst for the rapprochement between Seoul and Beijing. On February 29, 1984, Ye Fei, deputy chairman of the National People's Congress, revealed China's position on continuing sports exchanges with South Korea. In March 1984, Qian Qichen, deputy foreign minister, invited South Korea to attend the 1990 Beijing Asian Games, and Wu Xueqian, foreign minister, confirmed China's participation in the Seoul Olympic Games in 1988.[39] In June 1987, China announced that it would refer to South Korea as the Republic of Korea during the Fourth Asian Women's Volleyball Championship as well as during the 1990 Beijing Asian Games.[40]

## Patterns of Sino–South Korean Trade, 1979–1987

Until the late 1980s, studies of China's foreign policy and foreign economic relations provided little if any information on the burgeoning economic bilateralism between China and South Korea. Those few studies that did only offered some trade data for a year or two at best. This was largely understandable, since both China and South Korea had wished to conceal their "secret" economic relations, in order not to provoke North Korea and Taiwan. During this period, Sino–South Korean trade was mostly indirect; therefore, the official aggregate data was largely incomplete and inaccessible. Both governments sought to conceal the information by placing the relevant data in the category "Other."

South Korea's indirect trade with China adopted the form of re-exports from Hong Kong, Singapore, and Japan. Several kinds of intermediaries were utilized: American, Japanese, and overseas Chinese general trading firms; Hong Kong trading companies that maintained contacts with the branch offices of South Korean general trading firms; and trading firms owned by overseas Koreans with other than South Korean citizenship. The complicated routes of trade and the number of actors involved in the process generated problems with information collection for the Korea Trade Promotion Corporation (KOTRA), which was then responsible for monitoring South Korean exports to China.[41] South Korean firms often exaggerated their performance in the China trade in order to better position themselves for the possibility that the Seoul government, to reduce excessive competition among firms, might select only one or two firms in each industry to deal with China. Furthermore, the secretive nature of the paperwork further complicated the data-collection problem.[42]

TABLE 4.1 South Korea's Trade with China, 1979–1987 (in US$ millions)

| YEAR | TOTAL | EXPORT TO CHINA | IMPORT FROM CHINA | VIA HONG KONG |
|------|-------|-----------------|-------------------|---------------|
| 1979 | 19 | 4 | 15 | — |
| 1980 | 188 | 115 | 73 | 80 |
| 1981 | 353 | 205 | 148 | 219 |
| 1982 | 129 | 48 | 81 | 150 |
| 1983 | 134 | 51 | 83 | 160 |
| 1984 | 462 | 229 | 233 | 345 |
| 1985 | 1,161 | 683 | 478 | 604 |
| 1986 | 1,336 | 715 | 621 | 653 |
| 1987 | 1,679 | 813 | 866 | — |

Source: Korean government statistics reported in *Joong-ang Ilbo* [Joong-ang Daily], June 22, 1988; and *Xianggang jingji nianjian* [Hong Kong economic yearbook], 1982, 1984, and 1986.

If we revisit the studies on this theme published during the 1980s, we find that most of them worked with wrong data or at best very rough estimates.[43] With the official data at hand (see table 4.1), a more systematic assessment can now be made.[44] The data indicate that South Korea's trade with China during this period suffered serious setbacks in 1982 and 1983. Two factors account for this. First, between 1981 and 1982, China had vigorously sought to reduce imports to cool down its overheated economy. Second, between 1982 and 1983, despite the loosening of import controls, China restrained itself, due to North Korea's filing in 1982 of serious complaints over Sino–South Korean economic contacts.[45] Given that both exports to and imports from China were significantly reduced during these two years, the bilateral trade had been considerably affected by political factors.

### South Korea's Imports from China

In the "secret" trade between China and South Korea during this period, Chinese agricultural goods were a very important item. In 1984, when the Chinese found themselves with surplus feed grain, maize in particular, they sought to export it rather than consume or store it, and South Korea utilized the opportunity in the following way: The Korea Corn Processing Industries Association and the National Federation of Livestock Cooperatives put out tenders to South Korean general trading companies, which then telexed the pertinent information to traders in Hong Kong. South Korean general trading companies then located a third-country vessel, usually manned and owned by South Koreans but flying the flag of a third country. In the paperwork, the ultimate destination had to be obscured through the use of two bills of lading, one of which was destroyed later on. The port of destination was an open secret: As long as the Chinese did not see the name "South Korea" written anywhere, it did not matter.[46]

Interviews with a large South Korean corn importer, Samyang, added further evidence of the clandestine grain trade. The company's corn imports from China started in the latter half of 1984, and in that year and the first half of 1985, 24,120 metric tons worth US$3.16 million were imported. From July 1985 to June 1986, imports increased by 96.4 percent, with a total value of US$5.61 million. Between July 1986 and June 1987, imports again surged by 91.3 percent—90,625 metric tons, valued at US$7.76 million. The share of the imports from China constituted 77 percent of the company's total corn imports during 1985 and 1986, and the figure rose to 97.6 percent during 1986 and 1987. For six major South Korean corn-importing companies, which handled 81 percent of South Korea's corn imports during 1986 and 1987, the share of imports from China averaged 60 percent.[47]

Samyang arranged its corn purchases from China through South Korean or Japanese general trading firms, which in turn utilized traders in Hong Kong. During 1985 and 1986, the company received eleven shipments, six arranged by Mitsui, four by Hyosung, and one by Cargill. Whereas Samyang purchased 48 percent of its Chinese corn from Mitsui, the figure went up to 80 percent during 1986 and 1987. The corn containers revealed their Chinese origins but they did not disclose their final destinations, and they were disposed of upon arrival in South Korea.[48]

Coal was the most commonly mentioned item among Chinese exports to South Korea. The following two excerpts demonstrate the importance of the item.

Rumors that are too persistent to be ignored indicate that South Korea has been buying more than 200,000 tons of Chinese coal annually...mainly through third parties....But recently, the Chinese have been cracking down on the clandestine shipments.[49]

From the late 1970s to 1982, coal moved directly from the PRC to Korean ports, although the arrangements were made through brokers in Hong Kong. In response to complaints from North Korea, shipments were suspended in 1982. Since the official statistics never suggested that there were any imports from the PRC, it is impossible to determine the extent of such a trade.[50]

Interviews amplify these secondary sources. Table 4.2 leads us to three observations. First, the 1982 crackdown by China noted earlier affected the coal trade as well, but there was no suspension. Second, the huge increases in trade in 1985 and 1986 dramatically changed the overall trend. Third, during the initial period up to 1983, the volume of coal trade had been sufficiently small so as to permit the use of third-party contacts. As it increased dramatically after 1985, more direct contact was necessary. Both parties still used the name of a third party (a paper company), but according to sources in Seoul, the Korea Coal Corporation developed direct communication with the China National Coal Import and Export Corporation. After 1981, the nature of the shipping changed as well, with coal being shipped directly from the Chinese ports of Qinhuangdao, Dalian, Tianjin, and Shanghai to Korean ports, mostly Pusan, Inchon, and Pohang.[51]

TABLE 4.2 South Korea's Coal Imports from China

| YEAR | AMOUNT (1,000 METRIC TONS) | VALUE (US$ MILLIONS) | PERCENTAGE OF CHINA'S TOTAL COAL EXPORTS |
|------|------|------|------|
| 1979 | 188 | 7.7 | 4.1 |
| 1980 | 310 | 12.7 | 4.9 |
| 1981 | 158 | 6.5 | 2.4 |
| 1982 | 296 | 12.1 | 4.6 |
| 1983 | 110 | 4.5 | 1.7 |
| 1984 | 199 | 8.1 | 2.9 |
| 1985 | 820 | 33.5 | 10.8 |
| 1986 | 1,251 | 51.2 | 12.7 |
| 1987 | 1,960 | — | — |

*Source:* For the amount and value of imports, interviews in August 1987. For percentage of China's total, *Zhongguo duiwai jingji maoyi nianjian* [Almanac of China's foreign economic relations and trade], 1984 issue, 928; and 1986 issue, 1057. See also *Chosun Ilbo* [Chosun Daily], June 21, 1988; and Shi Hao, "Dalu meitan gongye xiankuang diaocha [Survey of the current situation of China's coal industry]," *Zhonggong yanjiu* [Studies of Communist China] 21, no. 5 (May 1987): 118.

South Korea's Exports to China

South Korea's ten top export items in 1984 included four types of textile materials (textile yarns, artificial fabrics, special fabrics, and cotton fabrics), three electrical devices, and paper, glass, and artificial fiber. Exports of artificial fabrics, paper products, steel, organic chemicals, and raw materials for textiles increased rapidly from 1984 to 1986, while exports in other categories—yarn, artificial fibers, television sets, and special fabrics—declined.

In the composition of Sino–South Korean trade during this earlier period, there seems to have been a vertical division, both inter- and intraindustry. South Korea exported semifinished and finished products such as electrical appliances, textile fabrics, and steel, while China exported natural resources, agricultural products, silk and cotton yarns, and other raw materials. A close examination of the trends within the textile industry at the time suggests that Chinese and South Korean industries were achieving a sort of specialization and vertical division of labor, with South Korea supplying synthetic fabrics and textile yarns for processing in Chinese weaving mills. The vertical trade within the textile industry between China and South Korea continued well beyond the period concerned.[52]

## South Korea's Investment in China, 1984–1987

Aside from the indirect trade during the period from 1984 to 1987, Sino–South Korean economic cooperation also encompassed a few joint ventures. While it certainly was a large step forward compared to the 1979 to 1983 period, when no investment from Seoul had been allowed by Beijing, political considerations always lurked in the background. The case of Daewoo's joint venture with Fujian Province, described below, well illustrates this point.

In February 1985, a New York–based company of Daewoo formed a joint venture with Ming Long Development Corporation, a subsidiary of Jujina Enterprise, which represented commercial interests of Fujian. The joint enterprise was named Kingwoo, and its mission was to build a television and refrigerator assembly plant in Fuzhou. The five layers of communication (Daewoo–Sovereign–Kingwoo–Ming Long–Jujina) testified to the amount of political sensitivity involved in this groundbreaking deal. The excessive caution proved of little use, however. The information leaked and, due to the opposition from Pyongyang, the construction of Daewoo's Fujian plant was suspended for a year, resuming only in early 1987.[53] In this case, moving from the signing of the agreement to the actual opening of the plant took almost three and a half years, due mainly to China's concern with North Korea.[54]

Another case also provides a persuasive account concerning how sensitive and vulnerable Beijing was to the complaints filed by Pyongyang during this period. The Korean Shipbuilding and Construction Corporation (KSCC), specializing in shipbuilding and construction engineering, had its first contact with China in 1982, through its Hong Kong subsidiary, regarding an unsuccessful project of constructing a cement plant in Fujian. In late 1984, three executives of KSCC entered China on the strength of an invitation letter from Shandong. The deal concerned harbor construction in Shandong, and the executives were hosted by the Shandong branch of the China Council for the Promotion of International Trade (CCPIT). The negotiations proceeded smoothly and a provisional contract was even signed by the two parties. While the deal was clearly not profitable for KSCC, since it was the first such project with China, the company was willing to build the harbor and receive coal in return.[55]

To the mystification of the Koreans, contacts with the Chinese partners were severed. When a Hong Kong–based KSCC executive went back to China in early 1985, he discovered that his Chinese interlocutors had been criticized and dismissed, and the deal was no longer mentioned in China. The executive soon learned unofficially from the Chinese side that the Ministry of Coal had not cooperated with the Ministry of Communication on the deal, and to resolve the interministerial policy discord, the State Planning Commission (SPC) had to get involved. Once the SPC got involved as a coordinating supra-agency, the Foreign Ministry also became an interested party, out of its concern for North Korea. It strongly objected to the project, and the deal was quietly dropped. The official excuse from the Chinese was that the project had not been included in the Seventh Five-Year Plan (1986 to 1990).

KSCC then began to think in terms of small-scale projects, one of which was a joint venture for fishing-rod production. In 1986, the China Light Industry Import and Export Corporation invited an executive from the company to discuss the proposal, but the negotiations bogged down over the KSCC's desire to station South Korean engineers in China. During the negotiations, the Chinese side made it clear that they did not want any South Koreans stationed in China.[56]

Yet another case suggests that confusion and a lack of pertinent information were widespread. A chief executive of a construction subsidiary of the Korean Airline Group visited China in early 1986, with the idea of constructing a parking structure near the Great Wall. The subsequent negotiation took place between the Chinese authorities and a Korean American who represented the firm. The talks foundered, however, because the company could not come up with a reasonable method by which to get paid for its construction work. During the interview, the executive confessed that he had not really known to whom to talk in China and which Hong Kong intermediary to rely on. He then concluded that the future for business in China was still very vague.[57]

There were several reports on various other joint venture projects pursued by Daewoo, Hyundai, Lucky-Gold Star, and other South Korean business conglomerates. Three additional projects by Daewoo were widely rumored, including a car plant in Fuzhou, in which General Motors would become a partner; a coal-mining venture in Shanxi; and a power-plant construction project in Nanjing. Right after the Kingwoo deal was struck between Daewoo and Fujian, the Lucky-Gold Star Group also sent a delegation to China to discuss deals involving electronics and chemicals.[58] Yet this period from 1984 to 1987 was largely one of testing the water, as big corporations were still highly uncertain about committing large investments out of a concern for investment guarantees—let alone profit returns.

## The Political Limits of Sino–South Korean Relations

China allowing economic contact—though mostly indirect—with South Korea meant a major breakthrough in Beijing's policy toward Seoul. This crucial shift from a "nonpolicy" to de facto economic diplomacy should be understood within the framework of post-Mao foreign-policy pragmatism. The desire of China's reformist leaders to modernize their economy and assume global responsibilities gave birth to three characteristics of post-Mao foreign policy. First, a peaceful international environment was absolutely necessary, in which China could devote itself fully to the task of economic modernization. Second, China would actively seek foreign capital and technology, without which the modernization plan could not be materialized. Third, post-Mao open policy, the logical extension of China's desire for external assistance, presupposed flexibility rather than the dogmatism of the Maoist era.

These three characteristics were made manifest in China's policy toward the Korean peninsula in the following ways. First, China would seek peace and stability on the peninsula, because any disruption of which would lead Beijing to an agonizing dilemma between either supporting North Korea and antagonizing the United States and Japan or standing by idly and losing North Korea to the Soviet Union. Second, China saw considerable benefits in continuing economic exchanges with South Korea, which could help China gain foreign currency and midlevel technology. Third, the opening and the maintenance of the contact presupposed an abandonment of China's hitherto dogmatic posture toward South Korea.

China's principal position in dealing with South Korea during this period was to develop economic and nongovernmental ties, along with athletic and cultural exchanges, in ways that would not excessively provoke North Korea. In retrospect, the Chinese crackdown on indirect trade with South Korea in 1982 and the closure of the first joint venture in 1986 were mere gestures with no lasting effect. They were, in fact, highly calculated moves on the Chinese side designed specifically to "give North Korea some face" (*gei beihan liudian mianzi*). In the short term, however, these sporadic interruptions worked against the smooth progress of Sino–South Korean economic ties.[59]

By 1987, many seasoned observers predicted that Sino–South Korean economic relations would further expand, although the same could not be said of political rapprochement or diplomatic normalization. In order to tap into South Korea's advanced midlevel technology, Beijing had to strengthen its economic ties with Seoul. Despite their low profile during this earlier period, Sino–South Korean economic relations already reached a point where any reverse direction would be clearly not in the interests of either party. Trade with South Korea constituted 2.3 percent of China's overall trade in 1986; South Korea was China's seventh-largest trading partner. Since 1984, the trade volume between China and South Korea also far surpassed that between China and North Korea.

In an interview with Japan's *Nihon Geizai Shimbun* (*Japan Economic Daily*), Hu Qili, a member of the Politburo Standing Committee, commented that China was willing to have direct trade with South Korea if North Korea was not opposed.[60] China also became increasingly more confident that North Korea was highly reluctant to tilt decisively toward the Soviet Union. Furthermore, to the surprise of many, there was a report that Kim Il-Sung, during his visit to China in May 1987, was asked by a Chinese official to give serious thought to the option of cross-recognition.[61] This report is very important, as it was China who initiated the proposal. This was a very different position than the one previously maintained by China, which was merely to repeat North Korea's position on reunification. Considering the Taiwan issue, it might have been a risky move, but one might speculate whether by then China had already come to the conclusion that Korea was one problem and Taiwan quite another.[62]

# 5

## The Political Economy of Rapprochement, 1988–1992

Having tasted the sweet success of initial economic cooperation, China became progressively more receptive to expanding contacts, exchanges, and transactions with South Korea from 1988 through 1992. While certain limits were clearly there, emanating largely from Beijing's perennial concern for Pyongyang, their grip gradually loosened over the years. Both the Seoul Olympic Games in 1988 and the Beijing Asian Games in 1990 provided convenient pretexts for further expansion of semiofficial contact, along with the dramatic increase in both bilateral trade and South Korea's investment in China.[1] The enormous growth of bilateral economic exchanges inevitably led to the establishment of trade offices in 1991 and eventually to the normalization of diplomatic relations in 1992.

### The Takeoff Phase, 1988–1990

The Sixth Republic's *nordpolitik* ("northern diplomacy" toward socialist states) officially began after Roh Tae Woo's election as president in December 1987. The Seoul government announced a large-scale development scheme—called the "Yellow Sea Plan" (*hwanghae gyehyaek*)—for its western region, which faced China's eastern coast. At about the same time, the Chinese government also publicized a crucial decision to open up the Shandong and Liaodong peninsulas. Although these two announcements had not been coordinated by the two governments in advance, the spirit embedded in both clearly pointed to a widening basis of cooperation between Seoul and Beijing.[2]

South Korea's scheme was welcomed by Pu Shan, president of the Chinese Association for International Economic Research (*Zhongguo shijie jingji xuehui*), who remarked that it would be beneficial for China to cooperate with newly industrializing countries, including South Korea, in developing its coastal regions.[3] In early 1988, Tian Jiyun, China's vice premier and Politburo Standing Committee member stated that China would develop "direct" trade with South Korea, the first time a top Chinese official had said so.[4]

There is no denying that the 1988 Seoul Olympic Games provided a valuable opportunity and timely catalyst for South Korea and China to further expand their economic cooperation. With China dispatching more than four hundred athletes to the event, South Korea scored a major diplomatic victory by taking China—and many other socialist countries, including the Soviet Union—further away from its northern competitor. Positive effects of the global sporting event were clearly demonstrated by the amount of the bilateral trade between South Korea and China, which almost doubled from US$1,679 million in 1987 to US$3,087 million in 1988.

In the immediate aftermath of the successful Olympic Games in Seoul, bilateral relations improved considerably. *Renmin ribao* (*People's Daily*) even carried commercial advertisements for South Korean products, as well as publishing positive reports on Seoul's economic accomplishments.[5] The China Council for the Promotion of International Trade (CCPIT) proposed to the Korea Trade Promotion Corporation (KOTRA) in January 1989 that they start negotiating for the exchange of trade offices. China also for the first time invited a South Korean cabinet member, Finance Minister Gyu-seong Lee, to participate in the General Assembly of the Asian Development Bank, in May 1989. Speculations soon abounded that the normalization of diplomatic relations between South Korea and China was imminent.[6] Such optimism was short-lived, however, as the world was awakened by the tragic events in Tiananmen Square in early June 1989.

The exploration of Sino–South Korean relations in this takeoff phase would not be complete without examining the repercussions in China of this traumatic event. In 1989, South Korea's trade with China was hit hard: South Korea's exports to China recorded a considerable drop (16 percent) for the first time since 1983, thereby slowing the growth of the bilateral trade.[7] The slowdown was facilitated by three factors. First, Sino–South Korean trade data on a monthly basis suggest that South Korea's exports had already begun to decrease in late 1988, after the Third Plenum of the Thirteenth Central Committee, where new import restrictions on many consumer goods were adopted.[8] Second, an additional restriction was imposed in 1989 on twenty consumer goods such as television sets, videotape recorders, and computers, all of which were major South Korean export items.[9] Third, from late 1989, the Chinese government also began to apply a new customs regulation, according to which all imported goods of neutral packing—applicable to most South Korean exports to China—were to be exempted from preferential duties.[10]

After the June 4 incident, the Seoul government reportedly adjusted downward its target of China trade for 1989 from US$4.3 billion to US$2.5 billion.[11] The actual trade turnover, however, surpassed the adjusted target by 28 percent and marked a 1.8 percent increase over that in 1988. South Korea also sent more than 2,500 business delegations to China in 1989 alone, marking a 70 percent increase over 1988.[12] A comparison of South Korea's China trade with that of Taiwan and Singapore, however, suggests that the effects of Tiananmen may have been more adverse for South Korea than for the other two. Although none of the three countries had diplomatic relations with China at the time, Singapore and Taiwan marked 28 and 46 percent increases in their trade with China, as opposed to South Korea's 1.8 percent.[13]

While the Tiananmen incident demonstrated that South Korea–China economic relations were indeed susceptible to various domestic and external factors, aside from the smaller-than-expected increase in trade, not much else was actually affected. Instead, important progress was made quietly in many areas. For instance, Seoul for the first time participated in a syndicated loan to China. Most of the cargo was also shipped directly between China and South Korea, although letters of credit were still exchanged in Hong Kong. South Korean efforts in the area of joint ventures, too, remained aggressive. In the first half of 1990 alone, nineteen joint venture projects with a total investment of US$35 million were signed, marking a 90 percent increase over the first half of 1989.[14]

China, too, seemed to conclude that maintaining and expanding economic cooperation with South Korea was in its best interests. In 1989, China's trade surplus with South Korea was US$267 million; in 1990, that rose to US$715 million. Besides, it was known that South Korea had been silent on the military suppression at Tiananmen Square and was more willing to resume business with China than were the United States, Europe, or Japan.[15] It was in June and August 1989 that Sino–South Korean ferry routes and charter flights were established for the first time. Furthermore, several South Korean business conglomerates went so far as to provide US$5 million and over four hundred passenger cars as goodwill donations, to show their support for China's hosting of the 1990 Asian Games.[16] These events provide the background for the rationale behind the crucial decision made in late 1990 to exchange trade representative offices between Seoul and Beijing.[17]

## The Normalization Phase, 1991–1992

It was no coincidence that South Korea–China trade reached a total of US$5,812 million in 1991, a 52 percent increase over that of 1990, and that in 1991 alone, South Korea invested US$425 million in China, in over sixty-nine projects, accounting for 66 percent of South Korea's accumulated investment in China. Behind this quantum leap lay an institutional breakthrough: the establishment of trade representative offices in 1991. Staffed mostly by career diplomats despite their nominally nongovernmental designations, the trade offices practically provided a political guarantee, which in turn boosted the level of economic cooperation between the two countries. In June 1991, the Customs Administration of China for the first time published official data on its trade with South Korea, which it referred to as the Republic of Korea.[18]

Despite many positive developments in Sino–South Korean relations, the establishment of trade offices had remained the most intricate issue of contention.[19] Although South Korea had been anxious to set up trade offices since 1988, as its economic stakes in China had significantly increased over the years, China had remained very cautious, due to the political repercussions this might create for its relations with North Korea.[20] The initial Chinese response was to allow South Korean firms to have their business representatives reside in China but to oppose any governmental representation. By June 1990, a total of fourteen South Korean firms had already set up branch offices in China, although only three of them—Samsung, Daewoo, and Lucky-Gold Star—received official endorsement from the Chinese government.[21]

In retrospect, China's rigid position had begun to soften in December 1987, when the State Council had designated Shandong as the "key-point province" (*zhongdiansheng*) in dealing economically with South Korea. This significant policy immediately led to the signing of trade agreements in August 1988 between the Shandong branch of the China Council on the Promotion of International Trade (CCPIT) and the Korea Trade Promotion Corporation (KOTRA). While the agreements stipulated the establishment of trade offices, that did not materialize, due to Seoul's strong preference for a national Beijing office over a regional office that would represent merely one or two provinces.[22]

Seoul's insistence on a Beijing office brought the negotiations to a stalemate, and the uncertainties raised by the Tiananmen incident deadlocked any further progress on the issue. When the negotiation eventually resumed in late 1989, China's position appeared more accommodating and flexible, however. Reportedly, on the basis of the highly beneficial nature of the bilateral economic relationship, the Chinese side adjusted their position from insisting on opening an office in Yantai, which would only represent Shandong Province, to considering the establishment of a Beijing office.[23] In June 1990, Yuan Mu, the spokesperson of the State Council, admitted that China and South Korea were negotiating for the establishment of trade offices.[24]

The next set of major disagreements concerned the official designation and the terms of formalization. While the South Korean side demanded that its office be designated as the "Trade Representative of the Republic of Korea," the Chinese insisted on using the unofficial designation "Beijing Office of the Korea Trade Promotion Corporation," out of concern for Pyongyang. While there was strong opposition to the Chinese proposal in South Korea, the Seoul government, eager to concretely improve relations with China while President Roh Tae Woo was in office, agreed on October 20, 1990, to the terms set by Beijing.[25]

Regarding the terms of formalization, Seoul demanded a formal exchange of documents, while Beijing insisted on tacit understandings only. The final outcome was to exchange a document of secret accord, the contents of which were to be classified for thirty years—until 2020.[26] With regard to the more practical terms of staffing and diplomatic privileges, however, most of South Korea's demands were satisfied. South Korean staff members were empowered to carry out consular duties and were protected with full diplomatic immunity. In communicating with the home government, use of secret codes and diplomatic pouches was also permitted.[27] When the trade office began its operation on the thirteenth floor of the China World Trade Center in Beijing, eleven of the twenty members of the South Korean staff at the trade office were officials from the Ministry of Foreign Affairs.[28]

After the establishment of trade offices, South Korea–China economic relations were further accelerated in early 1992, by the signing of formal agreements on trade, tariffs, and investment guarantees. Particularly, thanks to the trade agreement, South Korean exports to China enjoyed most-favored-nation (MFN) status, thereby avoiding differential duties. By March 1992, therefore, most of the thorny economic and institutional hurdles were cleared, with only the negotiation for diplomatic normalization pending. In retrospect, even the diplomatic normalization was accomplished much sooner than most seasoned observers had initially expected, highlighting the crucial spillover effects of economic interdependence on political rapprochement.

## Sino–South Korean Trade, 1988–1992

Trade continued to constitute the most important area of bilateral interaction between South Korea and China during this period. To a considerable extent, bilateral trade constantly upgraded the level of economic cooperation and even guided the overall path of rapprochement between Seoul and Beijing. Unlike the previous period (1979 to 1987), however, Sino–South Korean trade did not suffer serious setbacks, as the North Korean constraints had considerably weakened over the years.

Bilateral trade more than doubled from US\$3,087 million in 1988 to US\$6,380 million in 1992. Over the thirteen-year period since 1979, China had scored a total surplus of US\$3,265 million in trade with South Korea, while that of South Korea's was only US\$711 million. In short, Seoul had been paying special attention to its trade with China, since South Korea–China economic cooperation was driven as much by Seoul's political considerations as by its search for expanding export markets other than the United States and Japan.[29]

As the political constraints on economic cooperation gradually weakened, Chinese officials hinted at the possibility of having direct trade with South Korea.[30] Subsequently, the share of direct trade in Sino–South Korean trade increased rapidly. In 1991, the amount of the bilateral trade via Hong Kong was US$2.3 billion, accounting for 40.3 percent of the Sino–South Korean trade for that year, a significant reduction compared to the figure of 75 percent in 1984. The share of South Korea's direct exports to China in its total exports to China also rose from 22 percent in 1988 to 42 percent in 1991.[31]

By 1992, South Korea–China trade had reached a point where any move in the reverse direction was clearly not in the interests of either party. The share of South Korea–China trade in China's total foreign trade steadily rose from 0.06 percent in 1979, 0.3 percent in 1983, 2.2 percent in 1986, and 3.8 percent in 1988, to 4.3 percent in 1991. Similarly, the share of bilateral trade in South Korea's total foreign trade also increased from 0.05 percent in 1979, 0.3 percent in 1983, 2 percent in 1986, and 2.7 percent in 1988, to 3.8 percent in 1991.[32] In compara-

TABLE 5.1 Top Products in South Korea–China Bilateral Trade, 1988–1992

|  | 1988 | 1990 | 1992 |
|---|---|---|---|
| Chemical products | 1/4 | 2/2 | 2/4 |
| Primary products | 7/5 | 8/1 | 8/1 |
| Textiles | 3/1 | 1/3 | 3/2 |
| Steel | 2/2 | 4/5 | 1/6 |
| Electrical products | 5/7 | 3/7 | 4/5 |
| Machinery | 6/6 | 6/6 | 5/7 |
| Plastics and rubber | 8/– | 7/– | 7/– |
| Mineral products | 4/3 | 5/4 | 6/3 |
| Miscellaneous | 9/– | 9/– | 8/– |

*Note:* The figure to the left of the slash refers to the rank of each item in South Korea's export to China; the figure to the right, the rank of China's exports to South Korea.

*Source:* Liu Jinzhi et al., *Dangdai zhonghan guanxi* [Contemporary China's relations with Korea] (Beijing: Zhongguo shehuikexue chubanshe, 1998), 152–155.

tive terms, South Korea became China's eighth-largest trade partner in 1989, and its seventh largest in 1990 and 1991.[33]

During this period, Sino–South Korean trade continued to have a mutually complementary structure. According to the data on the types of goods involved in the trade between the two countries in 1988, 1990, and 1992 (table 5.1), South Korea's top export items were chemical products, steel, and textiles, while China's top export items consisted mainly of primary products (mainly agricultural), mineral products, and textiles.[34] The complementary nature of the trade was particularly well manifested in the sectors of textile and chemical products, which were top trade items for both sides. These sectors were characterized by a sort of vertical division of labor; that is, South Korea imported and processed textile raw materials and yarns for export to China. At this juncture, however, it was already suggested that the speed at which the complementary trade between China and South Korea would be replaced by competitive trade might constitute a long-term determinant of the bilateral economic relationship.[35]

## South Korean Investment in China, 1988–1992

South Korea's investment in China during this period had been somewhat overpublicized relative to its actual accomplishments. Much of the media fervor about Sino–South Korean joint ventures was more symbolic than substantive. During much of this period, the size of South Korea's investments committed in China was fairly marginal compared to the volume of its trade with China. According to the data presented in table 5.2, South Korean firms, particularly the larger ones, had been much more cautious in making investment decisions than in engaging in trade up until 1991, when the trade offices were exchanged between Seoul and Beijing. This was understandable considering the high risks involved in investing in a country with which South Korea had no diplomatic relations.

Though all South Korean investments had been made indirectly through front companies based in third countries in 1985 through 1987, two first cases of direct investment were made in 1988, with the Olympic blessing.[36] According to a Xinhua report in late 1988, Chu Baotai, deputy director of the Foreign Investment Bureau of the Ministry of Foreign Economic Relations and Trade (MOFERT), commented, "as far as Chinese policy is concerned, businessmen from South Korea enjoy equal treatment with other foreign businessmen."[37] China's *World Economic Herald* also called for a quick adoption of direct trade between China and South Korea.[38]

Once the inroads were made, South Korean direct investment in China increased very rapidly, from twelve projects worth US$9.8 million in 1989 to 112

TABLE 5.2 South Korea's Investment in China, 1985–1992 (no. of projects: US$ millions)

| YEAR | DIRECT INVESTMENT | INVESTMENT VIA THIRD COUNTRIES | NET TOTAL (US$ MILLIONS) | TOTAL |
|------|------|------|------|------|
| 1985 | — | 1: 0.1 | 1: 0.1 | 1: 0.1 |
| 1986 | — | 2: 1.8 | 2: 1.8 | 3: 1.9 |
| 1987 | — | 1: 6.0 | 1: 6.0 | 4: 7.9 |
| 1988 | 2: 3.4 | 3: 2.0 | 5: 5.4 | 9: 13.3 |
| 1989 | 12: 9.8 | 5: 4.9 | 17: 14.2* | 26: 27.5 |
| 1990 | 38: 54.5 | 3: 2.9 | 39: 54.6* | 65: 82.1 |
| 1991 | 112: 84.7 | 5: 3.6 | 116: 83.2* | 181: 165.3 |
| 1992 | 269: 221.4 | N/A | 269: 221.4 | 385: 386.7 |

*Notes:* The data presented are on the basis of approval by the Bank of Korea. The figures with asterisks do not round up, as there were some withdrawals of investment in that year.

*Source:* Bank of Korea, *Haewoe tuja tonggye yonbo* [Statistical yearbook of overseas investment] (Seoul: Bank of Korea, 1992), 29; Yang Pyongsop, "Hanguk eui daejung tuja chuyi wa teukjing [Trends and characteristics of Korea's investment in China]," *Bukbang gyungje* [Economies of the Northern Area] (May 1992): 33; Si Joong Kim, "Korean Direct Investment in China: Perspective of the Korean Private Sector," paper presented to the International Workshop on the Emerging Pattern of Foreign Investment in East Asia, Honolulu, May 1–2, 1992; and a statistical file by the International Private Economic Council of Korea (IPECK), September 1990, 2–3.

projects worth US$85 million in 1991, rendering the investment via third countries almost insignificant. With the cumulative total of 181 projects totaling US$165 million by the end of 1991, South Korean investment in China constituted 11.4 percent of South Korea's total number of foreign investment projects and 3.2 percent of its total overseas investment. Despite the swift pace at which South Korean investment in China was increasing, its share of the total foreign investment in China still remained fairly minimal.[39]

During much of this period, the South Korean business community, rather than aiming at the Chinese domestic market, was largely testing the waters with export-oriented pilot projects that utilized China's low labor costs.[40] The average size of South Korea's investment in China was also very small: US$0.9 million per project—even smaller than that of Japan's.[41] South Korea's business conglomerates were rather cautious about committing large investments, because pertinent institutional mechanisms for investment guarantees were then lacking. The signing of the investment guarantee agreement in May 1992 and, more importantly, the diplomatic normalization in August 1992 provided a crucial boost for South Korea's investment in China.[42]

## The Infrastructure of South Korea–China Bilateralism

Since economic exchanges had been the core of South Korea–China relations up to 1992, most of the institutional and organizational arrangements were also largely economic in nature, although their symbolic and political ramifications were by no means insignificant at the time. Around 1988, the watershed year when bilateral trade and direct investment began to shoot up, both sides—especially South Korea, being on the giving end of the investment dynamic—realized the necessity of a certain type of bilateral coordinating venue with sufficient authority.

### The Communication Dimension

The unprecedented direct negotiations during the hijacking incident in 1983 and the Kunsan torpedo boat incident in 1985 led to the creation of an important but contingency-specific channel of bilateral communication between Seoul and Beijing, namely, the hotline between the Korean Consulate General in Hong Kong and the Hong Kong branch of the New China News Agency.[43] It was also around 1985 that the Seoul government considerably expanded the size of its diplomatic corps at the Hong Kong General Consulate, to which high-level diplomats began to be assigned as mission chiefs. In 1991, Beijing also agreed to Seoul's proposal that South Korea's Consulate General in Hong Kong was to be maintained even after its return to China's sovereignty in 1997.[44]

A wide range of informal and private channels of communication were also created and maintained between high-level officials of both countries.[45] One significant derivative of these efforts to maintain venues of bilateral communication and coordination was the agreement signed in January 1990, facilitating direct consultation and cooperative arbitration in the case of conflicts involving fishery issues and maritime accidents.[46] The establishment, in 1990, of direct phone and facsimile communication, as well as direct postal exchange, also brought China and South Korea much closer.[47]

### The Transportation Dimension

When the number of people and the volume of cargoes flowing across the Yellow Sea became too large for the indirect means of transportation via Japan and Hong Kong to handle, arrangements were made to facilitate direct transportation. In September 1990, Golden Bridge, the 4,317-ton ferryboat of the Weidong Ferry Corporation—a joint venture between six Korean and two Chinese firms—made its much-publicized maiden voyage from Inchon, Korea, to Weihai, Shandong. The ferry service was soon extended to Qingdao.[48] In 1990, container service was also initiated, linking South Korea's Pusan and Inchon with China's Dalian and Qingdao on a biweekly basis. Direct container service was later extended to Shanghai and Tianjin on a weekly basis.[49]

In addition to the direct maritime linkages, similar changes took place with air routes. Since late 1988, with the Olympic blessing, there had been occasional charter flights connecting China with South Korea.[50] In August 1989, Seoul–Shanghai charter flights were permitted briefly. In June 1990, China allowed the Korean Air Line to use a Kunming route in its flights to Tripoli. After the Beijing Asian Games, China permitted Seoul–Beijing charter flights to run for an additional three months. In late 1991, irregular charter flights were also instituted between Seoul and Tianjin and Shanghai. In May 1992, these were regularized and flown on a weekly basis.[51] With the diplomatic normalization in 1992, direct flights between Seoul and Beijing, which China had strongly sought to avoid, were finally established.

Some procedural arrangements were also made to facilitate easier and wider access to each other. After the signing of a travel agreement in July 1988, Shandong Province permitted South Koreans to go on group tours to China and, in some cases, even individual trips were allowed.[52] The Shandong provincial government would first provide tourist visas and later report to the Ministry of Foreign Affairs. Moreover, the duration of the tourist visa was often extended from fifteen days to one to three months and, in some cases, even repeatedly extended to one year.[53] With the establishment of trade representative offices in January 1991, entry visas were more conveniently issued in Seoul and Beijing instead of Hong Kong and Tokyo.[54]

### The Transactional Dimension

Several positive developments took place to facilitate smoother economic exchanges between the two countries. The Bank of China for the first time opened a letter of credit on December 21, 1988, with South Korea's Foreign Exchange Bank. In 1989, correspondence agreements were signed between South Korean and Chinese banks, thereby simplifying the troublesome procedures involved in business transactions. In April and July 1992, respectively, the Korean Exchange Bank and the Bank of China opened offices in Beijing and Seoul.[55] Also in 1989, China agreed to accept patent and trademark filings by South Korean firms.[56] More importantly, both South Korea and China progressively relaxed their tight control over the establishment of branch offices and subsidiaries of each other's business firms and banks. By June 1992, nineteen branch offices of various South Korean firms were established in China, while nine Chinese corporations opened offices in South Korea.[57]

## The Institutional Dimension

As its economic stake in China steadily increased over the years, South Korea became anxious to set up trade offices. After a very complicated process of negotiations and bargaining, China finally agreed to exchange trade offices with South Korea in November 1990. In spite of their official designation as nongovernmental and economic missions, the trade offices were empowered to conduct consular duties and were staffed mostly by career diplomats.[58] Following the establishment of the trade offices, trade agreements were signed and put into effect in January 1992. These agreements abolished the differential duties imposed on South Korean exports to China. In May 1992, China and South Korea also signed an investment guarantee agreement, by which South Korean investment, either wholly owned or joint ventures, were to receive the same treatment as foreign firms owned by other countries.[59] Of course, the most important institutional breakthrough was the establishment of embassies in August 1992.

## The External Constraints on Sino–South Korean Bilateralism

From the beginning of Sino–South Korean economic cooperation in the late 1970s up to the normalization of diplomatic relations in 1992, North Korea was the most serious impediment. Without the perennial concern for its "friendship" with Pyongyang, Beijing would not have insisted so strongly on the principle of having only nongovernmental relations initially, and later, on semigovernmental and provincial contacts only. China's "special" relationship with North Korea proved to be the most persistent obstacle to the smooth development of Seoul-Beijing bilateralism.

The pace at which the Soviet Union and Eastern European countries had normalized relations with South Korea plainly demonstrates that China's concern for North Korea was special indeed. By March 1990, most of the Eastern European countries had already normalized their relations with Seoul.[60] In December 1989, the Soviet Union and South Korea agreed to establish consular offices and, in March 1990, direct flights between Seoul and Moscow were opened. The June 1990 summit conference between Mikhail Gorbachev and Roh Tae Woo and the subsequent normalization in September 1990 clearly distinguished Moscow from Beijing in their respective approaches to Pyongyang.[61]

The special relationship between Beijing and Pyongyang can be explained by several factors.[62] First, on a very general level, the combination of historical solidarity, cultural affinity, and ideological similarity—which North Korea–Soviet relations had largely lacked—may provide a partial explanation. The relationship was often referred to as "brotherhood" (*xiongdi zhi bang*), a concept that goes back to the traditional tributary system in which Korea had been generally regarded as the most reliable vassal (*neifan*), due to its sincere conformity to Confucian values.[63] Second, the Chinese contribution of men and material during the Korean War and, equally importantly, the restraints exercised by the Chinese, in stark contrast to the Soviet Union, in politically interfering with North Korea's domestic affairs were always highly appreciated by Pyongyang. Third, China has historically considered (North) Korea as the most crucial buffer against the advance by maritime powers with strategic aspirations for the Asian continent.[64]

On the basis of such a special relationship with Pyongyang, Beijing was willing to detain merchant ships carrying South Korean goods and limit its cooperative relations with South Korea to nongovernmental and economic relations.[65] Yet, in retrospect, China's gradual, phase-by-phase approach was in large part Beijing's calculated move to "give North Korea some face" (*gei beihan liu dian mianzi*). That is, the post-Mao Chinese leadership might have already reached a consensus on the desirability of having cooperative economic relations with South Korea, although a similar consensus remained to be made on when and how Beijing should translate its economic rapprochement with Seoul into political terms.[66] One intricate question in this regard was how to separate the "two Koreas" from the potentially flammable issue of the "two Chinas."

The only external opposition to South Korea's efforts to improve relations with China came from Taiwan, which was then still the only China that South Korea officially recognized.[67] Taipei, like Pyongyang, had been wary of the rapprochement between Beijing and Seoul out of fear that the eventual normalization would force it to lose a principal ally. Although Taiwan had refrained from outright criticism of South Korea—until the normalization in August 1992—its concern had been voiced on various occasions.[68]

Taiwan's resentment was largely threefold. First, Taiwan protested the "immoral" nature of South Korea's active search for rapprochement with China. From Taipei's perspective, Seoul's explicit courting of diplomatic normalization with Beijing was considered to be an outright act of betrayal. Considering that Taiwan had dispatched a psychological-warfare unit manned by more than 1,500 troops to aid South Korea during the Korean War, Seoul's overtures toward Beijing were unacceptable. Taipei's resentment at the time was sarcastically epitomized in that "South Korea is both anti- and pro-Communist" (*nanhan fangong ye jiaogong*).[69]

Second, Taipei's resentment was also grounded upon the concern that, given the "one-China" principle observed by the regimes on both sides of the Taiwan Strait, Taiwan's domestic legitimacy and international prestige would be severely damaged if South Korea normalized relations with China. The loss of a traditional ally to its prime competitor would no doubt have a highly adverse effect on domestic politics, by weakening the legitimacy of the incumbent Kuomintang and by encouraging the supporters of Taiwanese independence.[70] Taiwan allegedly even went so far as to suggest that South Korea, as a divided nation itself, adopt a "two-China" thesis.[71]

Third, to a certain extent, Taiwan's concerns were also economic in nature. As an economic archrival of South Korea, Taiwan was not happy about South Korea's gradual encroachment on the China market, which Taiwan considered its own backyard. Since Taiwan regarded itself largely as equal to South Korea in terms of the ability to transfer midlevel technologies to China, and more capable in providing the capital resources that China badly needed, Taiwan must have envied the successful inroads South Korean businesses were making in China at the time.[72]

In its efforts to prevent South Korea's diplomatic normalization with China, Taipei employed several different tactics. On the "stick" side, Taiwan adopted a sort of economic sanction, by restricting import quotas for South Korean automobiles. As a diplomatic "stick," Taipei also played with an idea of establishing economic links with North Korea as part of its increasingly aggressive "money diplomacy" (*yintan waijiao*).[73] On the "carrot" side, Taiwan sought hard to increase the volume of its trade with South Korea. The total volume of South Korea–Taiwan trade more than quadrupled, from US$531 million in 1985 to US$2,635 million in 1989, quite closely matching the volume of Sino–South Korean trade.[74] In 1991, Taipei even offered to purchase from Seoul sixteen Pohang-class corvettes for US$100 million.[75] Seoul, however, was much more interested in expanding cooperative relations, including diplomatic normalization, with Beijing, even at the expense of Taipei.

# 6

## The Politics of Normalization

### Actors, Processes, and Issues

Whereas the literature on Sino–South Korean relations has proliferated since the early 1990s, no study has to date been available that provides detailed accounts of the intricate process by which Seoul and Beijing came to the historic decision to normalize diplomatic relations on August 24, 1992.[1] This chapter seeks to fill that void by reconstructing the hitherto largely veiled process of negotiations for diplomatic rapprochement and normalization. To do so, this study first identifies the key actors and organizations involved on both sides and then examines the political dynamics of decision making in both Beijing and Seoul. While at the time of this writing much of the process still remains shrouded in secrecy, the present endeavor relies on a wide range of documented sources and interviews conducted by the author.[2]

## Top Leaders and Informal Channels

### The Beijing Dimension

China's policy making is generally understood as a process of constant negotiation and bargaining, due to the fragmented nature of authority in the system.[3] Negotiations are necessary and often unavoidable when there are different interests and values in conflict. Such conflicts are more likely when there is a newly emerging policy issue on which a consensus has yet to be reached among different groups and factions. Establishing ties with South Korea, China's former adversary, was undoubtedly one such thorny and sensitive issue, and, therefore, it required a broad consensus within the top leadership. How to minimize Pyongyang's resentment and at the same time maximize economic benefits from the ties with Seoul, in addition to isolating Taiwan, were the points at the core of the considerations at the Zhongnanhai.

While identifying the views of top leaders within the Chinese government is both necessary and desirable, the sheer lack of relevant and reliable information renders a systematic examination largely infeasible. Some efforts were made, however, to construct a sketch of the views that some Chinese leaders at the top held prior to and during the normalization with South Korea. Given the extreme sensitivity involved in China's rapprochement with South Korea at the time, Deng Xiaoping's personal approval and a broad consensus within the Politburo—and its Standing Committee—must have been indispensable.[4]

In March 1980, Deng Xiaoping told Japanese visitors, "it would not be in China's best interest to develop relations with South Korea."[5] However, in retrospect, this public comment might have been a diplomatic way to give North Korea some face, since his key lieutenants, Hu Yaobang and Zhao Ziyang, displayed much more positive attitudes toward Seoul at around the same time.[6] By 1985, if not earlier, Deng had altered his views on the South Korean issue and reportedly ordered a feasibility study on China's normalization with South Korea.[7] According to the memoir of Qian Qichen, China's foreign minister at the time, Deng had been pushing for an improvement of China's relations with South Korea since 1988.[8] In late 1991, after both Koreas joined the United Nations, Deng allegedly wanted to make sure normalization occurred before Roh Tae Woo stepped down as South Korea's president.[9] Given that China's top leaders often sought Deng Xiaoping's "opinion" on key policy issues, Deng's consent must have been critical in finalizing Beijing's decision to normalize its relations with Seoul.[10]

The specific views held and the roles performed by the octogenarian elders in supporting or constraining China's rapprochement with South Korea remain mostly unknown, despite their unique political status and authority in Chinese politics up to the mid-1990s. Chen Yun and Wang Zhen were allegedly very uncomfortable with the idea of "betraying" North Korea for economic gains from the rapprochement with South Korea.[11] The views of other elders—such as Li Xiannian, Bo Yibo, Song Ping, and Deng Yingchao—on the issue are simply not known.

Below the supreme leader and powerful elders were a handful of high-level generalists such as Hu Yaobang, Zhao Ziyang, Wan Li, Jiang Zemin, and Li Peng. The views of Hu and Zhao were considered generally favorable toward China's economic cooperation with South Korea, as discussed in chapter 3, although their political fate prevented them from taking part in Beijing's eventual normalization with Seoul. Wan Li's view toward the rapprochement was also allegedly positive, but its specifics remain virtually unknown.[12]

The views and role of Jiang Zemin, a 1989 arrival on the national stage, is not known. Li Peng's view on the issue also remains largely veiled, although some of his postnormalization activities with regard to South Korea were highly publicized. When the relevant Chinese materials and archives become accessible in the future, the role of Li as the head of the Central Foreign Affairs Leadership Small Group (*Zhongyang waishi lingdao xiaozu*) during the process of China's rapprochement with South Korea should be more properly evaluated.[13]

Two key figures who performed crucial roles in China's rapprochement with South Korea merit special consideration.[14] One is Qian Qichen, longtime foreign minister and later vice premier in charge of China's foreign affairs. Qian's role in China's diplomatic normalization with South Korea was certainly crucial, although his role must have been accentuated particularly since late 1991, when the formal organization—the Foreign Ministry—was put in charge of the actual negotiations.[15] The nature of the relationship that Qian as a member of the Foreign Affairs Leadership Small Group—Li Peng, too, for that matter— maintained with the informal and secret ad hoc group designed to deal with Seoul under the directing of Tian Jiyun remains unclear. However, once the official normalization talks were under way starting in April 1992, Qian became China's sole plenipotentiary for the clandestine task.[16]

Tian Jiyun is the most interesting figure with respect to China's rapprochement and normalization of relations with South Korea. As a close colleague of Zhao Ziyang and a Politburo member since 1985, Tian consistently demonstrated no-nonsense pragmatism and a reformist spirit.[17] Why he had been assigned to deal with the clandestine "foreign" affairs in the first place remains uncertain, but it may be speculated that Tian, as a native of Shandong, was deemed an appropriate person to oversee the initiation of nongovernmental economic relations between Shandong and South Korea. Since the State Council had secretly designated Shandong in December 1987 as the "key-point province" in economic dealings with South Korea, it might have been around this time (possibly after the 1988 Seoul Olympic Games) that the Small Group on South Korea (*nanchaoxian xiaozu*, hereafter SGSK), of which Tian was made chairman, was established.[18]

While sufficient information is lacking, the SGSK seems to have been a supra-agency whose function and staff spanned the party, government, and even the military. Other than Tian Jiyun, two additional members of the SGSK are so far known: Yue Feng and Liu Yazhou. Yue Feng was a retired senior colonel (*shangxiao*) of the People's Liberation Army. Having worked as the executive vice chairman for the China Association for International Friendly Contacts (*zhongguo guoji youhao lianluohui*) since 1985, under General Wang Zhen and later Huang Hua, Yue allegedly was in a family relationship with Zou Jiahua, son-in-law of Marshall Ye Jianying.[19]

Another key member of the SGSK, Liu Yazhou, was at the time a colonel (*daxiao*) affiliated with the General Political Department of the Central Military Commission. Liu also sat on the board of the nongovernmental China Association for International Friendly Contacts. Liu was also a member of the "princelings" (*taizidang*), since he was a son-in-law of Li Xiannian, state president of China.[20] Why military officers such as Yue and Liu were recruited to promote secret contacts with South Korea remains unclear. But their excellent connections with the top leaders (for example, Li Xiannian, Ye Jianying, Zou Jiahua, and possibly Li Peng) might have been an invaluable asset to the Chinese government, which needed people it could fully trust for the clandestine task at hand.[21]

## The Seoul Dimension

Political sensitivity and secrecy involved in the process of rapprochement necessitated diverse informal channels and networks in South Korea as well. President Park Chung Hee, who had laid the groundwork for "northern diplomacy" with his June 23 announcement in 1973, utilized his secret intelligence networks to make some overtures toward China (discussed in chapter 4). In 1974, President Park had also purchased a high-rise building in Sheung Wan on the Hong Kong Island as an outpost for China diplomacy. The building was later renamed the Korea Centre (*Hanguo zhongxin*), and it housed the Korean Consulate General, Korea Trade Promotion Corporation (KOTRA), and branch offices of Korean media organizations.[22] President Park allegedly also utilized several secret envoys to explore the possibilities of opening trade routes with China starting as early as 1976.[23]

A couple of fortuitous opportunities through which Seoul and Beijing came to engage in direct contact with each other—most notably the 1983 hijacking incident and the 1985 Kunsan torpedo boat incident—took place during Chun Doo Hwan's tenure (1981 to 1988) as South Korea's president. Available evidence suggests that Chun had shown a strong interest in improving relations with China and the Soviet Union. President Chun appears to have been particularly interested in developing close economic ties with China.[24] Deputy Prime Minister Shin Byung-Hyun remarked in his work report to the National Assembly in November 1981 that "while no direct trade is currently being conducted with China, the situation will improve in that direction."[25] Chun also allegedly passed a message to Deng Xiaoping in August 1985 through Takeyuri, head of the Japanese Gomeito Party, proposing the development of bilateral trade.[26] It was also during Chun's tenure that the Interagency Commission on the Promotion of Northern Policy (*Bukbang jongchaek chujin bonbu*) was established in 1985.[27]

Whereas the Chun Doo Hwan administration skillfully utilized the hijacking and torpedo boat incidents to initiate economic exchanges—though mostly indirect and nongovernmental in nature—with China, certain limits were clearly imposed. In retrospect, Chun appears to have been more strongly committed to the consolidation of South Korea's traditional alliance relationship with the United States. This was understandable, considering that his rise to power had been indebted to the military coup and bloody suppression of the Kwangju

Uprising and, therefore, America's formal endorsement of his rule was indispensable.[28]

Roh Tae Woo, who succeeded Chun as president in February 1988, was perhaps the most important figure in South Korea's rapprochement and normalization process.[29] Roh was popularly elected and therefore was not as constrained as Chun was by American perceptions of his legitimacy. During his presidential campaign in late 1987, Roh had already referred to the mainland as China and pledged that he would seek to improve Seoul's relations with most socialist countries, including the Soviet Union, China, and eventually North Korea. In the immediate aftermath of the election, on December 24, 1987, President-elect Roh even expressed his wish that South Korea normalize its relations with China during his presidential tenure.[30]

Roh Tae Woo maintained quite a few channels of communication with China in promoting rapprochement and seeking normalization of relations. At least three types of communication channels with Beijing were utilized by President Roh from 1988 through 1992. Of these three types of channels, only one was partly known about at the time of its operation; the existence of the other two was revealed only in the mid-1990s, after the diplomatic normalization had already occurred.

The first channel originated from the governmental intelligence establishment—mainly based in the National Agency for Security Planning (NASP). Yet formal organizations played a secondary role. The real locus was Park Chul-Un, who was at the time dubbed the "Royal Prince of the Sixth Republic." Park made it his priority to support the northern diplomacy pursued by President Roh. Being a nephew-in-law of Roh, Park not only wielded enormous power due to his privileged access to the president, but he also commanded certain groups of intelligence and research officers affiliated with various government agencies including NASP and their attachés to the Consulate General in Hong Kong. After leaving NASP, Park became policy advisor to the president.[31]

Park was deeply involved in Seoul's northern diplomacy toward both Eastern Europe and the Soviet Union. His role in the secret negotiations for the normalization with Moscow appears to have been much more crucial than with Beijing. As a matter of fact, his ambitious yet split interest in both the Soviet Union and China might have actually worked against his role regarding China, which took secrecy much more seriously than did the Soviet Union. According to some post facto reports, Park even sought to expedite the process of normalization with China in 1990, by proposing a package of economic aid worth US$2.5 billion.[32]

After May 1990, however, as later confirmed by Park himself, Park's political clout began to fade. In fact, once he became minister of political affairs in July 1989, he could not pay as much attention to the northern diplomacy as he had previously.[33] Park was slowly excluded from the core decision-making process concerning the northern diplomacy, which was then overseen by Noh Jae-Bong (the president's chief of staff) and Kim Jong-Whee (the president's national security advisor).[34] While Park tried hard to play some role in the process of normalization with China up to the last minute, once the negotiations became increasingly official and formal, there was little room for him.[35]

The second type of channel refers to the relatively unknown people who, owing to their special endowments and accesses, were asked to perform certain functions as go-betweens for Seoul's overtures toward Beijing. Two detailed examples are given here.[36] One concerns a Chinese-Korean doctor of traditional Chinese medicine named Han Shenghao (in Korean, Han Seong-Ho). According to a rare report published in a respectable Chinese media outlet, Han's relationship with President Roh went back to 1975, when Roh's family took him as their family doctor.[37] Reportedly, Han actively supported Roh during his presidential campaign in 1987. A few days after the inauguration, Roh met with Han at the Blue House and allegedly asked him to find a way to open contacts in Shandong as a "window to China."

Han first got in touch with Cheung Sek-kau, president of Yat-tung Corporation in Hong Kong and member of the Shandong People's Political Consultative Conference. Owing to Cheung's efforts, in April 1988, Han was able to make a secret trip to Jinan, Shandong, where he was received by Provincial Governor Jiang Chunyun and Li Yu, chairman of the Shandong branch of the China Council for the Promotion of International Trade (CCPIT). According to the aforementioned Chinese report, this visit paved the way for South Korea's fifteen-person delegation (including executives from Daewoo, Samsung, and Hyundai) to Shandong in June, which produced the first Sino–South Korean accord on economic cooperation. China soon reciprocated by sending a Shandong delegation led by Li Yu to Seoul in August. Five days before stepping down, on February 19, 1993, President Roh presented a medal of national honor to Han Shenghao for his important contributions to the northern diplomacy.

A Korean-American professor named Yeejay Cho was also reportedly President Roh's secret messenger in June 1990. Professor Cho, who was at the time vice president of the East-West Center in Hawaii, carried to Jiang Zemin President Roh's letter concerning the possibility of holding a summit between the two nations during the Beijing Asian Games. While the letter was delivered to a high-level official—presumably Song Jian, chairman of the State Science and Technology Commission—who hosted the conference in which Cho took part, it failed to reach Jiang mainly because the Chinese did not consider this particular channel of communication particularly credible.[38]

The third channel, completely secret at the time it was functioning, played the most important role in Seoul's normalization with Beijing. This channel of communication shared one key characteristic with the other two: the utilization of players who were very close to President Roh. The organization utilized in this channel was a legitimate business corporation that posed little political burden for the Chinese government, preoccupied with mollifying the resentments of North Korea. The name of the corporation was Sunkyung (later renamed SK), one of the largest conglomerates in South Korea. The eldest son of Choi Jong-Hyun, the chairman of Sunkyung, was married to Roh's only daughter.[39]

This particular communication channel was not developed solely by the Korean side. It was the Chinese—specifically the SGSK—that took the initiative in making contact in April 1990.[40] Lee Sun-Seok, president of Sunkyung, was invited to Beijing on April 25, 1990, where he was received by Tian Jiyun, vice premier and chairman of the SGSK. Though since the mid-1980s Lee had known Liu Yazhou and Yue Feng, two other key members of the SGSK, in Hong Kong, it was not just his friendship with them but, more importantly, his position as chief executive of a company closely related to President Roh that made this channel both reliable and acceptable to the Chinese.[41]

Through this secret channel, China's evolving positions on such key issues as inter-Korean relations, the establishment of trade offices, the two Koreas joining the United Nations, and exchanging special envoys for diplomatic normalization were allegedly relayed to the Korean side.[42] After the establishment of the trade offices in 1991 and, more importantly, after the two Koreas' accession to the United Nations, Beijing became willing and ready for a breakthrough in diplomatic normalization with Seoul. Once the direct negotiations for normalization began, however, the importance of the clandestine channel between the SKSG and Sunkyung quickly waned, as more official lines of communication between the ministries of foreign affairs of the two countries opened.

## Factors of Bureaucratic Politics

### The Beijing Dimension

It is more often than not a general rule in China that even if an overall policy direction is established at Zhongnanhai, it does not necessarily provide detailed guidelines as to how to go about implementing the policy. In fact, an intricate process of "policy remake" takes place, in which an evolutionary path of implementation is shaped at different layers of the government bureaucracy.[43] This is where the factors of bureaucratic politics among different organizations with conflicting institutional codes and missions come into play.

Aside from the top elites, the Politburo and their informal channels, the two most important organizational actors in the implementation of China's policy toward South Korea were the Ministry of Foreign Economic Relations and Trade (MOFERT, now the Ministry of Commerce) and the Ministry of Foreign Affairs (MOFA). MOFERT, as the ministry in charge of executing China's foreign economic relations, perceived as its mandate the enhancement of the overall size of China's foreign trade, the expansion of China's foreign investment, and the promotion of diverse forms of international economic cooperation.[44] Due to the geographical proximity and the complementary nature of economic cooperation, South Korea was naturally perceived by MOFERT as a desirable economic partner.[45] Although the China Council for the Promotion of International Trade (CCPIT) had been empowered to coordinate economic dealings with South Korea, CCPIT was under the general sponsorship of MOFERT and thus shared the same institutional interests with MOFERT in promoting South Korea–China economic ties.[46]

Whereas the organizational ethos of MOFERT was mostly economic in nature, that of MOFA revolved more around political and strategic rationales. The institutional mandate of maintaining smooth relationships with China's allies and friends equipped MOFA with a more reserved—if not reluctant—attitude toward Sino–South Korean economic cooperation, mainly out of its considerations for North Korea.[47] When North Korea's embassy in Beijing filed a formal complaint about economic dealings between South Korea and China, MOFA had to do something to mitigate Pyongyang's resentment.[48]

The difference in organizational ethos often put MOFERT and MOFA at loggerheads. Problems arising from the two-tiered foreign-policy system—one focusing on economic logic and the other on political rationale—were not confined to South Korea–China relations. As one analyst notes:

> The job of developing China's international economic contacts and attracting overseas investment, trade, and technology transfer has by and large not been entrusted to the existing foreign policy bureaucratic institutions. Instead...a separate foreign economic relations and trade bureaucracy has been created....[This] two-tiered system...has led to major contradictions in China's international relations. Part of the problem is that the Chinese try to play the game in two different ways. On the one hand, they emphasize that the development of economic relations will aid the development of diplomatic relations....On the other hand, when the development of economic ties may harm diplomatic relations elsewhere, the Chinese are quick to discount the impact of economic relations on political ties.[49]

The contradictions of this two-tiered system became increasingly manifest in Sino–South Korean economic relations. For instance, the failure halfway through the proceedings of the joint venture pursued by the Korea Shipbuilding and Construction Corporation discussed in chapter 4 clearly illustrates the adverse impact of MOFA's commitment to Beijing's smooth diplomatic relations with Pyongyang on its economic cooperation with Seoul.

The conflicting views of MOFERT and MOFA were also revealed at the Conference on the Korean Problem held by the Chinese National Association for Research on the Korean Economy (*Quanguo chaoxian jingji yanjiuhui*) in Fuzhou in November 1987. While the officials from MOFERT underscored the need to expand economic relations with South Korea, the delegates from MOFA reportedly kept silent.[50] Anecdotal as they may be, these episodes illustrate the reserved attitude of MOFA concerning China's rapprochement with South Korea. If the long delay in establishing trade offices was the result of MOFA's opposition, their eventual establishment in 1991 might have been facilitated by the enhanced status of MOFERT relative to MOFA in managing China's foreign economic relations.[51] According to a report, in 1988, MOFERT had been designated as the main central government unit in dealing with South Korea, although MOFA became the primary actor once official negotiations for normalization got underway in early 1992.[52]

Other than the party-to-party relationship,[53] the ties between China's People's Liberation Army (PLA) and North Korea's Korean People's Army (KPA) were probably the strongest of all; they were often dubbed the "brotherhood sealed in blood." The observation that China's PLA—the Korean War veterans in particular—might have played a pivotal role in obstructing the progress of Sino–South Korean rapprochement is derived from this "comrades-in-arms" relationship.[54] While the North Korean connections within the PLA might have constituted a strong interest group against Sino–South Korean rapprochement during its initial stages, once Deng's determination and the intra-Politburo consensus were secured in 1988, the PLA must have acceded to the decision.[55] The inclusion of the two well-connected PLA officers—Yue Feng and Liu Yazhou—within the Small Group on South Korea might also have been a calculated move on the part of the civilian leadership.

There is no firm evidence or strong ground to believe that different or opposing views were voiced by think tanks and research institutes in China concerning the rapprochement with South Korea. Particularly during the 1980s and in the aftermath of the Tiananmen incident, China's think tanks remained politically vulnerable and therefore had little influence on policy. However, the same cannot be said of China's foreign policy–related knowledge industry during and after the late 1990s.[56]

## The Provincial Dimension

After China embarked upon the path of economic modernization, Beijing conferred on the provinces a wide range of authority in the areas of planning, fiscal management, personnel decisions, foreign trade, foreign investment approval, lawmaking, and policy implementation.[57] Since the provinces were permitted to retain a portion of their foreign-currency earnings from trade and investment, they naturally strove to expand their dealings with the outside world. The provinces' craving for more foreign economic relations under the increasingly decentralized framework, however, often came into conflict with the priorities of the central government.[58]

Provincial overenthusiasm for foreign economic relations generated various problems that often required Beijing's direct intervention. First, excessive competition for exports among the provinces seeking to increase their foreign-currency earnings often resulted in the overall reduction of the competitiveness of Chinese goods overseas. Second, the central government occasionally found itself being pushed around by provincial demands for the expansion of overseas ties at a pace much faster than the central government had planned for. Third, the fast spread of local-global nexuses also produced concerns and difficulties related to the issue of national security—this in a country hitherto ruled so strictly by central authorities.[59] When Beijing occasionally moved in to reassert control over the provinces, conflicts ensued and deals were often aborted.[60]

When it came to promoting economic ties with South Korea, the story became much more complicated. Due to its perennial diplomatic concern for North Korea, the Chinese government had insisted on a novel system of leaving the task of dealing directly with South Korea to the provinces. This was Beijing's astute strategy—based on the "principle of separating politics and economics" (*zhengjing fenli de yuanze*)—designed specifically to be able to benefit from economic ties with Seoul and simultaneously maintain stable diplomatic relations with Pyongyang.[61]

While this strategy of allowing only provincial contacts had been both convenient and effective in shielding Beijing from Pyongyang's official complaints, the same system often generated unwanted problems for the central government.[62] When provinces were empowered to make decisions on foreign trade and investment related to South Korea, with which China did not have diplomatic relations, they were actually engaged in diplomacy as much as they were engaged in economic transactions. For both intelligence- and security-related reasons, Beijing often found it difficult to sustain such localized relationships with Seoul.[63]

Interprovincial competition was also prevalent. The central government had initially laid down a guideline for regional cooperation in 1987 by matching Guangdong with Hong Kong and Macau, Fujian with Taiwan, Shanghai with Europe, Liaoning with Japan, Heilongjiang with the Soviet Union, and so on.[64] In dealing directly with South Korea, Shandong was designated by the State Council, though secretly, as the key-point province (*zhongdiansheng*).[65]

The designation of Shandong was resented by other provinces, most notably Liaoning and Fujian, which also sought to secure their own foothold in Sino–

South Korean economic cooperation. Liaoning, for instance, established a liaison office in Seoul while Shandong was still negotiating over its own. Given that Shandong was the only province authorized by Beijing to do so, it was clearly a defiant act of the form "do it first and report it later" (*xianzuo houshuo*) on the part of Liaoning, to gain an edge in bargaining with the central government. Eventually, Liaoning was also designated by Beijing as a "key-point province" in dealing directly with South Korea.[66]

Liaoning's success by way of defiance was not repeated, however. Fujian, which had also expressed keen interest in developing economic ties with Seoul ever since hosting a Sino–South Korean joint venture with Daewoo in 1987, also defied Beijing by signing a second joint-venture agreement on manufacturing compressors, again with Daewoo. Subsequently, however, the central government reportedly vetoed the whole deal, with the official excuse that the provincial government had made the decision without Beijing's prior approval.[67]

The Fujian case illustrates how hard Beijing tried to keep the provincial ties with South Korea under tight control. Overall, however, Beijing's efforts were only partially successful. According to the geographical distribution of South Korean investment projects in China (table 6.1), the central government's efforts were not

TABLE 6.1 Number of South Korean Investment Projects per Chinese Province

|  | 1984–1989 | 1990–1991 | TOTAL |
|---|---|---|---|
| Shandong | 13 | 30 | 43 |
| Liaoning | 6 | 31 | 37 |
| Heilongjiang | 3 | 17 | 20 |
| Beijing | 5 | 13 | 18 |
| Jilin | 3 | 14 | 17 |
| Guangdong | 13 | 4 | 17 |
| Tianjin | 4 | 9 | 13 |
| Jiangsu | 2 | 3 | 5 |
| Fujian | 3 | −1 | 2 |
| Others* | 2 | 7 | 9 |

*Notes*: *Others include Hebei (3), Hainan (2), Zhejiang (2), Shanghai (1), and Shanxi (1).

*Source*: Statistical files from the International Private Economic Council of Korea (IPECK) document, January 12, 1990; and Sijoong Kim, "Korean Direct Investment in China: Perspectives of the Korean Private Sector," paper presented at the International Workshop on the Emerging Pattern of Foreign Investment in East Asia (Honolulu, May 1–2, 1992), 8.

that effective, as provinces other than Shandong and Liaoning, most notably Heilongjiang, Jilin, Beijing, and Tianjin, also attracted significant portions of South Korean investment. The central government might have made concessions to the provinces or, alternatively, this might have been a calculated move on the government's part to fill the gap generated by the steep downturn in economic relations with the United States and Japan after the Tiananmen incident.[68]

In accordance with the foreign-trade reform implemented in January 1991, all provinces in China were in principle placed on an equal standing as far as the rate of foreign-currency retention was concerned. Therefore, it became only natural for Beijing to relax its rigid control over the policy of regional designation and introduce the new concept of "eight northeastern provinces and municipalities" (*dongbei bashengshi*)—the three northeastern provinces plus Shandong, Hebei, Neimenggu, Beijing, and Tianjin—in promoting economic cooperation with South Korea.[69] One derivative was the gradual decline of southern China as a key location for South Korean investment, although the trend was to reverse once again later on.

### The Seoul Dimension

One of the most important goals of South Korea's foreign policy was to enhance the legitimacy and prestige of the Seoul regime with respect to Pyongyang. Since 1948, fierce diplomatic competition between the two Koreas resembled a zero-sum game, where an increase in the formal recognition of Seoul was perceived as causing a corresponding loss in Pyongyang's legitimacy.[70] Once the United States mended its relations with China in the early 1970s, Seoul had every incentive to improve relations with Pyongyang's old allies, such as China and the Soviet Union, which would then boost its prestige relative to Pyongyang's. This was precisely why the Sixth Republic under President Roh Tae Woo went so far as to characterize its foreign policy as "northern diplomacy."

The competition for prestige overseas soon manifested itself in domestic tugs of war among different arms of the government bureaucracy. As the rapprochement with socialist states became the regime's top priority under the Roh administration, many politicians and high-level officials competed for more say and influence over the pertinent policy processes. The cases of Park Chul-Un and Kim Bok-Dong, both relatives of President Roh, are good examples of this.[71]

As noted earlier, in much of South Korea's prenormalization contact with China, governmental units could not take part officially and, therefore, the role of non- or semigovernmental bodies was deemed crucial if not indispensable. Up until 1988, the Korea Trade Promotion Corporation (KOTRA), a semigovernmental organization under the Ministry of Trade and Industry (MTI), had been the only unit authorized to monitor, promote, and supervise South Korea's trade and other economic exchanges with socialist countries including China.[72]

As South Korea's economic relations with socialist countries were rapidly expanding, the Economic Planning Board (EPB), then the most powerful supraministerial agency in charge of economic and budgetary affairs, sought to establish its own institutional leg regarding Seoul's burgeoning contacts with socialist economies. It was in this context that a new quasi-governmental body called the International Private Economic Council of Korea (IPECK) was created by EPB, to compete with KOTRA under MTI.

IPECK, in effect, was born out of the marriage between EPB and the informal network run by Kim Bok-Dong, a retired army general and brother-in-law of President Roh Tae Woo. Since many relatives of President Chun had been implicated in a series of infamous financial scandals, President Roh sought to constrain the scope of political activities by his family members and relatives. While General Kim was thus prevented from involvement in domestic political affairs, President Roh nevertheless entrusted him with the task of promoting rapprochement with China. In close cooperation with EPB, Kim established IPECK as an influential quasi-governmental channel in dealing with China's CCPIT.[73]

The sudden doubling of South Korea's communication channels created much unnecessary competition and confusion.[74] The initial solution to this problem was to divide the labor: KOTRA was put in charge of trade relations with China; IPECK was placed in charge of investment there. However, this amplified rather than alleviated the confusion. Liaoning Province, for instance, was quick to take advantage of this bifurcation of the South Korean channel by contacting IPECK, in order to obtain a bargaining edge against Shandong, which was then in communication with KOTRA.[75]

CCPIT, China's designated window of communication with South Korea, was allegedly confused by this split in communication channels as well.[76] The Seoul government's interim solution was to give more authority to KOTRA, which was designated as the sole official representative for negotiating with China for the establishment of trade offices.[77] The problem was only resolved in November 1990, when it was decided that, beginning in January 1992, IPECK was to be merged into the Korean Institute of International Economic Policy (KIEP), another research arm of EPB, to engage exclusively in information gathering and data analysis.[78]

The timing was unmistakable, however. Since the Blue House and China's Small Group on South Korea had already set up a high-level secret channel via the Sunkyung Corporation, KOTRA could concentrate on its role as the implementer. Furthermore, once the trade office issue was resolved in November 1990, the Ministry of Foreign Affairs, which provided most of the staff of South Korea's trade office in Beijing, became a principal player, thereby dwarfing IPECK's importance as a go-between. Regarding elite politics, the influence of President Roh's relatives, such as Kim Bok-Dong and Park Chul-Un, was considerably curtailed and their informal networks for the northern diplomacy virtually decimated.[79]

## Operation East Sea: Facts and Lessons

The overall assessment of South Korea's northern diplomacy tends to be largely positive, as it considerably enhanced Seoul's legitimacy with respect to Pyongyang by normalizing relations with the Soviet Union, Eastern European countries and, most importantly, China. Nevertheless, it also suffered from certain flaws, the long-term implications of which are by no means insignificant. Concerning Hungary and the Soviet Union in particular, the stigma of "purchasing" diplomatic recognition in exchange for economic aid is hard to escape.

While there was no such "buying off" involved with regard to China, South Korea appears to have attached so much symbolic importance to the normalization with China that Seoul was willing to make unnecessary concessions just to obtain Beijing's diplomatic recognition.[80] The most serious problem was perhaps that once Roh made it clear that he wished to see the normalization take place and pay a state visit to China during his tenure as president, very little room was left for front-line negotiators to maneuver on their own.[81]

### On the Timing of Normalization

The timing of the normalization with China has long been considered controversial, although the normalization itself was generally viewed as both necessary and beneficial for South Korea. As described earlier, South Korea was more than explicit in expressing its willingness to normalize relations with China. Beginning in late 1991, China also became increasingly proactive in approaching the issue of normalization with South Korea. There were at least five reasons why a visible change took place in Beijing's position.[82] First, Seoul's successful normalization of relations with Eastern European countries and the Soviet Union in particular was a catalyst for China, which until that point had been merely sitting on the fence.[83] Second, under the tenet of "good neighborly policy" (*mulin youhao zhengce*), China was engaged in normalizing relations with many formerly antagonistic nations in Asia and elsewhere, namely Saudi Arabia (July 1990), Singapore (July 1990), Indonesia (August 1990), Brunei (September 1991), and Israel (January 1992). Third, the South Korea–Soviet

Union normalization made it impossible for Pyongyang to "play the Moscow card" on Beijing if China normalized relations with South Korea. Fourth, at around this same time, Taiwan embarked upon a path of "new diplomacy" (*xinwaijiao*), actively using "silver bullets" (that is, economic aid packages). Finally and perhaps most importantly, both South and North Korea joined the United Nations in September 1991, completely disentangling the "two Korea" issue from the "one China" principle once and for all.[84] As early as March 1990, Qian Qichen commented that the road to inter-Korean reunification did not have to be the same road as that for China's reunification with Taiwan.[85]

The first high-level meeting between foreign ministry officials of the two countries was held in Seoul, at the United Nation's Economic and Social Committee of the Asia Pacific (ESCAP) meeting in April 1991, between Lee Sang-Ok (South Korea's foreign minister) and Liu Huaqiu (China's deputy foreign minister). Minister Lee was highly supportive of the next ESCAP meeting, which was to be held in Beijing. Six months later, the foreign ministers of South Korea and China had their first ad hoc meeting at the United Nations, on October 2, 1991, one month after the two Koreas joined the United Nations.[86] Whereas this meeting did not explicitly touch on the issue of normalization per se, the second high-level meeting did, during Foreign Minister Qian Qichen's visit to Seoul to attend an Asia-Pacific Economic Cooperation (APEC) conference in November 1991, where Seoul worked out a win-win solution, facilitating the entry of China as a sovereign state and Taiwan and Hong Kong's entry as regional economies. During this visit, Qian was granted a meeting with President Roh, who allegedly revealed his wish for immediate normalization with China.[87]

South Korea had to wait another five months before the first meeting specifically convened to discuss normalization. During these months, China researched seriously how and on what terms to normalize relations with South Korea.[88] Certain signals nevertheless pointed to a clear trend toward diplomatic normalization.[89] In April 1992, Foreign Minister Lee Sang-Ok went to Beijing to attend another ESCAP meeting. During his stay, Lee was invited to the Diaoyutai, where he heard Foreign Minister Qian's proposal that the two countries open official negotiations for diplomatic normalization.[90] Foreign Minister Lee was afterward granted an audience with Premier Li Peng, who reportedly commented that "the constant flow of water eventually creates a canal" (*shuidao jucheng*), hinting that the timing was now ripe for normalization. Two specific conditions came with Beijing's proposal, however: (1) the Ministry of Foreign Affairs was to be the sole channel for official negotiations, and (2) the secrecy of the mission must be safeguarded at all times.[91]

The timing of the Seoul-Beijing normalization was the outcome of South Korea more or less following the terms set out by China, in addition to certain international conditions noted earlier. More specifically, President Roh's aspiration to fulfill his election pledge of completing the major goals of northern diplomacy during his tenure coincided with the upsurge of the Reformist drive in China, beginning with Deng Xiaoping's famous Southern Tour (*nanxun*) in early 1992. It appears that the Seoul government at the time did not fully understand the mindset held by its Chinese counterpart.[92]

### Operation East Sea

After South Korea expressed to China its official consent to normalization talks on April 24, 1992, Operation East Sea began by forming a taskforce. While Presidential National Security Advisor Kim Jong-Whee was designated as the chief representative for the negotiation, Ambassador Kwon Byung-Hyun, at the time affiliated with the Ministry of Foreign Affairs' research arm, the Institute of Foreign Affairs and National Security (IFANS), took charge of the actual negotiation process. For the sake of maintaining secrecy, Director in Charge of Chinese Affairs Shin Jung-Seung took a sick leave and was transferred to IFANS to work with Ambassador Kwon.[93]

During the three preliminary rounds and one main round of normalization talks between May 14 and July 29, a wide range of issues were discussed. Expectedly, the highest priority for China was the Taiwan issue. Beijing demanded that Seoul endorse the "one China" principle, sever diplomatic ties with Taipei, nullify all the treaties signed with Taiwan, and transfer all of Taipei's properties in South Korea to Beijing upon normalization. The Korean negotiators proposed in return that Beijing should not tilt toward Pyongyang, stop supplying North Korea with offensive weapons, and offer explicit support for the denuclearization of the Korean Peninsula.[94] These demands were rather abstract and not really substantive and immediate in nature and, potentially, China could always get around them if it wished to.

A close examination of these talks suggests that it was mostly the Chinese side that set the agenda and controlled the pace of negotiation. There is little evidence that leads one to believe that the South Korean negotiators took crucial initiatives or made any substantial gains from these negotiations. Overall, it was the South Korean side that conceded more to the Chinese. The bottom line for the South Korean negotiators was that the historic South Korea–China summit had to be realized during the tenure of President Roh, and unfortunately, their Chinese counterparts were well aware of that.[95]

During a June meeting, Ambassador Kwon, South Korea's chief negotiator, received instructions that President Roh Tae Woo wanted to visit China while still in office. After that, the South Korean negotiators became totally preoccupied with the task of realizing a summit between Seoul and Beijing. They even came up with an idea of holding a Roh-Jiang summit in July 1992, where diplomatic normalization would be announced. This radical proposal was quietly rejected by China.[96]

Seoul was willing to cast Taipei aside and nullify all treaties it had signed with it, as Seoul had for so long been eager to establish diplomatic relations with Beijing. It was even willing to turn over all of Taipei's South Korean properties to Beijing.[97] In return, however, South Korea gained little. There was no formal assurance that China would treat both Koreas equally. China discarded South Korea's demand for more attention to North Korea's nuclear program, on the basis of its noninterference principle. Seoul also failed to solicit an expression of regret or apology for Chinese intervention in the Korean War.[98] Furthermore, South Korea was unable to get China to agree on the establishment of a consulate general in Shenyang.[99] In sum, had it not been for President Roh's determination, it is not all clear why the normalization had to be agreed upon at that particular time.[100]

## The Taiwan Issue

As South Korea made improved relations with China a priority, Taiwan was left almost completely out of the picture. Both official complaints and informal messages of resentment from Taipei fell on deaf ears; the Seoul government was busy monitoring signals from Beijing.[101] Seoul's position on Taiwan appeared to oscillate somewhat in early 1991, in the immediate aftermath of the establishment of its trade office in Beijing. In March 1991, the South Korean government stipulated that it would not rush into diplomatic normalization with China. In June 1991, Seoul was quoted as saying that its relations with Taipei were important regardless of the rapprochement with Beijing. In early 1992, rumors circulated that diplomatic normalization with China would be deferred until 1993.[102]

In retrospect, all these were smokescreens, and Seoul's will to normalize relations with Beijing continued unabated. Two reasons account for Seoul's seeming oscillation on the Taiwan issue at the time. First, the rapidly expanding South Korea–Taiwan trade, which rose from US$0.5 billion in 1985 to US$3.1 billion in 1991, was one factor. The prospect of South Korea's taking part in various projects of Taiwan's Six-Year Economic Plan appeared attractive, although much of it was mere Taiwanese propaganda.[103] Second, around this time, the pro-Taiwan voice briefly gained strength in South Korea, and Taipei renewed its lobbying efforts, sending envoys to Korea and inviting Korean officials and scholars to Taiwan.[104]

Given that diplomatic normalization eventually occurred on August 24, 1992, the Seoul government was simply distracting popular attention away from the ongoing negotiations with China.[105] Seoul's decision to normalize relations with China was certainly the right move, as both Washington and Tokyo—South Korea's key allies—had already done so as early as two decades before. Yet the timing and process of normalization taught Seoul some valuable lessons. The issue of timing has already been discussed in connection with President Roh's personal determination and its adverse effect on South Korea's diplomacy.

The way Seoul handled the issues related to Taipei also provides abundant food for thought. While secrecy was the key to the sensitive negotiations for the normalization between South Korea and China, Seoul could have been more sophisticated about it. Most importantly, the effort the South Korean government put into attempting to attain a genuine understanding from Taiwan concerning the inevitability of normalization with China was no match for the strenuous effort China made to help North Korea "save face."[106] China's foreign minister, Qian Qichen, went to Pyongyang on July 15, 1992, and informed Kim Il Sung of the imminent normalization with South Korea. Seoul was apparently acting more secretively than Beijing.[107]

Considering that Taiwan was the first country to recognize the Republic of Korea in January 1949 and that South Korea and Taiwan had also maintained ideological and political solidarity on a par with an alliance for over forty years, Seoul should have done more to mitigate the resentment Taipei might harbor. Prior to their normalizing relations with China, the United States, Japan, and Saudi Arabia all sent special envoys to obtain Taiwan's understanding. South Africa even sent its ministers of foreign affairs and defense to explain the inevitability of normalizing relations with China. For the sake of safeguarding secrecy, Seoul chose not to do what it should have done.[108]

When Chiang Yen-shih, secretary-general to President Lee Teng-hui, visited Seoul as a special envoy on May 6, 1992, President Roh reportedly said, "South Korea will never do away with its old friend."[109] While the South Korean government had originally planned to notify Taipei of the normalization date one week prior to the event, it eventually ended up giving only a two-day notice.[110] According to Chin Shu-chi, Taipei's ambassador to Seoul at the time, Taiwan was notified at five in the afternoon on Friday and the normalization was to take place the following Monday moring.[111] The main reason was that Seoul had to keep Taiwan from selling its embassy buildings and other properties. If the South Korean government had not been pressed for time in pushing for the normalization with China, it could have allowed Taiwan to keep some of its properties, as the United States and Saudi Arabia had so graciously done.[112]

Counterarguments are available from the South Korean side. According to interviewees deeply involved in Operation East Sea at the time, Seoul's overall rationale was that, unlike China's normalization with Japan and the United States during the 1970s, Sino–South Korean normalization would do much less strategic harm to Taiwan, which was pushing for its own rapprochement with the mainland. If the costs had indeed been perceived to be that high by Taipei, then why, according to these interviewees, did Taiwan devote so little effort to keeping South Korea from normalizing relations with China? Despite Seoul's virtually open campaign to improve relations with Beijing, Taipei had not realized the seriousness of the problem until they assigned Chin Shu-chi, former deputy foreign minister, to be the ambassador to Seoul in 1992. Seoul's perception at the time was that Taiwan had taken its relations with South Korea for granted.[113]

The residue from the unpleasant experience of severing diplomatic ties persisted much longer in Taipei's subsequent handling of its relations with Seoul than was the case for many other countries. It took over eleven months from the severing of diplomatic ties before Seoul and Taipei agreed in Osaka to exchange nongovernmental offices. It should be noted, however, that South Korea did try its best to push China to allow Seoul to open the highest possible level of nongovernmental office in Taiwan—the Korean Mission in Taipei (*daibiaochu*)—rather than opening an opaque label such as "Cultural and Economic Office."[114] Yet for over a decade, South Korea's airlines were not permitted to fly to Taiwan. The way the Taiwan issue was handled in Seoul's pursuit of normalization with Beijing should be remembered, as it can offer useful lessons for South Korea's future diplomacy.

# 7

## Beyond Normalization

South Korea and China in the Post–Cold War Era

With the normalization of relations on August 24, 1992, South Korea–China bilateralism reached a point where sustaining stable long-term cooperation was both necessary and crucial. Important to note is that the Sino–South Korean diplomatic normalization materialized at a time when the cold war structure was being dismantled around the globe and, therefore, it introduced a key uncertainty into the international relations of Northeast Asia. This chapter, focusing on Seoul-Beijing relations of the post–cold war era, asks three questions: (1) What characterized the regional dynamics of Northeast Asia during this period? (2) How did South Korea–China economic dynamism play out in the postnormalization era? and (3) How can the potential for strategic and diplomatic compatibility between Seoul and Beijing be assessed?

## Post–Cold War Northeast Asia in Flux

Since the early 1990s, as the effects of the demise of the cold war were strongly felt in the region, Northeast Asia had been plunged into a volatile state. During the 1990s, in the wake of global strategic reconfiguration, the Northeast Asian region possessed the following characteristics: (1) structural uncertainties concerning the regional system under formation, (2) the continuing dominance of bilateralism along with some signs of multilateralism, (3) the end of ideology and the competition for primacy between economics and politics, and (4) the burgeoning of new ties and flexible choices hitherto deemed inconceivable or unthinkable.

### Polyarchy or Unipolarity?

A predominant projection for the post–cold war era was initially that "the sudden end of the conflict has, not surprisingly, given rise to a situation for which it is difficult to find a real precedent."[1] In stark contrast, Northeast Asia was in fact witnessing a gradual reversion to a familiar system of polyarchy quite reminiscent of the one that had existed during the late nineteenth and early twentieth centuries.[2] One notable difference between the two polyarchies, of course, was that China in the contemporary system was no longer the "sick man of the East."

The strategic matrix of Northeast Asia has been multipolar since the Sino-Soviet rupture in the early 1960s. While a tripolar structure remained largely intact even after the end of the cold war, the precise nature of this multipolarity was rather difficult to define, as its dynamics have continued to evolve. During the 1990s, it increasingly resembled a *ménage à trois*, a relationship of amity among the United States, Russia, and China—if not a quadrangular dynamic including Japan.[3] If it had indeed been a *ménage à trois*, the problem of that configuration was that the lack of a clear and present danger deprived the strategic triangle of a stable raison d'être.[4] While the Chinese and Russian stances since the September 11, 2001, tragedy have more converged toward than diverged from the stance of the United States, their durability remains uncertain. The strategic configuration of the Northeast Asian region, in tandem with evolving U.S.-China dynamics, is thus still very much in flux.[5]

The perception of a potentially "militarist" Japan constitutes another variable for the regional dynamics. As one analyst put it, "the mission of Japan's Self-Defense Forces to defend homeland and contiguous territorial waters is giving way to Japanese regional air and maritime power projection capabilities to wage limited offensive military strikes."[6] In the wake of the War on Terrorism and the second Gulf War, the overall trend is certainly in favor of Japan's increasingly strengthened military capabilities under tacit promotion by the United States.[7]

## The Primacy of Bilateralism

In Northeast Asia, bilateralism has continued to dominate during the period concerned. In marked contrast with Europe and Southeast Asia, Northeast Asia is a region that still lacks a regional identity or consciousness. Historically, all the formal security arrangements in the region have been bilateral in nature, such as the U.S.-Japan, U.S.–South Korea, U.S.-Taiwan, Soviet–North Korean, and Sino–North Korean alliances.[8] Whereas Southeast Asia (the Association of Southeast Asian Nations, or ASEAN), South Asia (the South Asia Association for Regional Cooperation, or SAARC), and the Southwest Pacific and Oceania (the South Pacific Forum, or SPF) possess intraregional organizations, Northeast Asia is virtually devoid of a meaningful equivalent.[9]

With a few exceptions, economic interactions in the region have also been mostly dyadic. The efforts toward the Pacific Economic Cooperation Council (PECC) and Asia-Pacific Economic Cooperation (APEC) encompassed a far broader scope than Northeast Asia per se. The idea of the "Northeast Asian Economic Sphere" (*Dongbeiya jingjiquan*) espoused by China was short-lived, although the concept of "Greater China" had a slightly longer life span.[10] While China, Japan, and Korea have separately signed free-trade agreements with ASEAN, no equivalent is yet available within Northeast Asia. The earlier assessment that the Northeast Asian region would most likely remain as a loose network of bilateral ties still seems valid at the dawn of the twenty-first century, although more efforts are certainly being made in the direction of promoting economic multilateralism.[11]

In retrospect, in Northeast Asia, recognizing the potential benefits of multilateral cooperation was one thing, and realizing them, quite another.[12] In the absence of a common perceived threat or a well-defined platform of common interests, the ever-expanding economic exchanges—especially those between South Korea and China and across the Taiwan Strait—are reinforcing rather than mitigating the predominantly bilateral nature of intraregional interactions in Northeast Asia.[13]

## Economics in Command Over Politics?

A gradual shift in the focus from military-strategic issues to economic ones is widely said to constitute another salient trend of the post–cold war era. Unlike security issues, economic cooperation was generally deemed less risky and more beneficial due to the low cost involved in the case of betrayal and the heightened willingness to reciprocate.[14] The shift from a military strategy to a trading strategy was manifest in the perceptions and behavior of China and Russia. Deng Xiaoping's "opening" of China strictly followed this trading strategy, and Yeltsin's failed reform measures were also directed at reversing the vicious cycle of internal decline caused by external overexpansion.[15] As the Soviet threat diminished considerably during much of the 1980s and evaporated in the early 1990s, a strategic rationale for Sino-U.S. relations also faded significantly.

This is not to suggest that the trading strategy is adhered to as the only rule of the game in Northeast Asia. In the case of U.S.-China relations, strategic and Taiwan issues dominated the agenda during the 1980s, and economic and human rights issues surged in much of the 1990s.[16] So far as the reunification is concerned, however, China has effectively demonstrated that it is more than willing to forego the trading strategy vis-à-vis Taiwan.[17] As the U.S.-led war on terrorism and the North Korean nuclear conundrum highlight, the military strategy and proliferation of weapons of mass destruction are still crucial factors in the regional dynamics of Northeast Asia.

## New Bilateralism and Flexible Choices

With the reduction of tension and antipathy, a wide range of opportunities for new bilateralism was generated for the region. Whereas the cold war structure in Northeast Asia had been characterized by a sort of "northern triangle" of the Soviet Union, China, and North Korea poised against the asymmetrical but largely amicable alliances among the United States, Japan, and South Korea, a series of new developments—most notably, Sino-Soviet détente, South Korea's diplomatic normalization with both Russia and China, and improved inter-Korean relations—facilitated crucial changes in the regional dynamics. Rigid security ties were considerably loosened and flexible choices loomed large.

One popular modus operandi was that adversaries initially sought to improve their relationships by way of engaging in economic cooperation, then by expanding nongovernmental relations across the board, and eventually by normalizing their diplomatic relations. South Korea's foreign-policy behavior during the 1980s and early 1990s—the "northern policy" or *Nordpolitik*—epitomized such an evolutionary process of rapprochement.[18] The new bilateralism was not monopolized by South Korea, however. China took full advantage of the changing regional atmosphere by improving relations with Russia, Vietnam, Singapore, Israel, Indonesia, South Africa, and even Taiwan. Of late, North Korea also appears to be emulating some of these experiences.

## Postnormalization Sino–South Korean Relations: Compatibility, Competition, and Cooperation

Despite the volatile nature of the regional strategic environment, economics continued to dominate South Korea–China relations during the 1990s. The diplomatic normalization in 1992 provided a further impetus for the burgeoning economic cooperation. The unabated increase in trade and investment was highly conducive to the sustenance of the bilateral relationship well beyond normalization. As is usually the case with complex interdependence, however, new tensions and conflicts were also generated, as best demonstrated by the Sino–South Korean "garlic war" in the summer of 2000.[19]

### South Korea–China Trade

In 1993, one year after normalization, China had already become South Korea's third-largest trading partner, after the United States and Japan. In 2001, China became the number-two destination for South Korean exports. In 2003, China (excluding Hong Kong and Macao) surpassed the United States as South Korea's top export market and in 2004, China replaced the United States as South Korea's top trading partner. The share of China trade in South Korea's total trade rose from 2.8 percent in 1990 to 7.7 percent in 1996, 10.8 percent in 2001, and 16.6 percent in 2004.[20] As table 7.1 illustrates, Sino–South Korean trade leapt from US$6.4 billion in 1992 to US$79 billion in 2004. Furthermore, whereas China had scored more surpluses prior to normalization, South Korea reaped huge successive surpluses from 1993 through 2004.[21]

Table 7.2 lists South Korea's ten top items of export to China for 1992 and 2001. The share of the top-ten items in total exports declined from 83.2 percent in 1992 to 74.7 percent in 2001, indicating a more diversity in South Korean exports to China. The total number of South Korean export items also rose from 750 in 1992 to 1,030 in 2001. Whereas the overall structure of South Korea's exports to China seemed largely unchanged, that of South Korea's imports from China was in important transition (compare with table 5.1). Unlike in 1992, the increased importance of industrial machinery and electronic devices from China was evident in 2001. That is, China was no longer simply exporting primary products and raw materials to South Korea.

TABLE 7.1 South Korea–China Trade After Normalization (in US$ millions)

| YEAR | TOTAL | EXPORT TO CHINA | IMPORT FROM CHINA | BALANCE |
|------|-------|-----------------|-------------------|---------|
| 1992 | 6,380 | 2,650 | 3,730 | −1,080 |
| 1993 | 9,080 | 5,150 | 3,930 | 1,220 |
| 1994 | 11,660 | 6,200 | 5,460 | 740 |
| 1995 | 16,540 | 9,140 | 7,400 | 1,740 |
| 1996 | 19,920 | 11,380 | 8,540 | 2,840 |
| 1997 | 23,690 | 13,570 | 10,120 | 3,450 |
| 1998 | 18,420 | 11,940 | 6,480 | 5,460 |
| 1999 | 22,560 | 13,690 | 8,870 | 4,820 |
| 2000 | 31,250 | 18,450 | 12,800 | 5,650 |
| 2001 | 31,490 | 18,190 | 13,300 | 4,890 |
| 2002 | 41,152 | 23,753 | 17,399 | 6,354 |
| 2003 | 57,019 | 35,110 | 21,909 | 13,201 |
| 2004 | 79,349 | 49,771 | 29,578 | 20,193 |

Source: *Hanjung sugyo sipjunyon eui gyungje songgwa wa munjejom* [The economic accomplishments and problems on the tenth anniversary of Korea's normalization with China] (Seoul: KOTRA, August 2002), 4. The data on 2002 through 2004 is from http://www.mocie.go.kr (last accessed on January 18, 2006).

TABLE 7.2 South Korea's Ten Top Export Items, 1992 and 2001 (% of Total Exports)

| RANK | 1992 | 2001 |
|---|---|---|
| 1 | Steel products (30.2) | Petrochemical products (18.3) |
| 2 | Petrochemical products (17.3) | Mineral raw materials (9.2) |
| 3 | Fabrics (10.1) | Electronic parts (8.9) |
| 4 | Leather/fur products (5.4) | Fabrics (8.8) |
| 5 | Textile raw materials (4.9) | Industrial electronics (7.9) |
| 6 | Industrial machinery (4.1) | Steel products (7.6) |
| 7 | Paper products (3.4) | Leather/fur products (3.7) |
| 8 | Mineral raw materials (3.1) | Home appliances (3.7) |
| 9 | Electronic parts (2.6) | Industrial machinery (3.4) |
| 10 | Chemical products (2.1) | Chemical products (3.2) |
| Total Percent of All Exports | 83.2 | 74.7 |

Source: *Hanjung sugyo sipjunyon eui gyungje songgwa wa munjejom* [The economic accomplishments and problems on the tenth anniversary of Korea's normalization with China] (Seoul: KOTRA, August 2002), 7.

While intraindustry trade still remains important, the revealed comparative advantage (RCA) of South Korea's export items has steadily declined over the years. For instance, none of South Korea's five top export items was considered "highly competitive" when compared to the Chinese products in the same category.[22] The problem of product competitiveness was already manifested in overseas markets during the early 1990s. South Korea's share in the American market declined from 3.7 percent in 1990 to 3.5 percent in 1991, while China's share rose from 3.1 percent to 3.9 percent during the same period.[23] The trend has continued well into the twenty-first century. Whereas South Korea's share in the American market has declined from 3.1 percent in 1999 to 2.8 percent in 2003, China's has risen from 8 percent in 1999 to 11 percent in 2003.[24]

Beginning in the late 1990s, South Korea witnessed a declining share in the China market as well. A close look at the data, as table 7.3 demonstrates, suggests that China's rapidly increasing imports from itself—mainly in the forms of re-exports from Hong Kong and overseas reprocessing by Chinese firms—has been the main cause. This, again, indicates the generally enhanced competitiveness of Chinese products when compared to South Korean goods. As

TABLE 7.3  Percentage of Exports to the China Market

|              | 1998 | 1999 | 2000 | 2001 |
|--------------|------|------|------|------|
| Japan        | 20.2 | 20.4 | 18.5 | 17.6 |
| Taiwan       | 12.1 | 11.8 | 11.3 | 11.2 |
| United States| 11.9 | 11.8 | 9.9  | 10.8 |
| South Korea  | 10.7 | 10.4 | 10.3 | 9.6  |
| Germany      | 5.0  | 5.0  | 4.6  | 5.6  |
| China        | 2.2  | 2.5  | 3.2  | 3.6  |

Source: *Hanjung sugyo sipjunyon eui gyungje songgwa wa munjejom* [The economic accomplishments and problems on the tenth anniversary of Korea's normalization with China] (Seoul: KOTRA, August 2002), 13.

of 2001, China boasted 753 global number-one products, while the figure for South Korea was only sixty-nine.[25] Furthermore, in 2004, concerning ninety-nine key technologies, the gap between South Korea and China was estimated to be only 2.2 years and shortening.[26]

Under these circumstances, where many of South Korea's key export items have been losing out to Chinese goods in the American, Japanese, and European markets, the South Korean business community became increasingly concerned with "boomerang effects." They were alarmed by the possibility that technology transfers made through their direct investment in China might eventually come back to hurt them. The Korean media even coined a new term, "Sinophobia" (*gongjungjeung*). In retrospect, however, technological concerns were not a dominant constraint on investment decisions, as many increasingly came to consider China as their future production base as well as their consumer market.[27]

## South Korea–China Investment

Investment is another pillar of Sino–South Korean economic bilateralism. As table 7.4 shows, the impact of normalization was clearly felt in 1992 and after. In 1993, South Korea was the tenth-largest investor in China.[28] By 1995, China became the top recipient of South Korea's foreign investment. In 1996, 46 percent of South Korea's total foreign investment was poured into China.[29] While negative growth was recorded for 1997 through 1999, due to the financial crisis that had engulfed East Asia, "China fever" soon returned to South Korean investors.[30] In 2002, South Korea's investment in China surpassed its investment in the United States, and in 2003, South Korea became the third-largest investor in China.[31] By 2004, South Korea's cumulative investment in China (US$17.9 billion) for the first time outnumbered South Korea's investment in the United States (US$17.1 billion).

The average per project size of South Korean investment in China increased, though only marginally, from US$616,000 in 1991 to US$977,000 in 2003. This figure was much lower than the average size of South Korean investment in the United States and Southeast Asia in 1993—US$2.6 and US$1.6 million, respectively.[32] For the period of 1992 to 2002, the average South Korean invest-

TABLE 7.4  South Korea's Investment in China, 1991–2004

| YEAR | NUMBER OF PROJECTS | INVESTMENT AMOUNT (IN US$ MILLIONS) |
|---|---|---|
| 1991 | 69 | 42.5 |
| 1992 | 170 | 141.1 |
| 1993 | 381 | 263.7 |
| 1994 | 841 | 634.5 |
| 1995 | 751 | 841.8 |
| 1996 | 738 | 921.6 |
| 1997 | 631 | 738.7 |
| 1998 | 262 | 695.1 |
| 1999 | 459 | 365.3 |
| 2000 | 777 | 710.3 |
| 2001 | 1,047 | 635.4 |
| 2002 | 1,381 | 1,019.5 |
| 2003 | 1,679 | 1,642.4 |
| 2004 | 2,149 | 2,290.7 |
| Total | 13,373 | 13,278.2 |

Notes: The data—both in number and amount—show investments that actually materialized. The total numbers do not add up precisely, due to investment withdrawals and the inclusion of pre-1991 figures.

Source: Data from the Korea Export and Import Bank, at http://www.koreaexim.go.kr/kr/oeis/m03/s01-0401.jsp (last accessed on January 23, 2006).

ment per project was US$880,000, while the average South Korean FDI per project was US$2.4 million.[33] However, in recent years—particularly since 2002—South Korean investment in China has involved more capital, as large corporations and their parts manufacturers have relocated to China. In 2004, the average size of South Korean investment per project was US$1.1 million.

The major destinations of South Korea's investment in China have also been changing over the years. While Shandong and the northeastern provinces (Heilongjiang, Jilin, and Liaoning) were the most popular up until the mid-1990s, South Korean investors' preference has been shifting toward Jiangsu, Shanghai, Beijing, Tianjin, Zhejiang, and Guangdong. Although Shandong still remains the most important, its share in South Korea's total investment in China fell from 38 percent in 2000 to 24 percent in 2005.[34] In terms of actually committed investment, Shandong and the three northeastern provinces accounted for 58 percent of South Korea's total in 1992, which declined to 33 percent in 2005. On the other hand, the share of Shanghai, Guangdong, Jiangsu, and Zhejiang rose from 14 percent to 34 percent in the same years.[35]

While the investment relationship had been mostly unidirectional up to the early 1990s, China also began to invest in South Korea.[36] China's investment in South Korea from 1988 to 1992 entailed only US$1.5 million, in eight projects. From 1993 to 1996, however, a total of 166 new projects were committed by China, with investments worth US$32.5 million.[37] China's investment has grown in both number and size since 1998, as well. China's accumulated total investment in South Korea by the end of 2004 was US$3,101 million, involving over 472 projects.[38]

## Other Postnormalization Developments

With the normalization of relations and the establishment of embassies, all possible formal channels of communication between Beijing and Seoul were set up. Accordingly, the relative importance of South Korea's consulate general in Hong Kong declined significantly over time, with South Korea opening a consulate general in Guangzhou (2001), in addition to Shanghai (1993) and Qingdao (1994). In 1994, Seoul and Beijing exchanged military attachés. In March 1999, after a long lapse, South Korea finally established its consular office in Shenyang, which was later upgraded to a consulate general in 2003. In 2005, another consulate general opened in Chengdu of Sichuan.[39]

In addition to the ever-expanding trade and investment, the number of people traveling across the Yellow Sea has increased considerably. By 2004, thirteen routes were opened for car-ferry transportation across the Yellow Sea.[40] The frequency of direct maritime container service increased, as did air transportation, with over 380 weekly flights in 2004.[41] China also relaxed its regulation over outbound tourism to South Korea. On June 2, 1998, residents of the four

TABLE 7.5  Visitor Exchanges Between South Korea and China (in 1,000s of people)

|  | KOREAN VISITORS | CHINESE VISITORS | TOTAL |
|---|---|---|---|
| 1988 | 6 | 3 | 9 |
| 1990 | 32 | 26 | 58 |
| 1993 | 112 | 40 | 152 |
| 1995 | 407 | 81 | 488 |
| 1996 | 530 | 104 | 634 |
| 1999 | 820 | 310 | 1,120 |
| 2001 | 1,290 | 480 | 1,770 |
| 2003 | 1,561 | 513 | 2,074 |
| 2004 | 2,850 | 630 | 3,480 |

Sources: Hanguk gyungje sinmun [Korea Economic Daily], October 21, 1991; Munhwa Ilbo [Munhwa Daily], February 20, 1997; Chosun Ilbo [Chosun Daily], August 25, 1992, August 24, 1997, and January 5, 2003; and http:// www.knto.or.kr (last accessed on January 22, 2006).

centrally administered municipalities (Beijing, Shanghai, Tianjin, and Chong-qing) and five eastern provinces were allowed on group tours to South Korea.[42]

The number of visitors between South Korea and China increased at a very rapid pace. As table 7.5 demonstrates, the total number of visitors between the two countries surged from 9,000 in 1988 to 3.5 million in 2004. In 2005, over 250,000 South Koreans were long-term residents in China.[43] The number of Chinese residents in South Korea also increased quickly. The Chinese share in the total number of alien long-term residents in South Korea rose from 11,264 (12.3 percent) in 1995, to 30,836 (18.7 percent) in 1997, and to 153,930 (30.6 percent) in 2000.[44] The increase also generated the thorny problem of Korean-Chinese illegal residents, who settled without legal permission from the Seoul government. As of April 2000, 62 percent of Korean-Chinese long-term residents were estimated to be illegal.[45]

## Beyond Economics: Strategic Compatibility?

From Seoul's viewpoint, the three most important yet uncertain variables in the post–cold war regional dynamics of Northeast Asia are China, Japan, and North Korea.[46] The main focus here is on Japan, North Korea, and their ramifications for South Korea–China relations. South Korea's perceptions and choices regarding the future role of China are discussed in chapter 9.

## Cooperation Over "Japan's Rise"?

Many strategic analysts have argued for some time that Japan's military capabilities have already gone well beyond that of merely defending the Japanese homeland and contiguous territorial waters. While the projections of an era of "Pax Nipponica" have long lost their audience, Japan's increasing military involvement overseas—mostly under the banner of the United Nations and the auspices of the United States—has often generated serious concern among its neighbors. From South Korea's viewpoint, with the fourth-most-powerful navy and the third-largest defense spending in the world, Japan has become a formidable military presence.[47]

Both historical memories and contemporary frictions underlie South Korea's perceived Japanese threat. While psychological bitterness toward Japan and perceptions of threat are to a considerable extent shared between South Korea and China, for South Korea, the threat of Japan may be more real and serious than for China, which is larger and a nuclear power. According to a multinational survey carried out in 1996, only 10 percent of the South Korean respondents and 23 percent of the Chinese respondents replied that Japan had been sincerely repentant of its militarist past, and 78 and 63 percent of the South Korean and Chinese respondents, respectively, hoped South Korean–Chinese strategic relations would improve in the future.[48]

The fundamental question for Seoul concerns how to protect South Korea's vital security interests vis-à-vis Japan given circumstances where Washington has been assigning an increasingly expanded military-strategic role to Tokyo regardless of how such a move would be viewed by Seoul.[49] Regarding Japan, there appears to exist a huge perceptual gap between the United States on the one hand and South Korea and China on the other. According to two nationwide surveys conducted in South Korea in 1995 and 1997, Japan was viewed as the nation most threatening to South Korea's security interests.[50] However, in stark contrast, Americans have maintained much more favorable perceptions of Japan, which they regard as quite unique among Asian countries.[51] According to a survey conducted in 1999, 46 percent of the American general public and 62 percent of the "elite" (represented by the Luce Foundation Fellows) were in favor of Japan's rearmament.[52] According to two nationwide surveys in 1997 and 2000, however, over 90 percent of the South Korean general public responded that preventing Japan's militarism should be Seoul's top foreign-policy priority.[53]

While South Korea has managed to sustain an amicable official relationship with Japan under the auspices of the United States, security concerns have always lurked in the background.[54] While there appear to be some shared perceptions between China and South Korea (and North Korea, for that matter) of the latent threat Japan may pose, the possibility of an anti-Japan "united front" remains highly unlikely under the current circumstances.[55] In the long run, however, South Korea, which has been increasingly eager to achieve a status as partner—as opposed to client—in its security relationship with the United States, even by shouldering huge defense burdens, may seek to add a meaningful security dimension to the already burgeoning Sino–South Korean bilateralism.[56] China, which has begun to view the United States as unshackling Japan militarily, may also develop room for such ideas.[57]

What merits our attention in this regard is the gradual expansion of military ties between the two countries. The establishment of military attaches in Beijing (December 1993) and Seoul (April 1994) was followed by bilateral exchanges of military personnel within the context of sports and educational exchanges. Later, high-level South Korean military officers paid low-profile visits to China—though these visits were not always reciprocated. As time went on, what ranks these visiting officers held tended to get higher. For instance, in May 1997, General Park Yong-Ok, assistant minister of defense for policy planning, visited China; he was soon followed by Lee Jeong-Lin, deputy minister of defense, in November 1997.[58]

In August 1999, Cho Sung-Tae, South Korea's defense minister, for the first time met with Chi Haotian, the Chinese defense minister, in Beijing, and the latter reciprocated the visit in January 2000. In October 2001, a South Korean naval vessel made a port call in Shanghai and in May 2002, a Chinese naval ship visited Inchon. Again in September 2005, South Korea's frigates visited Zhanjiang. While the overall extent of reciprocity has not been ideal (it currently stands at the ratio of three South Korean delegations to one Chinese), the gradual but steady expansion of military-to-military cooperation between Seoul and Beijing has been indicative of the "comprehensive cooperative partnership" (*quanmian hezuoxing huoban guanxi*) being forged between the two countries.[59]

## Cooperation Over the North Korean Nuclear Conundrum

Unlike the former Soviet Union, which had expanded its spheres of influence in every corner of the world, China's strategic aspirations have to date been more modest and limited. Not only has China's role of representing the entire Third World faded over the years, but the rise of East Asia has also induced Chinese foreign policy to concentrate more on that dynamic region.[60]

The United States as a global power and China as an Asian power, therefore, share several nexuses. Other than Taiwan, the Korean issue has been most salient—particularly North Korea's clandestine nuclear programs.

If there were an Asian country that has made more headlines than China since the early 1990s, it would certainly be North Korea. North Korea's refusal to allow special inspections by the International Atomic Energy Agency (IAEA) and the subsequent withdrawal from the Non-Proliferation Treaty (NPT) in 1993 generated enormous concern in the international community.[61] Whether it was for Pyongyang's bargaining leverage vis-à-vis the United States in eliciting economic aid and talks on normalization or for a "strategic equalizer," North Korea's nuclear weapons program would be highly destabilizing. Were North Korea to enter the exclusive nuclear club, Japan would perhaps be the first to follow. If this took place, the United States might find it difficult to dissuade South Korea from going nuclear.[62] Reactive proliferation as such would then have highly adverse effects on overall strategic balance and economic cooperation in Northeast Asia.

Three options were considered by the United States during the crisis of 1993 and 1994: military strikes, economic sanctions, and diplomatic negotiations. In order for the United Nations to engage in military action against North Korea's nuclear facilities, China's endorsement at the Security Council was a prerequisite. Given China's "special" relationship with North Korea, such an endorsement was highly unlikely. Furthermore, how China would respond to a military sanction unilaterally carried out by the United States remained uncertain.[63] While the United States could have resorted to a military strike without the UN banner—an option that was seriously considered by Washington—such action would have surely vitiated all the economic accomplishments South Korea had made. Furthermore, throughout the process of assessing the military option, Seoul was apparently not consulted very closely.[64]

Generally speaking, a country like North Korea would be highly vulnerable to economic sanctions, due to its extremely weak economy and its heavy dependence on one or two countries. Given that 28 percent of Pyongyang's trade was then conducted with Beijing, and China's provision of food and energy for North Korea was on highly preferential terms, no economic sanctions would work properly without Beijing's cooperation. But China was consistent in opposing any sanctions against North Korea. Given that, cutting off the financial pipeline from the overseas Koreans in Japan—a yearly remittance of eighty billion yen—would be only partially effective.[65] In the end, owing to timely mediation by Jimmy Carter, the diplomatic option was adopted, which led to the Agreed Framework in Geneva in November 1994.

Since China had long considered the NPT as discriminatory and unfair and had suffered dearly from America's nuclear blackmail during the Korean War,

Beijing might have been tacitly sympathetic to those with aspirations of nuclear self-reliance.[66] China had also initially regarded the problem fundamentally as a bilateral issue between Pyongyang and Washington, dissociating itself from the American view that it was a regional problem.[67]

China's ambivalence was manifested in its consistent opposition to any measure of sanctions on the one hand and its conspicuous abstention at the International Atomic Energy Agency (IAEA) and the United Nations meetings on the other, where warnings to Pyongyang were meted out. On the other hand, while stressing its "limited" capacity, Beijing was nevertheless involved in dissuading Pyongyang from going nuclear by sending several high-level envoys. In ambassadorial talks with the United States and Japan, Beijing reportedly conveyed to South Korea the message that if the threats of military and economic sanctions were withdrawn, China would do more to resolve the problem.[68] To what extent China's efforts proved successful in pressuring North Korea to forego its nuclear program in 1994 is difficult to assess, however.[69]

In retrospect, China did not abandon its longtime ally for the sake of satisfying the United States and its new partner South Korea. In a sense, it was a game that China could not lose in any event. It appeared as if Beijing had done its due share of protecting Pyongyang and, at the same time, had successfully looked like a fair mediator. And when Beijing's efforts did not produce visible effects, China could always point to the lack of trust between the United States and North Korea and to the limited nature of its capacity as a convenient justification.

Eight years later, in the fall of 2002, many observers had a strong sense of deja vu when North Korea claimed that it was "entitled to have nuclear programs" and subsequently withdrew from the NPT in December 2002. A considerable number of similarities exist between the events of 1993 and 2002, including the sequence of Pyongyang's actions and Washington's concern over a two-front conflict (the other being Iraq). This time around, however, China's calculus and response appeared somewhat different. Above all, it did not call for noninterference by other powers. Instead, Beijing took the position that North Korea's nuclear program had become an international concern.

If China had mostly sat on the fence during the first crisis, it was mainly because Beijing had not been convinced that Pyongyang had then possessed the pertinent technologies. Not surprisingly, China even vetoed a UN condemnation of North Korea's nuclear program.[70] Yet that was happening precisely when China's relations with North Korea had begun to cool significantly, China's continued economic assistance to North Korea notwithstanding. China's gradual "socialization" with the international community during the 1990s also made South Korea increasingly more attractive relative to North Korea, although that did not induce China to abandon North Korea's core interests.[71]

In the second nuclear crisis, initially China did not accept America's assessment of North Korea's progress on its nuclear weapons program.[72] Chinese officials repeated their standard position that China possessed only limited influence over North Korea and that the United States should do more to resolve the problem.[73] At the same time, however, it should be noted that China appeared to enjoy the enormous attention the world was paying to its potential role in the looming crisis.[74]

China's stance made a crucial about-face in early 2003, roughly in late February. It was around this time that Beijing became more receptive to the American intelligence assessments of North Korea's nuclear programs.[75] The change was also facilitated by China's perception that North Korea's relationship with the United States was heading toward a clash that would be disastrous for China. Not only did the Chinese express grave concerns about the increasingly hostile exchanges between Washington and Pyongyang, but they were also extremely alarmed by the close encounter between North Korean MIG fighters and an American RC-135S reconnaissance plane on March 2.[76]

In February, China's deputy foreign minister, Wang Yi, went to Pyongyang and reportedly made a straightforward plea for Pyongyang to terminate immediately its nuclear provocation. Again in March, Qian Qichen, China's foreign-policy giant, flew to Pyongyang to demand that North Korea stop its nuclear brinkmanship.[77] In stark contrast with its response during the first crisis, this time around, Beijing chose to support a resolution put forward by the IAEA in January 2003, which demanded an immediate termination of Pyongyang's nuclear weapons programs. Furthermore, China even voted in favor of referring the North Korean case to the UN Security Council for discussion in February 2003.[78]

More critical signs came in the subsequent months. In late February, oil pipelines from China to North Korea were shut down for almost three days, although this unprecedented incident was officially attributed to "technical difficulties."[79] Shortly afterward, when China offered to host a three-party talk in Beijing to provide a venue for direct dialogue between Washington and Pyongyang, North Korea did not hesitate to accept the invitation.[80] In August, China again showed off its importance in the proceedings, by hosting the six-party talk in Beijing where, for the first time, the United States, China, Japan, Russia, and the two Koreas gathered to exchange views. Once again, China emerged as a crucial mediator for the region, significantly boosting its image as a "responsible great power."[81]

China's "constructive role" in managing the North Korean nuclear problem does not seem to have been an outcome of Sino–South Korean coordination. It had more to do with its own assessments of the North Korean problem and its potential effects on the region, as well as with the newly announced tenet of "great-power diplomacy with responsibilities" (*fuzeren de daguo waijiao*). Nevertheless, Beijing's evolving positions on Pyongyang—and not just those regarding its nuclear aspirations—are bound to create more room for diplomatic coordination between China and South Korea.[82] In fact, South Korean and Chinese officials often stated that no discernible differences existed between themselves as far as the North Korean nuclear issue was concerned.

## The South Korean Variable: Divided Allegiance?

While North Korea's nuclear problem was highly visible, the South Korean variable remained largely opaque. Seoul's strenuous efforts to normalize relations with Moscow and Beijing were fundamentally directed at first isolating Pyongyang and then bringing it to the negotiation table. Such efforts on the part of Seoul, especially for the rapprochement with China, were conducted fairly independently of American direction.[83]

What led Seoul to seek room for a more independent foreign policy?[84] In strategic terms, Seoul's desire to reduce its perpetual dependence on the United States played a crucial role, given that America's changing threat perceptions had been the sole determinant of its defense commitments regardless of South Korea's position.[85] South Korea's growing national pride also played a key role in facilitating Seoul's pursuit of a less U.S.-dependent foreign policy. South Korea wished to break out of its role as an "American client state" and assume a position on a par with its economic performance, domestic democratization, and diplomatic pluralism.[86] As an analyst aptly put it, "leaders in Seoul display a new appreciation that security means more than perpetuating the U.S. connection. . . . It still remains vital, but so are Seoul's new-found diplomatic levers."[87]

Seoul's desire to attain some authority of its own vis-á-vis Washington was expressed in its dealing with Beijing in particular. Of course, it does not mean that there was at the time a firm consensus within the South Korean leadership on whether and how to adjust its relations with the United States. As a matter of fact, disagreement and confusion more aptly described Seoul's strategic thinking during the Kim Young-Sam administration (1993 to 1997). Given that Seoul had rarely made explicit suggestions for "diversified diplomacy" (*woegyo dabyonhwa*) away from its exclusive dependence on Washington, a small "incident" in the spring of 1994 permitted a rare glimpse of a possible bifurcation of Seoul's diplomatic allegiances.

At a press briefing on the night of March 29, concerning President Kim Young-Sam's state visit to China, Hwang Byung-Tae, South Korea's ambassador to China, commented that "South Korea–China cooperation over the issue of North Korea's nuclear program should go beyond the current level of simply notifying Beijing what has already been decided between Seoul and Washington.... South Korea's diplomacy should break out of its heavy reliance exclusively on the United States." In less than two hours, upon strong request by the national security advisor, the ambassador canceled his remark and commented that it only represented his personal view.[88]

Not surprisingly, the incident was widely publicized in the Korean media, which in turn generated heated debate. Interesting is the fact that, despite the media's one-sided characterization of the incident as a "diplomatic mishap," a large number of South Koreans—including diplomats, politicians, and policy analysts—tacitly endorsed Ambassador Hwang's view.[89] Given the centrality of China's role in the resolution of the North Korean nuclear crisis, this incident might have simply been an expression of Seoul's wishful thinking about China playing a more active role. In hindsight, however, it was clearly a harbinger of the long-term possibility that South Korea was to maintain a certain balance of its own vis-à-vis the United States and China.[90]

# 8

## The Rise of China and the U.S.–South Korean Alliance Under Strain

The decade of 1990s began with the demise of the Soviet empire, leaving the United States searching for a new mission in Northeast Asia. While Washington had initially sought to scale down its involvement in East Asia in the early 1990s, its East Asian Strategic Initiative (EASI) was rather short-lived. The "rise of China" debate, the heightened tension across the Taiwan Strait during 1995 and 1996, North Korea's nuclear brinkmanship and missile challenges, latent irredentism, and the economic dynamism of Northeast Asia have all led the United States to reaffirm its pivotal role in the region.[1] The redefinition of American strategic interests in the region has in turn consolidated the U.S.-Japan alliance, exemplified by the 1997 Defense Guideline revision, and led to the establishment of the trilateral coordination and oversight group (TCOG), involving the United States, Japan, and South Korea.

The increasingly proactive posture taken by Washington has caused some strategic concerns in Beijing and Moscow. Both China and Russia have sought to circumscribe America's "hegemonic parameters" in Asia both bilaterally and multilaterally (for example, with Sino-Russian joint military exercises, the formation of the Shanghai Cooperation Organization and the Boao Asia Forum, and China's proactive engagement with the ASEAN).[2] The U.S. bombing of the Chinese embassy in Belgrade in 1999, the missile defense (both TMD and NMD) controversies, and the reconnaissance plane (EP-3) incident in 2001 have all added to the prevailing concerns with America's unilateral actions and their strategic implications.[3]

Other events also shed light on the highly volatile state of affairs in the region: the election of pro-independence Chen Shui-bian as Taiwan's president and Japan's increasingly "rightist" drift. More importantly, the new administration of George W. Bush described China as America's "strategic competitor," in sharp contrast to Bill Clinton's efforts to build a "strategic partnership."[4] Furthermore, North Korea's revived aspirations for nuclear weapons capability and America's vow to eliminate weapons-of-mass-destruction programs pursued by all "failed" and terrorist states in the wake of the traumatic September 11 have painted a grim picture of this crucial region at the dawn of the new millennium.

Most alarmed by the changing atmosphere and confrontational signals was the South Korean government. Just as German unification was made possible by the tacit acceptance of the Soviet Union and active persuasion of the concerned European states by the United States—as well as the sincere efforts of the two German states—so too might Korean reunification require consensus building among the four major powers in Northeast Asia.[5] Consensus is best reached when all concerned parties maintain amicable relationships among themselves. Unfortunately, *ménage a six* in Northeast Asia is highly unlikely, which poses a serious problem for Seoul, which has to elicit support—or at least no objection—from the four major powers, the United States and China in particular.[6] Given that South Korea is structurally tied to the United States by an alliance framework, equating the rise of China with a Chinese threat will undoubtedly constrain the range of strategic options available for Seoul in its pursuit of reunification.

China is increasingly more important to South Korea's foreign relations in both economic and strategic terms. At the same time, Seoul has to sustain an amicable and beneficial relationship with Washington not only for economic reasons but also for its strategic and reunification goals.[7] Maintaining amicable relationships with both the United States and China, however, may become increasingly difficult if the overall capability gap between the two, in real or perceptual terms, gets smaller and smaller, eventually producing a typical case of "power transition," a "clash of civilizations," or even both.[8]

More noteworthy are the evolving perceptions of South Koreans toward the United States and China. The emergence of highly favorable views of China among the general public in South Korea marks a stark contrast with the plummeting popularity of America there. Despite South Korea's crucial strategic and economic importance to the United States, which has nevertheless paled before Japan's importance, little attention has been paid to these important changes.[9] The sheer disparity in the amount of attention Seoul and Washington have assigned each other constitutes the largest hurdle in South Korea–U.S. relations in the long run. Owing to the much-shared cultural and historical heritages, geographical proximity, and rapidly expanding bilateral ties, China is becoming a crucial variable that may drive a wedge into South Korea–U.S. relations.[10]

## China's Rise Over South Korea

Given the brief history of South Korea–China relations, it is rather surprising to find that the "shadow" of China has been cast over South Korea across the board, in economic, diplomatic, cultural, and military domains. The size of Sino–South Korean trade increased 4,176 times in just twenty-five years, from US$19 million in 1979 to US$79 billion in 2004. Much of the trade expansion occurred prior to the diplomatic normalization in 1992. China replaced Japan as South Korea's second-largest export market in 2001, and it replaced the United States as its number-one export destination in 2003. In 2004, China became South Korea's top trading partner. In 2005, the bilateral trade passed the US$100 billion mark, three years ahead of the initial plan. In a sense, as table 8.1 illustrates, South Korea has become "addicted" to the highly profitable trade with China over the years. The China trade marked 15.3 and 16.6 percent of Korea's total trade, and 88 and 69 percent of Korea's total trade surplus in 2003 and 2004, respectively.[11]

As of 2002, China also replaced the United States as South Korea's number-one destination for outbound investment. In 2003 alone, Seoul invested US$1.6 billion in China, surpassing the United States and Taiwan and becoming the third-largest investor in China, after Hong Kong and Japan.[12] The trend is likely to continue, as 80.3 percent of the midsize and small firms surveyed in South Korea in late 2003 preferred to relocate themselves to China. Considering that many conglomerates and their parts manufacturers have already moved their assembly lines to China, South Korea's economic dependency on China will certainly continue to increase.[13] In sum, China matters dearly to South Korea in economic terms.

Does China matter militarily? This remains largely opaque. Few South Korean security experts are publicly negative about the military implications of

TABLE 8.1  South Korea's Trade Dependency on China

|  | CHINESE SHARE OF SOUTH KOREAN TRADE (%) | SOUTH KOREA'S TRADE SURPLUS (US$ MILLIONS) |
|---|---|---|
| 1985 | 1.9 | 205 |
| 1990 | 2.8 | −715 |
| 1995 | 6.4 | 1,740 |
| 2000 | 9.4 | 5,656 |
| 2001 | 10.8 | 4,887 |
| 2002 | 13.1 | 6,354 |
| 2003 | 15.3 | 13,201 |
| 2004 | 16.6 | 20,193 |

*Source*: http://www.kotis.or.kr/tjgb (last accessed on January 16, 2006).

the rise of China, although it has never been a taboo subject. Considering that China was South Korea's military adversary some fifty years ago, it is all the more interesting to hear a wide range of calls for the expansion of bilateral military cooperation, resulting in the defense ministers' visits and exchanges of port calls by naval vessels since the late 1990s.[14] Seoul has so far maintained a sort of strategic ambiguity as to whether and under what circumstances China is likely to pose a grave and direct threat to South Korea and how to cope with such contingencies.[15]

Most specialists in South Korea echo what their American counterparts have long argued: the People's Liberation Army (PLA) is big but outdated.[16] However, these discussions that China's conventional forces are weak, outdated, and powerless even against Taiwan may not be directly applicable to South Korea. If it wishes, China may not necessarily need Dongfeng-41, Su-27, or SSBN for military action against Korea. With its J-8s, brown-water navy, and "rapid-reaction forces" (*quantou budui*) stationed in the Beijing, Shenyang, and Jinan Military Regions, China could pose a formidable threat to South Korea. In sum, China may matter militarily even though such concerns have not yet been officially voiced by the Seoul government.[17]

Does China matter diplomatically? Undoubtedly. Korea is one of the few places over which the Chinese shadow had traditionally been cast very heavily irrespective of the ebbs and flows of Beijing's influence. The Sino-Japanese War in 1895 over the suzerainty of Korea, Mao's painful decision in 1950 to intervene in the Korean War despite the continuing civil war and grave domestic problems, and Beijing's agreement in 1997 to participate in the four-party talks testify to China's persistent and unequivocal interests in the Korean peninsula.[18] Now with much more power, wealth, prestige, and influence than ever before, China has become a formidable diplomatic presence to be reckoned with, as far as the Korean question is concerned. Needless to say, Beijing's real and potential influence over Pyongyang, as well as its new initiatives to host the three- and six-party talks, further adds to China's pool of resources that can be employed when dealing with the Korean problem at large.[19]

Does China matter in cultural and perceptual terms? Absolutely. Prior to the Asian financial crisis, about six hundred thousand South Koreans visited China in 1997. The figure rose to over 2.8 million in 2004. As of 2005, thirty thousand Korean corporate offices were in operation and over half a million South Koreans were long-term residents in China, including 43,000 students, which accounted for 48 percent of all foreign students in China. Bilateral educational exchanges were only officially permitted in 1993, but the pace at which the number of South Korean students in China has risen has been dramatic indeed. The "China fever" in South Korea—along with the "Korean fad" (*hanliu*) in China—has been as much cultural as economic.[20]

## South Korea's Views of China and the United States

On the basis of nineteen nationwide opinion surveys conducted from 1988 through 2005, the following trends and characteristics are evident. First, as the data below demonstrate, South Korean perceptions of China have become increasingly favorable during the period concerned. Second, in stark contrast, South Korean views of the United States have generally declined. Third, of the nineteen nationwide surveys considered here, all except five indicate that South Korean perceptions of China were more favorable than perceptions of the United States.[21] Fourth, as tables 8.2 through 8.5 indicate, South Koreans' favorable perceptions of China were inversely correlated with age, while favorable perceptions of the United States were positively correlated with age. The older generations, with more immediate memories of the Korean War and the cold war, expressed less affinity for China, while the younger generations were much more positive about it. The comparison between the data in tables 8.2 and 8.3 on the one hand and the data in table 8.4 through 8.6 on the other also

TABLE 8.2  South Koreans' Attitude Toward China by Age Group, 1989/1990 (%)

|          | 20s       | 30s       | 40s       | 50s AND OLDER |
|----------|-----------|-----------|-----------|---------------|
| Positive | 43.9/46.3 | 31.6/36.6 | 28.9/33.8 | 22.3/26.8     |
| Neutral  | 36.1/35.7 | 45.2/37.8 | 41.6/44.8 | 51.4/46.6     |
| Negative | 20.0/17.7 | 23.3/25.1 | 29.5/21.0 | 26.3/26.4     |

*Note*: The figures to the left of the slash refer to 1989; those on the right refer to 1990.

*Sources*: *Chonhwangi ui han'guk sahoe: 1989 kungmin uisik chosa* [The Korean society in transition: 1989 national perception survey] (hereafter 1989 IPD survey; N=1,500) (Seoul: Institute of Population and Development, 1990), 153; and 1990 IPD survey (N=1,500), 184.

TABLE 8.3  South Koreans' Attitude Toward the United States by Age Group, 1989/1990 (%)

|          | 20s       | 30s       | 40s       | 50s AND OLDER |
|----------|-----------|-----------|-----------|---------------|
| Positive | 28.2/29.5 | 30.0/34.1 | 44.3/47.8 | 54.2/48.6     |
| Neutral  | 26.8/27.3 | 33.5/33.1 | 32.1/30.8 | 26.2/35.9     |
| Negative | 44.9/43.2 | 36.5/32.6 | 23.6/21.4 | 19.7/15.3     |

*Note*: The figures to the left of the slash refer to 1989; those on the right refer to 1990.

*Sources*: 1989 IPD survey, 153; and 1990 IPD survey, 181.

TABLE 8.4 South Koreans' Choice for a National Cooperative Partner for the Twenty-first Century, by Age Group, 1993 (%)

|  | UNITED STATES | CHINA |
|---|---|---|
| 20s | 22.8 | 34.8 |
| 30s | 36.4 | 34.4 |
| 40s | 39.0 | 36.4 |
| 50s and older | 54.8 | 27.7 |

*Source*: 1993 IPD survey (N = 1,545), 158.

TABLE 8.5 South Koreans' Guesses as to Which Country Would Be Their Closest Partner in the Year 2006, by Age Group, 1996 (%)

|  | UNITED STATES | CHINA |
|---|---|---|
| 20s | 19.3 | 46.6 |
| 30s | 21.3 | 50.4 |
| 40s | 26.5 | 50.2 |
| 50s and older | 32.1 | 41.0 |

*Note*: Although a specific N value is not available, this survey was conducted by a reputable survey institution.

*Source*: Ministry of Information (MOI), *Hangukin ui uisik kach'igwan chosa* [Survey of national consciousness in Korea] (hereafter MOI survey) (Seoul: Ministry of Information, 1996), 354.

TABLE 8.6 South Koreans' Opinions as to Which Country Is More Important, 2004 (%)

|  | UNITED STATES | CHINA |
|---|---|---|
| 20s | *52.7 | **45.6 |
| 30s | *58.8 | **52.7 |
| 40s | *44.3 | **44.8 |
| 50s | *38.4 | **29.2 |

*Note*: Although specific N values are not available, these surveys were conducted by reputable survey institutions or agencies.

*Sources*: *Dong-A Ilbo* [Dong-A Daily], May 4, 2004; ***Hanguk gyungje sinmun* [Korea Economic Daily], October 12, 2004.

suggest that the positive perceptions of China became increasingly less dependent on age after the 1992 normalization.

Public views concerning what needs to be done with respect to South Korea's relations with the four major powers—the United States, China, Japan, and Russia—also suggest that the United States is not necessarily viewed most positively (table 8.7). Nearly 9 percent of the respondents in the 1997 survey recommended that South Korea weaken its relationship with the United States; the comparable figure for China was only 1.3 percent. Thirty-one percent called for a strengthened South Korea–U.S. relationship, while 56 percent called for a consolidated South Korea–China relationship.[22] Certain preferences emerging from the general public tend to assign a higher priority to a new partner like China instead of the United States and Japan.

Whether and to what extent popular perceptions should be reflected in foreign-policy decisions are philosophical questions with no straightforward answers. Yet this poses a crucial question as to whether the election of Roh Moo-Hyun as South Korea's new president in December 2002—engineered primarily by the voters in their 20s and 30s—has led to a South Korean foreign policy with stronger Chinese and weaker American components. The American government initially thought that South Korea's "China fever" was mainly economic in nature, although that may not necessarily hold true in the coming years.[23]

Table 8.8, formulated on the basis of eleven different (that is, non-time-series) nationwide opinion surveys conducted from 1996 to 2005 provides additional insights. The survey data highlights that China has indeed been rising in the minds of South Koreans, possibly at the expense of the United States.

TABLE 8.7 South Koreans' Opinions on How to Manage Future Diplomatic Relations with Major World Powers, 1997 (%)

|  | WEAKEN RELATIONSHIP | MAINTAIN STATUS QUO | STRENGTHEN RELATIONSHIP | NO OPINION |
|---|---|---|---|---|
| With the United States | 8.7 | 59.9 | 30.7 | 0.7 |
| With China | 1.3 | 41.9 | 55.6 | 1.1 |
| With Japan | 11.1 | 62.8 | 25.3 | 0.9 |
| With Russia | 2.9 | 49.3 | 45.2 | 2.6 |

*Note:* N = 1,500, sampling error at ± 2.6 percent.

*Source:* 1997 Sejong survey, 12.

TABLE 8.8 South Korean Popular Preference for China or the United States, 1996–2005 (%)

| | PERCENT CHOOSING CHINA | PERCENT CHOOSING THE UNITED STATES |
|---|---|---|
| 1996[a] | 47 | 24 |
| 1997[b] | 56 | 31 |
| 1999[c] | 33 | 22 |
| 2000[d] | 45 | 43 |
| 2000[e] | 53 | 8 |
| 2002[f] | 41 | 30 |
| 2003[g] | 48 | 33 |
| 2004[h] | 61 | 26 |
| 2004[i] | 24 | 53 |
| 2005[j] | 39 | 54 |
| 2005[k] | 29 | 55 |

*Note*: Although specific N values are not available, these surveys were conducted by reputable survey institutions or agencies.

*Sources*:

a. MOI survey, 354. The question: "Which country will become closest to Korea in ten years?"

b. 1997 Sejong survey, 11–13. The question: "With which country should Korea strengthen its relations?"

c. *Dong-A Ilbo* [Dong-A Daily], January 1, 1999. The question: "With which country will Korea be closest to in the twenty-first century?"

d. *Hangook Ilbo* [Korea Daily], June 9, 2000. The question: "With which country should Korea cooperate most for the success of the inter-Korean summit?"

e. *Dong-A Ilbo*, December 5, 2000. The question: "Which country will become most influential in Asia?"

f. *Sisa Journal*, March 2002. The question: "Which of the four major powers do you feel most favorably toward?"

g. *Joong-ang Ilbo* [Joong-ang Daily], February 12, 2003. The question: "Where should South Korea's foreign-policy focus be placed?"

h. *Dong-A Ilbo*, May 4, 2004. The question: "Which country should South Korea regard as most important?"

i. *Global Views 2004—Comparing South Korean and American Public Opinion and Foreign Policy* (Chicago: CCFR, 2004), 19. The question: "With which country should South Korea cooperate most?"

j. *Chosun Ilbo* [Chosun Daily], January 1, 2005. The question: "Which of the four major powers do you feel most favorably toward?"

k. *Dong-A Ilbo*, November 7, 2005. The question: "On which country should South Korea's foreign-policy focus be placed?"

Of course, this does not necessarily imply favorable views of China are the result of anti-Americanism, although that certainly is a possibility. In fact, South Korea was not alone in witnessing a decline in the favorable views of the United States.[24] Much of the survey results from the early 1990s (tables 8.3 and 8.4) were prophesies that have come true in recent years. Given the younger generations' more favorable and hopeful views of China, Beijing's shadow over South Korea will likely expand. Perceptually, the rise of China has had a profound effect on Korea. However, it should be noted at this juncture that after the eruption of the history controversy in the summer of 2004, South Korean views of China soured, as is clearly demonstrated in the last three surveys in table 8.8. How long this new trend will continue, however, is uncertain.[25]

## Perceptual Ambivalence Toward China

There appears to have been a fine line between the South Korean general public and the policy elite in their respective views of China and the United States. In contrast with Japan and the United States, where the general public was more concerned with the rise of China, in South Korea, the elite felt much more uneasy than did the general public.[26] While the origin of such perceptual variations cannot be properly explained, the South Korean policy elite appear to have generally been more status-quo oriented—that is, preferring to remain within the U.S.-aligned structure—and thus more likely to fear that the rise of China would be destabilizing.[27] Embedded in the elite's ambivalence is their deep-seated concern with the uncertain intentions of China regarding South Korea. For good geopolitical reasons, South Korea cannot help but wonder whether the rise of China is likely to engender a malignant neighbor with *parabellum* dispositions.

On the basis of semistructured interviews conducted in 1997 and 1998 with twenty opinion leaders in South Korea's foreign-policy community, the following findings are reported.[28] All twenty interviewees regarded America's role in maintaining regional security in Northeast Asia as absolutely necessary. Eighteen of them, however, predicted that such a situation would change within ten to thirty years, and twelve of them specifically attributed the expected change to the rise of China. Ten interviewees (50 percent) chose China as potentially the most threatening country, while six selected Japan (the remaining four either chose Russia or gave no response). This was in sharp contrast to the general public's views of China and Japan. According to two nationwide surveys conducted in 1995 and 1997, Japan was viewed as most threatening by 53 percent and 23 percent of the respondents, respectively, while China ranked second by 24 percent in the 1995 survey, and ranked third, at 8 percent, in the 1997 survey.[29]

In the surveys jointly conducted by *Dong-A Ilbo* and *Asahi Shimbun* in 1999 and 2000, Japan was viewed by South Koreans as more threatening than China, by 31 percent to 14 percent in 1999 and 21 percent to 8 percent in 2000.[30] The South Korean elite's strategic ambivalence is further amplified when discussing the unfortunate possibility that containing China should become the principal function of the U.S.-Japan alliance. Regarding Seoul's strategic choices in such an event, five interviewees favored active cooperation with the United States and Japan against China; another five recommended a considerable detachment from the U.S.-Japan axis, to protect South Korea's expanding interests in China; and the rest proposed issue-variant support, maximum neutrality, reliance on multilateral institutions, and so on.[31]

The ambivalence of South Korea's elites is also embedded in their evolving views of China's role in the resolution of the "Korean problem." Ever since the June 23 pronouncement in 1973, the successive administrations in Seoul have held that Beijing could perform a meaningful role by wielding a constructive influence over Pyongyang, and South Korean presidential visits to China have always been preceded by such wishful signals. Over the years, however, an increasing number of experts have come to question Beijing's willingness to press Pyongyang on behalf of Seoul. Some have dubbed it as "separating politics [with Pyongyang] from economics [with Seoul]" (*zhengjing fenli* in Chinese).[32] Others go so far as to label it as a "China myth." Despite its unexpected decision in 1997 to join the four-party talks, which had initially been viewed by Pyongyang as a three-on-one formula, China managed not to tilt toward Seoul at Pyongyang's expense.[33] Similarly, Beijing has not sacrificed Pyongyang just for the sake of Seoul, its proactive efforts during the three- and six-party talks since 2003 notwithstanding.[34]

South Korea's ambivalence also has significant bearings upon the so-called uncivil faces of China. Maritime piracy and territorial intrusion by Chinese fishing vessels are very often pointed out as areas of grave concern.[35] China is also often portrayed as a serious violator of environmental protections, particularly regarding airborne pollutants.[36] Human-rights concerns have also loomed large in reinforcing the South Korean elite's ambivalence toward China. China not only branded all those who had fled North Korea as "escapees" rather than "refugees," but it also argued that Seoul's characterization of them as a human-rights problem was in effect an act of interference with China's sovereignty. On several occasions since 2000, Beijing even extradited some of these "refugees" to North Korea without any assurance of their safety.[37] As South Korean human-rights awareness has generally been enhanced in recent years, their perceptions of China as "uncivil" have also increased accordingly.[38]

Finally, the "audacity" of Chinese diplomats has often reinforced the ambivalent views held by the South Korean elite toward China. Concerning the Dalai

Lama's first visit to South Korea scheduled for 2000, Wu Dawei, China's ambassador to South Korea, warned that "permitting his entry would jeopardize the bilateral relationship, though not to the extent of severed ties." His comments were strongly resented, given that the Dalai Lama paid visits to more than forty countries with which China maintained diplomatic relations.[39] Another example concerns an incident in which the Chinese embassy phoned and faxed the members of the National Assembly to prevent them from attending Chen Shui-bian's presidential inauguration in May 2004. The press secretary reportedly even threatened to "remember those who insisted on attending it."[40]

Many in Seoul are afraid that a stronger China may become increasingly audacious and imposing on South Korea, just as the Ming and Qing courts did with Chosun. Particularly given that China carried out the so-called Northeast Project (*dongbei gongcheng*) in an effort to incorporate much of Korea's ancient history—Kokuryo in particular—into China's "local histories" (*difangshi*), South Korea's concern with China's "imperial" aspirations are not totally ungrounded.[41]

Despite the sentiments of reservation and ambivalence toward China, it should be noted that the South Korean policy elite itself has been going through crucial generational—and orientational—changes.[42] According to the interviews with a new generation of South Korean opinion leaders, conducted by an American think tank in 2002, 86 percent of the interviewees wished to see South Korea's future ties with China further strengthened, while the comparable figure for the United States was only 14 percent.[43] According to a survey on 138 newcomers to the National Assembly in 2004, 55 percent chose China as a more important foreign-policy target than the United States.[44] According to a similar survey conducted with 187 members of the Assembly one year later, 68 percent chose the United States.[45] As with the general public's view, the history controversy might have affected the South Korean elite's recent views of China. In any event, it is clear that China has become a key variable in the U.S.–South Korean alliance.

## The U.S.–South Korea Alliance Under Strain: Room for Wedging?

With the surge of popular hopes and expectations for China, favorable views of the United States have generally declined in South Korea (tables 8.2 through 8.8). Although it is not clear whether the decline is directly correlated with the rise of South Korea's favorable view of China, the South Korea–U.S. alliance has certainly been under strain in recent years. While the South Korean elite has held some skepticism and ambivalence toward the rise of China as a benign power, the multifaceted troubles in Seoul's relations with Washington have considerably expanded the room for China to wedge into the South Korea–U.S. alliance.[46]

During the last half century, the Korean-American alliance has endured the ebbs and flows expected of an "asymmetrical" alliance between two states with markedly different capabilities. During the 1950s and 1960s, the alliance was very close, because the North Korean threat was grave, South Korea's domestic economy was fragile, the United States was willing to exercise benign neglect, and neither Japan nor China constituted a significant variable in the Seoul–Washington relationship.[47] During this period, the "primary alliance dilemma"—whether or not to ally—was totally irrelevant, as South Korea had had no other option but to choose "external balancing" (that is, allying with the United States), even at the expense of Seoul's sovereignty and with increased military dependence on Washington.[48]

South Korea did not remain simply a loyal "client," however. Even during the cold war, as the South Korean economy grew at an extraordinary pace, the Seoul government often tried to transform itself into an "agent" with more discretion and issue-based roles commensurate with its enhanced capabilities.[49] Such efforts proved largely futile, due not only to structural constraints inherent in the asymmetrical alliance but also to the present danger emanating from North Korea. The "legitimacy debts" of South Korea's successive authoritarian regimes during the 1970s and 1980s further contributed to the perception that the costs of dependency were largely expendable so long as Seoul's ultimate security objectives were accomplished.[50]

The durability of the Korean-American alliance has been attributed in significant part to the vivid memories of America's military and economic assistance during the Korean War and afterward. With the passing of the older generations, however, those memories are fading fast. Instead, unpleasant recollections of America's support for the military dictators (and the suppression of the Kwangju Uprising in 1980), the crimes committed by American soldiers, and Washington's arrogance toward Seoul have introduced new strains in the U.S.–South Korean relationship.[51]

With Korea's democratic transition in 1987, its government has no longer faced the problem of "omnibalancing" typical of Third World alliances.[52] With little internal threat to regime stability, the Seoul government has been able to focus more explicitly on "external balancing." Furthermore, the post–cold war environments have opened new possibilities and options, most notably the rapprochement with socialist states, including that with China, under the Roh Tae Woo presidency (1988 to 1993). As an analyst has aptly put it, "leaders in Seoul display a new appreciation that security means more than perpetuating the U.S. connection.... It still remains vital, but so are Seoul's new-found diplomatic levers."[53]

Despite the steadily declining popularity of the United States among South Koreans, the view concerning the stationing of American forces gradually improved during the 1990s (see table 8.9). While 74.5 percent of the respondents in the 1988 IPD survey preferred the withdrawal of the U.S. forces sooner or later, the comparable figure gradually dropped to 60.2 percent in 1990, 51.5 percent in 1995, and 37.4 percent in 1997.[54] The change must have reflected the heightened security concerns reignited by the North Korean nuclear crisis in 1993 and 1994. The 2003 survey outcome (bottom row of table 8.9), however, suggests that the South Korean perceptions of the U.S. forces have somewhat worsened in recent years. The death of two schoolgirls in the summer of 2002 must have had a considerable effect on South Korea–U.S. relations thereafter.

There appears to be a widening gap between the public foreign-policy preferences in South Korea and America's strategic interests in the region. For instance, the 1997 Sejong survey asked the respondents to rank eleven foreign-policy goals in terms of their importance. Among the military-strategic goals listed, the top priority selected was the maintenance of peace on the Korean peninsula (64.2 percent), followed by the prevention of Japan's militarization (51.2 percent). Checking the "rise" of China was a distant fifth (34.4 percent), after attaining South Korean self-reliant defense (50.7 percent) and expanding

TABLE 8.9 South Koreans' Attitude Toward the U.S. Forces in Korea (%)

| | EARLY WITHDRAWAL | GRADUAL WITHDRAWAL | MAINTAIN STATUS QUO | REINFORCEMENT | NO OPINION |
|---|---|---|---|---|---|
| 1988* | 10.0 | 64.5 | 25.1 | — | 0.4 |
| 1989* | 9.8 | 61.7 | 28.2 | — | 0.3 |
| 1990* | 12.0 | 48.2 | 38.9 | — | 0.9 |
| 1995** | 5.9 | 45.6 | 36.8 | 4.7 | 6.9 |
| 1996** | 4.8 | 41.6 | 38.7 | 7.3 | 7.6 |
| 1997** | 2.9 | 34.5 | 49.1 | 8.9 | 4.6 |
| 2003*** | 13.8 | 42.8 | 41.5 | 2.0 | 1.4 |

Note: The IPD survey series did not have the "status quo" or "reinforcement" categories, and therefore the figures for the "withdrawal unacceptable" category were listed under "status quo."

Sources: * Denotes the IPD survey series. See 1989 IPD survey (N= 1,500), 70; and 1990 IPD survey (N= 1,500), 49 (the 1993 IPD survey did not ask the question about the U.S. forces). ** Denotes the Sejong survey series. See 1995 Sejong survey (N= 1,800), 68; 1996 Sejong survey (N= 1,200), 56; and 1997 Sejong survey (N= 1,500), 9. *** Refers to the survey conducted by *Joong-ang Ilbo* [Joong-ang Daily], February 12, 2003.

Korea's role at the United Nations (36.1 percent).[55] According to a multinational survey conducted in 2000, South Korean respondents ranked North Korea (54 percent) and Japan (21 percent) as their top two threats, while Americans chose China (38 percent) and Russia (21 percent).[56] As the improvement in inter-Korean relations becomes more visible and genuine, the "Japan question"—what Tokyo will become and how its relationship with Washington will evolve with regard to Beijing—will no doubt surface as a key variable.[57]

Most importantly, during the Kim Dae Jung presidency (1998 to 2003), the "Sunshine Policy"—engaging and assisting North Korea without making *quid pro quo* a prerequisite—landed Seoul in the driver's seat as far as inter-Korean relations were concerned. The "Sunshine Policy" was apparently supported more actively by China than the United States. Even the historic inter-Korean summit in June 2000 highlighted that South Korea's search for a proactive and pivotal role in mitigating tension on the Korean peninsula was more in line with Beijing's policy framework than it was with Washington's.[58] These developments, however, made Washington feel as if it was being increasingly sidelined.

South Korea's approach to the second North Korean nuclear crisis beginning in October 2002 has also underscored the diverging threat perceptions of Seoul and Washington.[59] While the Bush administration took South Korea out of the driver's seat, Seoul has been singing Beijing's tune of peace and stability, in an effort to prevent Washington from employing nonpeaceful measures against Pyongyang. According to a *Joong-ang Ilbo* survey in 2003, over 60 percent of the respondents believed that South Korea's relations with the United States need a complete rethinking, or at least that South Korea should move away from its exclusive dependence on Washington.[60] The heated debates and painstaking decisions related to the size, location, and timing of dispatching South Korean forces to Iraq in early 2004 were also indicative of the state of the alliance.

If an alliance between a great and a small power is healthy, the weaker partner generally has little incentive to seek changes in the relationship.[61] The key question concerns what has made the weaker partner—South Korea in this case—look for readjustments to its strategic map. As noted earlier, Seoul's growing desire to establish a foundation for its own defense without perpetual dependence on Washington constitutes one factor, especially considering that America's commitment to defending South Korea has been constantly subject to Washington's changing strategies and perceptions regardless of Seoul's.[62] While South Korean elites have traditionally acknowledged their psychological dependency on U.S. protection—often characterized as "separation anxiety"— changes have occurred during Kim Dae Jung's presidency, and the succeeding administration under Roh Moo-Hyun has come up with the concept of "cooperative and independent national defense."[63]

Many of these changes have been hard for the United States to swallow, given its belief that South Korea should always be grateful for what America did for it during and after the Korean War. The sheer disparity in capabilities between the United States and South Korea has been replicated in many areas of importance. In the global, strategic aims of the United States, Korea is only a small part of the Asian region. In stark contrast, Washington takes up a huge chunk of Seoul's policy horizon.[64] While a wide array of problems and tensions in the alliance—the Status of Forces Agreement (SOFA), the use of bases, everyday street-level conflicts involving American GIs, and so on—were simply taken for granted in the past as the cost of accepting America's defense shield, it is no longer as tolerated.[65]

The core problem appears to have more to do with the tendency of most Americans to be poorly informed on world affairs and mostly indifferent to South Korea.[66] Very few Americans, experts and the general public alike, are aware that South Korea is America's seventh-largest trading partner. According to a Gallup survey conducted in 1995, less than 10 percent of American respondents knew the name of South Korea's president at the time, while the comparable figures for Japan and China were 20 percent and 66 percent, respectively. Concerning the extent of interest in South Korea, the Gallup survey revealed that 58 percent of American respondents replied negatively and only 6 percent expressed substantial interest.[67] A 2001 survey by Harris Interactive also found that 60 percent of American respondents held no opinion whatsoever regarding the question, "how do you perceive South Korea?"[68]

A rare survey finding by Harris Interactive (table 8.10) provides useful comparative information as to how South Korea is perceived by the United States, Japan, and China. The United States and Japan appear almost identical in their perceptions of South Korea, in that a quarter of respondents possessed favorable views of South Korea, while the comparable figure for Chinese respondents was higher by 12 to 15 percent. On the other hand, the same survey also

TABLE 8.10 Perceptions of South Korea in the United States, Japan, and China, 2000 (%)

|  | FAVORABLE | UNFAVORABLE | NO OPINION | NOT SURE |
| --- | --- | --- | --- | --- |
| United States | 23 | 15 | 60 | 3 |
| Japan | 20 | 17 | 60 | 3 |
| China | 35 | 16 | 45 | 5 |

Source: Harris Poll #8, January 31, 2001.

shows that, with regard to Japan, South Korea and China held almost identical views: their favorable views accounted for 17 and 19 percent, while unfavorable views were 42 and 43 percent, respectively.

Crucial discrepancies are also discernible in terms of threat perceptions the United States and South Korea hold concerning Japan and China.[69] Most startlingly, with regard to future projections of dominance—that is, the question, "which country will be most influential in Asia in the next ten years?"—South Korean perceptions differed significantly from those of the American respondents. While only 19 percent of the Americans chose China, 53 percent of the South Korean respondents did so.[70] In the minds of South Koreans, China weighs increasingly heavily.

Anti-Americanism is not unique to South Korea, nor is it a new phenomenon there. In fact, it is rapidly spreading around the globe, particularly in recent years. The fundamental question is whether South Korea's relationship with the United States will worsen to the extent that there is actually room available for a third party to wedge in.[71] In geopolitical, economic, cultural, and perceptual terms, China may be waiting in the wings. Whether Seoul wishes to consider Beijing as its strategic alternative—or strategic supplement—is one thing, while China regarding such a contingency as a real possibility is quite another.

# 9

# Between Dragon and Eagle

## Korea at the Crossroads

Does history repeat itself? It appears so at least from the vantage point of the two Koreas, which unfortunately have been geopolitical pawns of their great-power neighbors for the last century. As Qing diplomat He Ruzhang had recommended in 1880, despite sporadic efforts directed at self-strengthening and realignment, Chosun (Korea's official designation during the Yi Dynasty) had largely remained the last bastion of the Sinic world order.[1] "Allying with the Qing" (*qinzhong*) while "aligning with Japan" (*jieri*) and "liaising with America" (*lianmei*) to counter Russia did not create room for Chosun's autonomy, but instead led to loss of sovereignty and colonization by Japan.

Over a century later, in the wake of the post–cold war thaw, South Korea—and to an increasing extent, North Korea as well—is likely to confront a familiar dilemma concerning which side, the United States' or China's, it should take. History may repeat in a similar pattern, but perhaps not precisely the same way. This time around, a reversed order of preference is equally possible, if not likely to prevail. The rise of China, with whom South Korea has already attained diplomatic normalization and been rapidly expanding cooperative relations on all fronts, is gradually making the Seoul government reconfigure its cold war–based strategic thinking and readjust its half-century alliance relationship with the United States.[2]

Three dimensions in particular highlight the ultimate strategic dilemma South Korea faces. First, if opinion surveys (see chapter 8 for details) are any useful guide at all, South Korea's formal alliance ties with the United States are likely to loosen, regardless of Seoul's preferences, due either to Washington's global posture review (GPR) or to anti-Americanism in South Korea.[3] Second, South Korea's perceptions of and expectations for China are somewhat too favorable, even though Beijing's genuine intentions regarding the Korean peninsula still remain largely unspecified.[4] Third, much of the Washington-Beijing relationship evolves independently of Seoul, even though it is the most crucial determinant of South Korea's external relations. How to find a suitable middle ground while maximizing the benefits of maintaining good relations with both the United States and China therefore is the key to South Korea's principal foreign-policy goals—namely, survival, development, and unification.

What should South Korea's options and strategies in dealing with both China and the United States be? Much of the answer to this fundamental question lies in one's assessment of China's future.[5] Should China become a friendly, benign power, Sino-American relations will cause less of a strategic problem for South Korea, which has to maintain good relationships with both. On the other hand, if China should become an aggressive and imposing challenger to the status quo, Washington-Beijing dynamics will no doubt constitute an extremely intricate problem for Seoul. In this regard, we first need to explore the future of China as a crucial determinant of South Korea's strategic environments and options.

## The Future of China: Beyond Simple Dichotomy

During the 1990s, in the aftermath of the collapse of the Soviet Union, some foreign observers were alarmed by the heightened prospect of China's political and even territorial disintegration.[6] Currently, however, China is being portrayed as a rapidly emerging great power with the potential to reshape the regional and global order.[7] All discussions concerning what China will become in the future are bound to be inconclusive at best, irrespective of their long lists of conditions, projections, forecasts, and caveats. Statistics on past performance, while useful, are not sufficient to offer accurate predictions for the future. Given the proven possibilities that the growth process can be telescoped or, alternatively, economic crises may interpose at any time, any future projection stands on a shaky ground.

Much of the debate on the future of China has been overly dichotomized, focusing mostly on China's military buildup or on the structural fragility of China's economy, thereby positing mostly the two possibilities of "China as threat" and the "collapse of China." It should be noted, however, that China's final destination still remains an open-ended question, as there has not been a consensus even on how to define the current state of the Chinese system.[8] To a considerable extent, the future of China is in the eyes of the beholder. That is to say, those who focus more on the structural problems of its economy and societal governance have tended to view China's future more negatively, whereas those who emphasize the resilient "adaptability" of the Chinese leadership are likely to portray it in more positive terms.[9]

At least eight scenarios can be conceived with regard to the future of China. The first scenario, the Yugoslavian model of the 1990s, is perhaps the worst of all possibilities, since it presupposes a nondemocratic, poor, and weak government in power, incapable of preventing the fragmentation of the state.[10] The ethnoterritorial disintegration or regional secession of China is one possibility, though not very likely, if a fatal combination of nationwide popular unrest, local militaries, and foreign aggression occurs simultaneously.[11] Since China differs significantly from the former Soviet Union in terms of its ethnic minority composition, history of national integration, respective reform strategy, and so on, a simple analogy of collapse does not hold well for China. Furthermore, China has been keenly aware of the crucial ramifications of the Soviet experiences.[12]

The second contingency refers to the Indonesian scenario, which presupposes a weak China that fails to accomplish the dual task of economic development and democratic transition.[13] Economic stagnation and authoritarian rule would reproduce social discontent and ethnic unrest. Yet the inefficient giant may continue to muddle through, but with highly explosive potentials for political, social, and economic instability.[14] The interposition of a gigantic financial crisis—if it should indeed occur in China as many have projected—may actually create fertile ground for this sort of contingency. Of course, the case of East Timor's secession also offers abundant room for reflection in relation with China's Taiwan conundrum.

Third, next on the continuum lies the Latin American model (*lameihua*). The nondemocratic, corrupt, and brutal regime may effectively rein in ethnic conflicts but fail to bridge the widening income disparities to the extent where political suppression and social instability become an indispensable part of everyday life. The rupture of a balance-of-payment problem, a "crash," or "long landing" of China's economy may actually facilitate such a situation.[15]

Fourth, we can also think of an Indian (of the 1990s) scenario. This particular contingency refers to a state of affairs where China has managed to attain democratic transition but failed to sustain high levels of economic growth for some reason: for example, severe constraints imposed in terms of energy and the environment.[16] The outcome would be an India-type imbalance: namely, a democratic but stagnant and discontented China.[17] At the time of this writing, India is gradually entering into a phase of high economic growth, due particularly to its IT sector. While the extent of similarity between the two remains uncertain, this scenario posits that China, like India, will constitute at least a formidable regional power with regional influence.[18]

Fifth, an open-ended scenario termed a "China model" may also be conceived of. While the so-called East Asian model or variants of developmental authoritarianism may share some key threads with this scenario, the sheer size of China and its relentless search for indigenized—that is, non-Western, quasi-socialist, and "undemocratic" but market-based—forms of political and economic transitions puts it in a league of its own.[19] China's search is not yet over, and it will continue, although the final destination of such search remains unspecified. It should be duly noted that China's preoccupation with local innovation and indigenization certainly goes well beyond mere rhetoric.[20]

Sixth, a more successful contingency presupposes a China that becomes both economically advanced on a par with the OECD nations and politically democratized to a considerable extent. This scenario, possibly termed the French model, depicts China as a top-notch leading nation in world affairs just short of being the hegemonic power, which is nevertheless capable of vetoing the hegemon once in a while.[21] The "deficiency" in this case—what prevents China from becoming a hegemon itself—is perhaps the relative inferiority of hard power as well as the lack of global soft power.

The remaining two contingencies refer to the most optimistic scenarios, which project China as one of the most powerful nations in the system—the hegemon or a hegemonic competitor. The main difference between these two scenarios lies in their respective aspirations for power and prestige in the global system. The seventh scenario—termed here the "coexister"—depicts China as a cooperative "bigemon" that seeks to maintain a cooperative if not symbiotic relationship with the United States. In this case, China may not necessarily strive to develop and diffuse its own soft-power components; that is, China may not be so much geared to spreading its own norms and values to counter those of the United States.[22]

The last scenario is somewhat ominous but perhaps more likely, given the numerous historical precedents readily available. All those debates on the "China threat," in fact, originate from the assessment that China is and will necessarily become able and willing to constitute a revisionist challenge against the United States and the existing international order.[23] Given that domestic developmental processes of continental states were rarely interfered with effectively by outside forces, China is likely to become much stronger than it is now.[24] Will China's strength then be threatening to others? It will certainly depend on whose viewpoint you take, since the *perceived extent* of the threat is the most crucial determinant of all. It seems that the core issue is not what China's future holds but whose viewpoint to take.[25]

Which of these eight scenarios is most likely to materialize? The ultimate answer is in the eyes of the beholder, as the current assessment of China's future is akin to a glass both half full and half empty. Some of these scenarios could even possibly be viewed as stages in a sequential process through which China has been moving since the demise of the Qing Dynasty. If China were to take one of the first four paths, South Korea's strategic dilemma—how to position itself between Washington and Beijing—would be considerably mitigated. However, an economically frail China with internal governance problems is not necessarily less of a grave threat.[26] The former Soviet Union's global power was not founded on its per capita indicators, nor was China's accession to the United Nations in 1971 rooted in its economic accomplishments. In this vein, the alliance with the United States will remain important to South Korea.

If the past track records can offer any useful guide, China is more likely to embark on one or some combination of the latter four paths.[27] That is, whether democratic or not and whether Western or Chinese style, China will become wealthier and more powerful. Will China's strength then be destabilizing or threatening? While for now, since the events of September 11, China appears to have been "co-opted" by the United States, Sino-American relations will inevitably resemble a relationship between competitors, if not enemies, rather than friends. Certainly, Washington casts wary eyes on the growth of China.[28]

It seems that the core issue is not *how* to predict China's future but *from whose point of view*. Certainly, there is more to the world than a simple juxtaposition of the West and China (or the "rest"). In the regional context of East Asia, while China is generally regarded as the object of engagement, significant variations are nevertheless found in the particular responses to the "rise" of China by Japan, Taiwan, Indonesia, Singapore, India, and so on. While South Korea has been highly successful in engaging China—in fact, successful beyond anyone's best guess—that very success has become the source of a grave strategic dilemma. The dilemma centers on the blending—if not the choice—between maintaining the status quo by remaining within the U.S.-centered alliance system or by embarking on a hopeful but uncertain journey into the orbits of a Sino-centric system. Certainly, South Korea is not alone in having to ponder how the rise of China will affect its future.

## The Menu of Choices and Rational Constraints

Given the acute strategic dilemma that the "rise" of China—that is, a stronger China at loggerheads with the hegemonic United States—may pose, what would be the best choice for South Korea to opt for? Theoretically, the range of choices is quite wide, and there seem to be at least ten options for Seoul to consider. They include: (1) preventive war, (2) distancing/downgrading, (3) neutrality, (4) self-help, (5) bandwagoning, (6) binding, (7) engagement, (8) balancing/containment, (9) hedging, and (10) issue-based support.[29] Given the premise that Seoul seeks to maximize economic gains while safeguarding its security interests and, at the same time, aims to maintain good relations with both Washington and Beijing, the following assessments are offered for each of the ten options.

South Korea is not and will not be in any position to contemplate a preventive war against the rising China.[30] In view of the ever-expanding economic, diplomatic, cultural, and even military cooperative relationships between the two, as well as for the sake of maintaining peace and stability on the peninsula, even joining in another country's preventive war against China also appears to be a totally unrealistic alternative for South Korea.

Neither distancing nor downgrading—that is, reducing the scope and intensity of cooperation—is deemed a desirable option from South Korea's viewpoint not only for the obvious geopolitical reasons (China's support—or at least, not vetoing—is essential for attaining reunification) but also, more importantly, because of its rapidly increasing economic stake in the China market.[31] The disastrous effect of China's import ban on the two Korean-made products, mobile phones and polyethylene, during the "garlic war" in the summer of 2000 suggests that as long as China sustains its remarkable growth, the distancing/downgrading option is unlikely to be considered by Seoul except under extraordinary circumstances.[32]

Viewed from any geopolitical angle, South Korea is more of a buffer state than a "rim state." Therefore, a declaration of neutrality does not appear to be an attractive or viable option for South Korea.[33] While South Korea's overall capabilities would make it a "pivotal state" in some other, more favorable strategic landscape, in the Northeast Asian context, leaning toward one or two of its stronger neighbors seems a more sensible alternative for Seoul, unless it is both willing and able to become a major power itself.[34] Replacing the U.S.-centered alliance system with self-declared neutrality in the absence of concrete and workable security supplements will be not only difficult but also too risky for Seoul to accept.

Nor does relying solely on "self-help"—opting for internal balancing to attain a self-reliant defense capability—look palatable, as it is invariably too costly in both economic (requiring at least additional US$1.5 billion per year) and political (extra efforts to mitigate domestic opposition) terms, and it certainly lacks a "competitive advantage" with respect to the major powers surrounding the Korean peninsula. Some of its independent "spirit" can, however, be utilized in combination with relying on diplomacy vis-à-vis its great-power neighbors. In fact, the "cooperative independent national defense" promoted by President Roh Moo-Hyun since 2003 contains a similar thread in this regard.[35]

The option of bandwagoning with China—leaving the current U.S.-based alliance system and joining the Sino-centric world—seems unrealistic as it stands now.[36] For the foreseeable future, the rise of China certainly appears more probable than the collapse of China.[37] Yet the rise of China will undoubtedly be an elongated process estimated to take at least twenty to fifty years.[38] If the *primus inter pares* status of the United States should remain unchanged until 2020 at the earliest, and particularly given the indispensable contribution the American forces make in deterring North Korea and maintaining stability in the region, it is deemed far too premature for South Korea to now opt for bandwagoning with China.[39]

Another commonly discussed idea is that of "binding"—constraining China with a bilateral alliance or embedding it within a multilateral framework of collective security. In light of the traditional ties between Beijing and Pyongyang, previously dubbed as the "brotherhood sealed in blood," Seoul's forming an alliance relationship with Beijing is a remote possibility at best.[40] Inducing China into a multilateral security arrangement in the context of Northeast Asia is also equally daunting, if more plausible than a Sino–South Korean alliance. China has long regarded Northeast Asia as a "semiregion" (*ciquyu*) where the mechanisms of collective security would not fit as neatly as they did in Europe or Southeast Asia.[41] "Incremental institutionalization," particularly given China's zeal for the Six-Party Talks framework, is certainly a possibility, but China will hold strong reservations if such schemes are pushed mainly by the United States.[42]

Compared to the six options discussed thus far, the remaining four seem more realistic and usable. Seoul has either already been utilizing some of these options or at times is seeking or has sought to implement others. The alternative of "engagement" needs no elaboration, as it has the second-longest history—twenty-some years—second only to that of "balancing/containment."[43] Evidence abounds that it has worked quite successfully for both South Korea and China and, therefore, will continue to be used extensively.[44]

Two points of caution need to be noted at this juncture. One concerns the gradual transformation of South Korea–China economic relations from one of complementarity to competition, which may eventually complicate the use of further engagement in the future.[45] The other refers to the structural and perceptual limits imposed on Seoul-Beijing engagement by the Korean-American alliance which, along with the U.S.-Japan alliance, is often viewed as an instrument of containing China.[46]

Balancing/containment has the longest history among all the options available for South Korea.[47] South Korea has been utilizing this option jointly with the United States and Japan since the Korean War, although much of Seoul's balancing role has been overshadowed by its zeal for engagement in recent years. Although there is ample room for the Korean-American alliance to be conscripted for the task of checking China, the "comprehensive cooperative partnership" (*quanmian hezuo huoban guanxi*) forged between Seoul and Beijing in 2003 makes the explicit use of a containment option much more difficult if not impossible.[48] Yet certain specific contingencies may put this view to a test: a military dispute between the United States and China over Taiwan would be a key example.[49]

The possibility of Seoul's increasingly split allegiance to Washington and Beijing leads us to the next option, hedging (minimizing risk by betting on both), which Seoul has occasionally experimented with.[50] In retrospect, Ambassador Hwang Byung-Tae's controversial comment made in 1994 that "Korea's cooperation with China on the issue of North Korea's nuclearization must go beyond the current level...to match that of mutual consultation between Seoul and Washington" was an important harbinger of what was to come within a decade.[51] In 1998, President Kim Dae Jung remarked in Hong Kong that Seoul was considering a trilateral military dialogue with Beijing and Pyongyang, which, a year later, led to the historic first meeting between the defense ministers of South Korea and China.[52]

The utility of hedging is often cancelled out by the high cost associated with having to please two players at the same time. The option of hedging thus demands a considerable degree of prudence on the part of its practitioner. If it should go wrong, the practitioner could be distrusted and even abandoned by both, which would be the worst outcome, and one that should be avoided by all means. The case of South Korea getting caught between the United States and Russia over the controversy involving the antiballistic missile (ABM) treaty in 2001 is a case in point.[53] It is not clear if hedging is a useful strategy at all for South Korea.

Hedging is often indistinguishable from the last option, issue-based support—siding with either depending on the issue concerned. If hedging requires prudent action with a certain amount of "hidden information," issue-based support presupposes more transparent and consistent rules of decision making, rules known to all of the players involved. In a sense, it can be said that issue-based support works from a proactive position, while hedging seems a bit more reactive and defensive in nature. A couple of examples are offered below to illustrate Seoul's occasional strategy of issue-based support in recent years.

In negotiations during the Uruguay Round (1986 to 1994), South Korea often sided with China in efforts to protect its agricultural produce market. In coping with Japan's "whitewashing" of history, Seoul tacitly cooperated with Beijing, while the position of Washington on that score remained largely unspecified.[54] On the other hand, with regard to issues of nonproliferation, South Korea was generally in support of the United States as opposed to China, which has often viewed some of America's demands as infringements on its sovereign rights.[55] In this vein, South Korea's controversial decision not to join the Theater Missile Defense (TMD) plan in 1999 was not merely the outcome of its concern for China but, more importantly, a consistent issue-based decision as well.[56] Concerning the U.S.-led United Nations resolution on human-rights conditions in China, on the other hand, Seoul has almost always abstained.

## Parameters of South Korea's Choice: Where the United States and China Converge

Both the United States and China have the same pronounced tenet concerning the Korean Peninsula—namely, "peace and stability" (*heping yu wending*). While there is no room for contention regarding the "peace" component, it remains largely unclear whether Beijing and Washington mean precisely the same thing by "stability." By stability, the United States refers to the maintenance of the status quo—that is, America's continuing predominance in South Korea and against North Korea. Then the question concerns: it that what China also prefers?[57]

As noted earlier, Seoul's interest is best served by maintaining good relations with both Washington and Beijing. When U.S.-China relations remain amicable, South Korea will not face the dilemma of having to choose one against the other. If Sino-American relations should get bumpy, however, South Korea, allied with the United States, would find itself in a very intricate position. The more tense and confrontational they become, the more likely Seoul would be forced to explicitly define its position with respect to the two powers. What parameters are then available for South Korea to consider?

I argue here that such parameters are most likely to be set by the congruence of the strategic interests of China and the United States, although the ultimate decision will be made by the South Korean leadership largely within the boundary of these parameters. In identifying the specific boundary of these parameters—where the strategic interests of the two great powers converge and diverge—the views of American and Chinese policy experts were solicited and decoded.[58]

Decoding elite opinion is always a daunting challenge. No royal method is readily available for randomly sampling experts and opinion leaders, nor is there a magic number for the sample size. Intensive face-to-face interviews utilizing both structured and open-ended questions were conducted with fifty-six American experts in Washington during 2002 and 2003, and with thirty-three Chinese experts in Beijing and Shanghai during 2004. Despite the potential problems of selection bias—although efforts were made to minimize it—these interviews may provide a useful sketch of where the strategic preferences of the United States and China tend to converge concerning South Korea.

What would be the timeframe within which South Korea's strategic soul-searching must be completed? Of the fifty-six American interviewees, 63 percent believed that by 2030, China would become a real competitor against the United States, while the comparable figure for the Chinese respondents was only 33 percent (the remainder either chose 2050 or replied that China would never be able to compete with the United States). In addition, 57 and 61 percent of the American and Chinese interviewees, respectively, chose the economy as the main area of Sino-American competition. In sum, these experts projected that U.S.-China confrontation would be quite unlikely within twenty years, particularly in strategic-military terms, except for the Taiwan contingency discussed later.[59]

China may nevertheless emerge as a key challenger for the whole Asian region sooner than the usual projections. Particularly given that 54 percent of the American interviewees and 76 percent of the Chinese interviewees saw U.S. soft power declining since September 11, 2001, there is ample room for China to exploit.[60] In fact, 67 percent of the Chinese experts interviewed were confident that China would be able to generate "alternative norms" that would eventually supplant those of America's.[61]

The American elite appear to be less confident than they should be concerning the future of U.S.–South Korean relations compared to Sino–South Korean relations. Most (95 percent) of the American interviewees replied that China considers the Korean peninsula its core sphere of influence, while the comparable figure for the Chinese interviewees was only 42 percent. As for the question regarding South Korea's number-one trading partner, 41 percent of the American interviewees responded, wrongly, that China had already replaced the United States in overall trade.[62] Furthermore, 87 percent of the American interviewees replied that China would be voted as possessing the biggest influence in ten years from now if a nationwide poll were conducted in South Korea today, whereas the comparable figure for the Chinese interviewees was 71 percent.

With both the real and perceived rise of China, what specific contingencies are likely to force South Korea into a situation where taking a side becomes unavoidable? Two such contingencies can be conceived of: one mid- to long-term contingency and the other more short-term. Regarding the former, with 2030 as its timeframe, the interviewees were asked what South Korea's strategic choice ought to be in case Sino-American hegemonic rivalry should indeed occur.

As table 9.1 illustrates, the American interviewees' predominant (67 percent) recommendation was that South Korea sustain its alliance with the United States but join in no hostile action against China. A follow-up question was posed: "Will such behavior be swallowed by America?" While 90 percent of the American experts replied positively, Washington's overly simplistic "friend-foe" dichotomy and, more importantly, the ongoing transformation of the U.S. forces in South Korea—from a fixed deterrent force against North Korea to a mobile balancer for the region as a whole—make it increasingly hard to hold up. The Chinese interviewees, on the other hand, were almost equally divided between replacing the alliance with a multilateral security framework (42 percent) and South Korea maintaining the alliance with the United States but joining no hostile action against China (40 percent).

TABLE 9.1 American and Chinese Elites' Preferences for South Korea's
Foreign-Policy Choices (%)

| OPTIONS | SUSTAIN THE U.S. ALLIANCE BUT JOIN NO FORCE AGAINST CHINA | BUILD MULTI-LATERAL SECURITY | REMAIN IN THE U.S. ALLIANCE EVEN IF IT INVOLVES FORCE AGAINST CHINA | DEVELOP A SELF-HELP SYSTEM | BAND WAGON WITH CHINA | OTHER OPTIONS |
|---|---|---|---|---|---|---|
| United States | 67 | 17 | 9 | 2 | 0 | 4 |
| China | 40 | 42 | 0 | 12 | 6 | 0 |

*Note*: The category "American Elites" comprises fifty-six American foreign-policy experts interviewed for the data presented here in 2002 and 2003. The category "Chinese Elites" comprises thirty-three Chinese foreign-policy experts interviewed in 2004.

The more immediate contingency refers to the possibility of U.S.-China confrontation over the Taiwan Strait. Concerning this issue, the difference in their respective preferences between Washington and Beijing appears much more manifest. Sixty-four percent of the American interviewees responded that the United States would certainly ask South Korea to provide support in such a contingency, and the same percentage suggested that the support requested by America would be in the form of military—combatant or non-combatant—assistance. Sixty-seven percent of the Chinese interviewees also replied that the United States would ask for support from South Korea, but only 12 percent believed that it would be in the form of dispatching military forces. The predominant majority (85 percent) of the Chinese experts thought that America would demand the use of military bases in South Korea. More importantly, 58 percent of the Chinese interviewees replied that South Korea should deny this request and, otherwise, it would be regarded by China as an act of aggression.[63]

Normally, the alliance-induced risk of abandonment and entrapment tends to vary inversely.[64] As the weight of the Korean-American alliance gradually shifts from deterring North Korea to supporting the U.S.-Japan division of security responsibilities in East Asia—possibly against China—Seoul's risk of abandonment (that is, the United States abandoning Korea's primary strategic interests for the sake of reducing its own burden by enhancing Japan's regional strategic position) and, more importantly, of entrapment (that is, Korea being sucked into U.S.-Japan collusion, possibly against China) may become positively correlated.[65] Given that alliances are "formal associations of states for the use of military force... against specific other states, whether or not these other states are explicitly specified," against whom is the newly adjusted Korean-American alliance as a regional security balancer to be poised?[66] This is the question that Seoul has to ponder seriously.

Since 2003, Seoul and Washington have in fact been negotiating the "strategic flexibility" of the American forces in South Korea—that is, on what terms the U.S. forces can be freely deployed in and out of South Korea to cope with regional contingencies. While maintaining that it understands and respects the U.S. need for strategic flexibility in its global military management, Seoul does not wish to be sucked into an unwanted conflict in Northeast Asia. An interim agreement meted out at the first South Korea–U.S. Strategic Dialogue in January 2006 was that Washington understood Seoul's concern while the latter accepted strategic flexibility in principle. Yet South Korea's preference for including a "prior consultation" regarding force mobility was not reflected in the agreement. Ample room for future friction remains.[67]

## Walking the Tightrope: The Choice of Not Making Choices

On the surface, history looks as if it is repeating itself. Even South Korea's stronger neighbors are precisely the same powers as those one hundred years ago. Much of the similarity stops there, however. This time around, a reversed order of preference may prevail in this familiar dilemma. If Chosun had clung to the crumbling Sinic world order against the rising West, South Korea is currently holding on to the U.S.-led security structure and norms in the midst of China's rise. The crux of the matter is whether the cost of South Korea's departure from the U.S.-aligned structure outweighs the benefit of opting for something else. Until concrete peace-assuring mechanisms are securely installed on the Korean peninsula, it will certainly be cheaper and more reasonable for Seoul to side with Washington, as Beijing has no intention or incentive to support Seoul at the expense of Pyongyang. Furthermore, not only will America's support be indispensable for reunification and postreunification reconstruction, but South Korea's economic relationship with the United States is also much too intimately intertwined with its strategic ties.[68]

Nor can China be dispensed with. Assessing China's power solely in per capita terms misses the whole point of its rise.[69] The former Soviet Union's global status was not premised on its per capita indicators, nor was China's accession to the United Nations Security Council over thirty years ago rooted in its economic caliber. China's fast-growing presence, influence, and shadow over the Korean peninsula can no longer be refuted. The bottom line for Seoul, therefore, is not to antagonize China and, in this regard, the aforementioned scenario of South Korea being sucked into a U.S.-China conflict over Taiwan or elsewhere in the region must be avoided under all circumstances.

The future of North Korea constitutes a crucial variable. If North Korea should become a nonnuclear open state, which is hinged upon some sort of leadership or regime change, trade, investment, development assistance, and tourism may pour into Pyongyang. This will in turn further open up the nation. If a rapprochement should occur between Washington and Pyongyang, the dynamics will become even more complicated.[70] Alternatively, the rise of a nuclear North Korea most likely would strengthen the traditional alliance ties among South Korea, the United States, and Japan, but what China's specific reaction to that eventuality would be remains to be specified.[71] Worse yet, the collapse of North Korea may fully open the stage for great-power politics on the Korean peninsula. Despite China's tendency to accommodate its position to that of the United States and South Korea, perceptual and behavioral inertia may continue to push Beijing to offer minimum-security assurance for Pyongyang.[72]

Absolutely necessary at this juncture is for South Korea *not* to make any specific choice prematurely, lest it should limit the range of strategic options available to itself. Not making choices entails enhancing the transparency of the knowns and maintaining strategic ambiguity with regard to the unknowns. That is, Seoul must maximize what it already has—the security alliance with the United States and economic and diplomatic cooperation with China—while trying not to commit itself to issues well beyond its control. Not making choices also presupposes carrying out comprehensive independent assessments of its security environment and future contingencies, to which the Roh Moo-Hyun administration appears to be strongly committed.[73] Strategic "soul-searching" includes that of exploring the boundaries of its own foreign-policy discretion with much needed prudence. Such explorations may often prove risky but may nevertheless offer valuable lessons and useful guidelines for the future.

For the first time since 1948, South Korea might have found a widened window of opportunities to create some "breathing space" of its own, by diversifying its key partners of economic and diplomatic cooperation to actors other than the cold war allies, that is, the United States and Japan. Yet the equation has never been simple for Seoul. How will the "China factor" fit into the future Korean-American alliance? Should China be viewed as a potential strategic supplement? Will "strategic bifurcation" become a serious possibility in the future?

It is search for security...which compels [a small power] to ally with a potential protector. This situation prevails particularly when the international system is marked by the presence of two mutually opposed dominant powers. As other potential powers enter the system and challenge the dominance of the superpowers, the small powers get more leeway to manipulate the international situation and thereby resist the pressures of the great powers.[74]

Seoul will closely monitor the specific behavior of the United States and China in order to determine which is likely to be more benign toward it. Assuming that the capabilities of the United States and China may eventually become more balanced in the future, which of the two will be deemed more benign will constitute a crucial variable.[75] Whether South Koreans' favorable perceptions of and positive expectations for China will actually outlive the eventual rise of China also remains to be seen. In the years to come, however, South Korea may find it increasingly difficult to locate a suitable middle ground between the United States and China without offending either of the two.

Northeast Asia is full of uncertainties and contradictions.[76] The interests of the major actors in the region do not necessarily coincide, and neither are they well aligned across the board. Quite the contrary is the case.[77] As a matter of fact, parallel interests necessitate the rise of diverse groupings or lineups depending on the policy issue concerned. Viewed in this vein, increasing the level of interdependence—often skewed and asymmetrical—in the region seems most crucial, as it is the only way to transform the major mode of behavior from norm-based to interest-driven. After all, interests are more transparent and predictable, while norms take time to share and internalize. Yet, common norms may become a prerequisite for Northeast Asia to become a "region" or "regional community" in the genuine sense of the term.

In conclusion, the future of South Korea–China relations is as difficult to predict as that of any other set of relationships in Northeast Asia, a region that is becoming increasingly diverse and complex. As China's shadow gets larger and South Korea's search for "national dignity" (*gukgyok*) continues, with the United States maintaining its superiority, the room for frictions may also expand. One is freshly reminded of the ultimate cause of conflict espoused by Thomas Hobbes: "In the nature of man, we find three principal causes of quarrel: first, competition; second, diffidence; third, glory."[78] As China is gradually becoming fixated on the third component—glory—South Korea's "breathing space" with respect to China may be significantly constricted, putting cultural amity to a real test and bringing the United States back in as the ultimate balancer. Then again, this is only the first chapter on contemporary Korea-China relations.

# Notes

## 1. The Rise of Korea-China Relations and the United States

1. See David Shambaugh, ed., *Power Shift: China and Asia's New Dynamics* (Berkeley: University of California Press, 2005).

2. Sino–South Korean relations had initially been designated as a "cooperative partnership" during President Kim Dae Jung's state visit to China in 1998. Although Seoul and Beijing had agreed upon upgrading it to a "*comprehensive* cooperative partnership" during Premier Zhu Rongji's visit to South Korea in 2000, it became official when President Roh Moo-Hyun visited China in 2003. According to Chinese sources, the latter is the second-best designation—second only to "traditionally amicable ties" (*chuantong youhao guanxi*)—accorded by Beijing. See Zhang Jianhua, ed., *Jiejue zhongguo zaidu mianlin de jinyao wenti* [On resolving the urgent problems China has faced again] (Beijing: Jingji ribao chubanshe, 2000), 523–524.

3. See Wang Gungwu, "The Fourth Rise of China: Cultural Implications," *China: An International Journal* 2, no. 2 (September 2004): 311–322.

4. "Special on China's Industrial Revolution," *Financial Times*, June 25, 2004; John T. Shaplen and James Laney, "China Trades Its Way to Power," *New York Times*, July 12, 2004; Gary Duncan, "No Need to Slay the Chinese Dragon," *Time*, December 20, 2004; Deepak Lai, "How Foreign Reserves Could Make China Yet Stronger," *Financial Times*, December 28, 2004; and Stephen Green, "China's Surfeit of Riches," *Asian Wall Street Journal*, March 2, 2005.

5. See John Mearsheimer, *The Tragedy of Great Power Politics* (New York: Norton, 2001), 32.

6. See *Joint Vision 2020, Asia Vision 2025, Quadrennial Defense Review* (2001, 2005), and *Mapping the Global Future* (2004). For the concept of "regional peer competitor," see Michael A. McDevitt, "The China Factor in Future U.S. Defense Planning," in *Strategic Surprise*, ed. Jonathan D. Pollack (Newport, R.I.: Naval War College Press, 2003), 153.

7. See Chen Xiangyang, *Zhongguo mulin youhao—sixiang shijian qianjing* [China's good neighborly policy: thoughts, practice, and prospects] (Beijing: Shishi chubanshe, 2004); Evan S. Medeiros and M. Taylor Fravel, "China's New Diplomacy," *Foreign Affairs* 82, no. 6 (November–December 2003): 22–35; and Avery Goldstein,

*Rising to the Challenge: China's Grand Strategy and International Security* (Stanford, Calif.: Stanford University Press, 2005), chaps. 5–6.

8.  Richard Betts, "Wealth, Power, and Instability: East Asia and the United States After the Cold War," *International Security* 18, no. 3 (Winter 1993–1994): 34–77; Aaron Friedberg, "Ripe for Rivalry: Prospects for Peace in a Multipolar Asia," *International Security* 18, no. 3 (Winter 1993–1994): 5–33; and Mearsheimer, *The Tragedy of Great Power Politics*, chap. 10.

9.  For the former view, see Michael D. Swaine and Ashley J. Tellis, *Interpreting China's Grand Strategy: Past, Present, and Future* (Santa Monica, Calif.: RAND, 2000), chap. 3. For such unintended consequences in regional power transition, see William R. Thompson, "Dehio, Long Cycles, and the Geohistorical Context of Structural Transition," *World Politics* 45, no. 1 (October 1992): 131–132.

10.  See, for instance, David Shambaugh, "China Engages Asia: Reshaping the Regional Order," *International Security* 29, no. 3 (Winter 2004): 64–99.

11.  Robert G. Sutter, *China's Rise in Asia: Promises and Perils* (Lanham, Md.: Rowman & Littlefield, 2005).

12.  David Kang, "Getting Asia Wrong: The Need for New Analytical Frameworks," *International Security* 27, no. 4 (Spring 2003): 57–85.

13.  G. John Ikenberry, "American Hegemony and East Asian Order," *Australian Journal of International Affairs* 58, no. 3 (September 2004): 353–367.

14.  For such an assessment, see Barry Buzan, "How and to Whom Does China Matter?" in *Does China Matter? A Reassessment*, ed. Barry Buzan and Rosemary Foot (London: Routledge, 2004), 152–154.

15.  See the individual country chapters in Alastair I. Johnston and Robert S. Ross, eds., *Engaging China: The Management of an Emerging Power* (London: Routledge, 1999). See also Herbert Yee and Ian Storey, eds., *China Threat: Perceptions, Myths, and Reality* (London: Routledge Curzon, 2002); Tsedendamba Batbayar, *Mongolia's Foreign Policy in the 1990s: New Identity and New Challenges* (Ulaanbaatar: Institute for Strategic Studies, 2002), 123–156; Zainal A. Yusof, "Malaysia's Response to the China Challenge," and Shigeyuki Abe, "Is 'China Fear' Warranted?" in *Asian Economic Papers* 2, no. 2 (Spring/Summer 2003): 46–131; Buzan and Foot, eds., *Does China Matter?*; John Kerin, "Canberra's Catch-22: The U.S. or China," *Weekend Australian*, May 8–9, 2004; and Shambaugh, *Power Shift*.

16.  See David I. Steinberg, ed., *Korean Attitudes Toward the United States: Changing Dynamics* (Armonk, N.Y.: M. E. Sharpe, 2005); and Jae Ho Chung, "Dragon in the Eyes of South Korea: Analyzing Evolving Perceptions of China," in *Korea: The East Asian Pivot*, ed. Jonathan Pollack (Newport, R.I.: Naval War College Press, 2005).

17.  See Michael Mastanduno, *Economic Containment: COCOM and the Politics of East-West Trade* (Ithaca, N.Y.: Cornell University Press, 1992); and Joan Edelman Spero and Jeffrey A. Hart, *The Politics of International Economic Relations* (New York: Wadsworth Publishing Co., 1996), chap. 10.

18.  To a considerable extent, the evolution of China–South Korea relations reflects the cultivation of an interest-based foreign policy behavior largely independent of prevailing ideologies. In this regard, see Joanne Gowa, *Ballots and Bullets: The*

*Elusive Democratic Peace* (Princeton, N.J.: Princeton University Press, 2000), chap. 1.

19. See, for instance, Richard N. Haass and Meghan L. O'Sullivan, *Honey and Vinegar: Incentives, Sanctions, and Foreign Policy* (Washington, D.C.: The Brookings Institution Press, 2000); and Robert S. Litwak, *Rogue States and U.S. Foreign Policy: Containment After the Cold War* (Baltimore, Md.: Johns Hopkins University Press, 2000), chap. 3.

20. See Helen Milner, "International Theories of Cooperation Among Nations," *World Politics* 44, no. 3 (April 1992): 469; and Michael H. Shuman and Hal Harvey, *Security Without War: A Post–Cold War Foreign Policy* (Boulder, Colo.: Westview, 1993), 144–148.

21. Whether the war on terrorism—which might perhaps replace the cold war—will eventually alter this cooperative paradigm remains to be seen.

22. Robert Axelrod, *The Evolution of Cooperation* (New York: Basic Books, 1984), chaps. 1 and 7.

23. For the potential benefits of regional cooperation in East Asia, see Norman D. Palmer, *The New Regionalism in Asia and the Pacific* (Lanham, Md.: Lexington Books, 1991), chaps. 3 and 10; and Murray Weidenbaum and Samuel Hughes, *The Bamboo Network: How Expatriate Chinese Entrepreneurs Are Creating a New Economic Superpower in Asia* (New York: Free Press, 1996).

24. See Gilbert Rozman, *Northeast Asia's Stunted Regionalism: Bilateral Distrust in the Shadow of Globalization* (Cambridge: Cambridge University Press, 2004); and Jae Ho Chung, "China and Northeast Asian Cooperation: Building an Unbuildable?" in *China Into the Hu-Wen Era: Policy Initiatives and Challenges*, ed. John Wong and Lai Hongyi (Singapore: World Scientific, 2006).

25. Zhang Liangui, "Chaoxian bandao de tongyi yu zhongguo [The Korean reunification and China]," *Dangdai yatai (Contemporary Asia-Pacific)*, no. 5 (2004): 29–36.

26. See Nicholas Eberstadt and Richard J. Ellings, "Assessing Interests and Objectives of Major Actors in the Korean Drama," in *Korea's Future and the Great Powers*, ed. Nicholas Eberstadt and Richard J. Ellings (Seattle: University of Washington Press, 2001), 331–340; and Jae Ho Chung, "Korea and China in Northeast Asia: From Reactive Bifurcation to Complicated Interdependence," in *Korea at the Center: Dynamics of Regionalism in Northeat Asia*, ed. Charles Armstrong, Samuel S. Kim, Stephen Kotkin, and Gilbert Rozman (Armonk, N.Y.: M. E. Sharpe, 2006), chap. 12.

27. See, for instance, Li Qiang, "Chaoxian bandao wenti sifang huitan de xianzhuang yu qianjing [The current situation of and prospects for the four-party talks over the Korean problem]," *Dangdai yatai (Contemporary Asia-Pacific)*, no. 3 (1999): 33–37; and Chen Fengjun, "Ershiyi shiji chaoxian bandao dui zhongguo de zhanlue yiyi [The strategic importance of the Korean Peninsula to China in the twenty-first century]", *Guoji zhengzhi yanjiu* [Study of International Politics], no. 4 (2001): 5–11.

28. See Chae-Jin Lee and Stephanie Hsieh, "China's Two-Korea Policy at Trial: The Hwang Chang Yop Crisis," *Pacific Affairs* 74, no. 3 (Fall 2001): 364–387.

29.  See Jae Ho Chung, "South Korea Between Eagle and Dragon: Perceptual Ambiva-
     lence and Strategic Dilemma," *Asian Survey* 41, no. 5 (September–October 2001):
     778–779.
30.  While Johnston and Ross characterize Seoul as shying away from hedging be-
     tween Washington and China, different empirical findings are available. Compare
     "Conclusion," *Engaging China*, 288; with Jae Ho Chung, *The Korean-American
     Alliance and the "Rise of China": A Preliminary Assessment of Perceptual Changes
     and Strategic Choices* (Stanford, Calif.: Institute for International Studies, February
     1999), available at http://ldml.stanford.edu/aparcpubsearch.
31.  See Zbigniew Brzezinski, Lee Hamilton, and Richard Lugar, eds., *Foreign Policy
     into the Twenty-first Century: The United States Leadership Challenge* (Washington,
     D.C.: CSIS, 1996), 49; Robert Dujarric, *Korean Unification and After: The Chal-
     lenge for U.S. Strategy* (Washington, D.C.: The Hudson Institute, 2000), 42–46;
     Eric A. McVadon, "China's Goals and Strategies for the Korean Peninsula," in
     *Planning for a Peaceful Korea*, ed. Henry D. Sokolski (Carlisle, Penn.: Strategic
     Studies Institute, February 2001), 149, 169; Kurt M. Campbell and Mitchell B.
     Reiss, "Korean Changes, Asian Challenges, and the U.S. Role," *Survival* 43, no. 1
     (Spring 2001): 59–60, 63; Alan Romberg, "The US-PRC-ROK Triangle: Managing
     the Future," (2004), available at http://www.stimpsoncenter.org, last accessed on
     June 28, 2004; and Jae Ho Chung, "America's Views of China–South Korea Rela-
     tions: Public Opinions and Elite Perceptions," *Korean Journal of Defense Analysis*
     17, no. 1 (Spring 2005): 213–234.
32.  For an enlightening piece on this, see Tang Shiping, "Zailun zhongguo de dazhan-
     lue [China's grand strategy revisited]," *Zhanlue yu guanli* [Strategy and Mange-
     ment], no. 4 (2001): 29–37.
33.  For an exemplary effort as such, see the National Security Council of the Republic
     of Korea, *Pyonghwa bonyong gwa gukga anbo* [Peace, Prosperity, and National
     Security] (Seoul: NSC, 2004).
34.  See, for instance, Jonathan Pollack, "U.S.-Korea Relations: The China Factor,"
     *Journal of Northeast Asian Studies* 1, no. 3 (Fall 1985): 24–36.
35.  Korean language materials on the Sino–South Korean rapprochement began to
     appear in the mid-1980s, several years earlier than the explosion of the English-
     language literature on the subject.
36.  For details, see chapters 4 and 5. Chapter 6 also demonstrates that secrecy was one
     of the two conditions demanded by China—the other being the designation of
     the Foreign Ministry as the only channel of formal communication and negotia-
     tions—for its proposed talks on the diplomatic normalization with South Korea.
37.  Such methodological difficulties are noted in Jae Ho Chung, "South Korea–China
     Economic Relations: The Current Situation and Its Implications," *Asian Survey* 28,
     no. 10 (October 1988): 1032, 1034–1036.
38.  See Hieyeon Keum, "Recent Seoul-Peking Relations: Process, Prospects, and
     Limitations," *Issues and Studies* 25, no. 3 (March 1989): 100–117; To-Hai Liou,
     "Sino–South Korean Relations Since 1983: Toward Normalization?" *Journal of
     East Asian Affairs* 5, no. 1 (1991): 49–78; Samuel S. Kim, "China's Korea Policy in a

Changing Regional and Global Order," *China Information* 8, no. 1/2 (1993): 74–92;
Jia Hao and Zhang Qubing, "China's Policy Toward the Korean Peninsula," *Asian
Survey* 32, no. 12 (December 1992): 1137–1156; Yi Xiaoxiong, "China's Korea Policy:
From 'One Korea' to 'Two Koreas,'" *Asian Affairs* (Summer 1995): 119–143; Fei-
ling Wang, "Joining the Major Powers for Status Quo: China's Views and Policy
on Korean Reunification," *Pacific Affairs* 72, no. 2 (Summer 1999): 167–185; and
Quansheng Zhao, "China on the Korean Peace and Unification Process," *Pacific
Focus* 17, no. 2 (Fall 2002): 117–144.

39. Studies on the bilateral economic cooperation were the most numerous. Examples
include Chung, "South Korea–China Economic Relations"; David Dollar, "South
Korea–China Trade Relations: Problems and Prospects," *Asian Survey* 29, no. 12
(December 1989): 1167–1176; Jang Won Suh, "South Korea–China Economic Relations: Trends and Prospects," *Journal of Northeast Asian Studies* 13, no. 4 (Winter
1994): 22–28; and Lee Chang-kyu, "Economic Relations Between Korea and
China," in *Korea's Economy 2004* (Washington, D.C.: Korea Economic Institute,
2004), 65–73.

40. See Robert E. Bedeski, "Sino-Korean Relations: Some Implications for Taiwan,"
*Asian Perspective* 13, no. 1 (Spring–Summer 1989): 99–115; and Robert E. Bedeski,
"South Korea's Diplomatic Normalization with China and Its Impact on Old Ties
Between South Korea and Taiwan," *Journal of East Asian Affairs* 7, no. 2 (Summer/
Fall 1989): 371–403.

41. Liu Hong, "The Sino–South Korean Normalization: A Triangular Explanation,"
*Asian Survey* 33, no. 11 (November 1993): 1083–1094.

42. Jae Ho Chung, "Sino–South Korean Economic Cooperation: An Analysis of Do-
mestic and Foreign Entanglements," *Journal of Northeast Asian Studies* 9, no. 2
(Summer 1990): 59–79; Samuel S. Kim, "The Making of China's Korea Policy in the
Era of Reform," in *The Making of Chinese Foreign and Security Policy*, ed. David M.
Lampton (Stanford, Calif.: Stanford University Press, 2001), 371–408; and Jae Ho
Chung, "From a Special Relationship to a Normal Partnership: Interpreting the
'Garlic Battle' in Sino–South Korean Relations," *Pacific Affairs* 76, no. 4 (Winter
2003/4): 549–568.

43. For a very rough sketch, see Hakjoon Kim, "The Establishment of South Korean–
Chinese Diplomatic Relations: A South Korean Perspective," *Journal of Northeast
Asian Studies* 13, no. 2 (Summer 1994): 31–48.

44. Exceptions are Chung, "South Korea Between Eagle and Dragon"; and Victor D.
Cha, "Engaging China: Seoul-Beijing Détente and Korean Security," *Survival* 41,
no. 1 (Spring 1999): 73–98.

45. These are Ilpyong Kim and Hong Pyo Lee, eds., *Korea and China in a New World:
Beyond Normalization* (Seoul: The Sejong Institute, 1993); and Chae-Jin Lee, *China
and Korea: Dynamic Relations* (Stanford, Calif: The Hoover Press, 1996).

46. Most notable Chinese-language materials include Song Chengyou, Jiang Yi, and
Wang Lei, *Zhonghan guanxishi—xiandaijuan* [History of Sino-Korean relations—
the volume on the contemporary period] (Beijing: Shehui kexue wenxian chubanshe, 1997); Liu Jinzhi, Zhang Minqiu, and Zhang Xiaoming, *Dangdai zhonghan*

*guanxi* [Contemporary China-Korea relations] (Beijing: Zhongguo shehui kexue chubanshe, 1998), which also provides an annotated bibliography; the memoirs of Qian Qichen, China's foreign minister at the time of normalization, *Waijiao shiji* [Ten stories of China's diplomacy] (Beijing: Shijie zhishi chubanshe, 2003), chap. 5; and the memoirs of Zhang Tingyan (China's first ambassador to South Korea), *Chushi Hanguo* [Being the ambassador to Korea] (Jinan: Shandong daxue chubanshe, 2004). Noteworthy Korean-language materials include Hong Duckhwa, *Dugae eui jungguk gwa silli oegyo* [This China, that China] (Seoul: Jajak Academy, 1998); Lee Ho, *Han jung so gan eui bukbang woegyo silche* [The real story of Korea's northern diplomacy with China and the Soviet Union] (Seoul: Cheil Media, 1997); Lee Sang-Ok (South Korea's former Foreign Minister), *Jonhwan'gi eui han'guk oegyo* [Korea's diplomacy in an era of transition] (Seoul: Life and Dream, 2003); and Park Chul-un, *Bareun yoksa reul wihan jeungen* [Testimonies for correct history] (Seoul: Random House Joong-ang, 2005).

47. Lee's *China and Korea*, for instance, does not delve into this crucial dynamic.

48. See chapters 2, 3, and 8 for details on this cultural/perceptual dimension.

49. For instance, all China-related reports in *Chosun Ilbo* [Chosun Daily], *Dong-A Ilbo* [Dong-A Daily], *Joong-ang Ilbo* [Joong-ang Daily], and *Hanguk gyongje sinmun* [Korea Economic Daily] for the period from 1948 to 2004 were closely examined. The South Korean government's declassified foreign-policy document files—housed in the Institute for National Security and Foreign Affairs (IFANS)— were also consulted for the period from 1948 through 1974.

50. For these elite surveys, see chapter 9.

51. It should be noted that the diplomatic normalization between China and South Korea was one outcome of Beijing's "normalization drive" during the 1990s. See, for instance, Jonathan Goldstein, ed., *China and Israel 1948–1998: A Fifty-Year Perspective* (Westport, Conn.: Praeger, 1999); Rizal Sukma, *Indonesia and China: The Politics of a Troubled Relationship* (London: Routledge, 1999); and Chris Alden, "Solving South Africa's China Puzzle: Domestic Foreign Policy-Making and the 'Two-China' Question," in *South Africa's Foreign Policy: Dilemmas of a New Democracy*, ed. Jim Broderick, Gary Burford, and Gordon Freer (Basingstoke: Palgrave, 2001).

52. Chinese sources suggest that Korea-China relations go back five millennia. See Yang Shaoquan and He Tongmei, *Zhongguo-Chaoxian Hanguo guanxishi* [History of China's relations with Korea] (Tianjin: Tianjin renmin chubanshe, 2001), 1:4–6.

53. For the importance of cultural perceptions and identity for the making of foreign policy, see Valerie M. Hudson, ed., *Culture and Foreign Policy* (Boulder, Colo.: Lynne Rienner, 1997); and Michael C. Desch, "Culture Clash: Assessing the Importance of Ideas in Security Studies," *International Security* 23, no. 1 (Summer 1998): 141–170.

54. See Chung, "South Korea Between Eagle and Dragon"; and Piao Jianyi, "Zhonghan jianjiao shinian lai zhengzhi yu waijiao guanxi shuping [Overview of the China–South Korean political and diplomatic relationship in the last ten years

since the normalization]," *Dangdai yatai (Contemporary Asia-Pacific)*, no. 8 (2002): 58–62.

55. The heated controversy in 2004 over China's efforts—the Northeast Project (*dongbei gongcheng*)—to incorporate Kokuryo as China's "local history" and Beijing's "imposing" stance on South Korea have often stirred negative public opinions of China in South Korea. For such concerns, see Nan Liming, "Hanguo dui zhongguo de wenhua kangyi [South Korea's cultural objection to China]," *Yazhou zhoukan* [Asia Weekly], July 25, 2004; *Dong-A Ilbo*, December 3, 2003 and December 25, 2004; *Joong-ang Ilbo*, December 4, 2003; and *Washington Post*, September 23, 2004.

56. See his recommendation for "allying with China, aligning with Japan, and liaising with the United States [*qinqing jieri lianmei*]" in Huang Zunxian, *Chaoxian celue* [The strategy for Chosun] (Seoul: Kunkuk University Press, 1977), 47, for the original Chinese text.

57. See, for instance, Andre Schmid, *Korea Between Empires, 1895–1919* (New York: Columbia University Press, 2002). Of course, Seoul's long-term reaction may as well go to the opposite direction if the rise of China is deemed by Korea as a serious threat that has to be contained.

## 2. A Sketch of Sino-Korean Relations

1. See Jack Levy, "Too Important to Leave to the Other: History and Political Science in the Study of International Relations," *International Security* 22, no.1 (Summer 1997): 22–33.

2. For a fascinating study of reputation in international affairs that goes beyond conventional wisdom, see Jonathan Mercer, *Reputation and International Politics* (Ithaca, N.Y.: Cornell University Press, 1996), chaps. 1 and 2.

3. See Alvin Z. Rubinstein and Donald Smith, "Anti-Americanism: Anatomy of a Phenomenon," in *Anti-Americanism in the Third World*, ed. Alvin Z. Rubinstein and Donald Smith (New York: Praeger, 1985); and Robert Wistrich, *Anti-Zionism and Antisemitism in the Contemporary World* (New York: New York University Press, 1990).

4. See Rita R. Rogers, "Intergenerational Transmission of Historical Enmity," in *The Psychodynamics of International Relationships*, ed. Vamik D. Volkan et al. (Lexington, Mass.: Lexington Books, 1990), 91–96.

5. Joyce Marie Mushaben, "A Search for Identity: The 'German Question' in Atlantic Alliance Relations," *World Politics* 40, no. 3 (April 1988): 395–417; and Gerrit W. Gong, ed., *Remembering and Forgetting: The Legacy of War and Peace in East Asia* (Washington, D.C.: Center for Strategic and International Studies, 1996).

6. Taiwan's Japanophilic disposition compared to China and Korea remains to be closely scrutinized in this regard. See, for instance, Shelley Rigger, *Politics in Taiwan: Voting for Democracy* (London: Routledge, 1999), chaps. 1 and 2; and Leo T. S. Ching, *Becoming Japanese: Colonial Taiwan and the Politics of Identity Formation* (Stanford, Calif.: Stanford University, 2001).

7.  More details on this dimension, including nationwide opinion surveys, are provided in chapter 8.

8.  While the demand for a formal apology has been a constant issue of contention in South Korea–Japan relations, not even a sign of "regret" was officially offered by the Chinese side for its military involvement against South Korea during the Korean War. The political dynamics over this issue during the South Korea–China diplomatic-normalization negotiations are discussed in chapter 6.

9.  For South Koreans' favorable views of China compared to their views of Japan and the United States, see Jae Ho Chung, "South Korea Between Eagle and Dragon: Perceptual Ambivalence and Strategic Dilemma," *Asian Survey* 41, no. 5 (September/October 2001): 783–785.

10. See Mark Mancall, "The Ch'ing Tribute System: An Interpretive Essay," in *The Chinese World Order: Traditional China's Foreign Relations*, ed. John King Fairbank (Cambridge, Mass.: Harvard University Press, 1968), 63–89; Michael H. Hunt, *The Genesis of Chinese Communist Foreign Policy* (New York: Columbia University Press, 1996), 3–28; and Michael D. Swaine and Ashley J. Tellis, *Interpreting China's Grand Strategy: Past, Present, and Future* (Santa Monica, Calif.: RAND, 2000), 22–79.

11. See Yang Shaoquan and He Tongmei, *Zhongguo-Chaoxian Hanguo guanxishi* [History of China's relations with Korea] (Tianjin: Tianjin renmin chubanshe, 2001), 1:4–6; Huang Zhilian, *Yazhou de huaxia zhixu* [China's world order in Asia] (Beijing: Zhongguo renmindaxue chubanshe, 1992), chap. 2; and Peter Yun, "Confucian Ideology and the Tribute System in Chosun-Ming Relations," *Sachong* [Historical Review], no. 55 (September 2002): 67–70.

12. See Hae-jong Chun, "Sino-Korean Tributary Relations in the Ch'ing Period," in *The Chinese World Order*, 90–91; and Yang and He, *Zhongguo chaoxian hanguo guanxi*, 2:542–579.

13. See Alexander Woodside, *Vietnam and the Chinese Model* (Cambridge, Mass.: Harvard University Press, 1971), 237.

14. See Huang, *Yazhou de huaxia zhixu*, 167–174. Also see Pow-key Sohn, "Power Versus Status: The Role of Ideology During the Early Yi Dynasty," *Dongbanghakji* [Studies of the East], no. 10 (1969): 211–217; and Chun Hae-jong, *Hanjung gwangyesa yongu* [Study of the history of Korea-China relations] (Seoul: Ilchogak, 1970), 24.

15. See Zhang Yongjiang, *Qingdai fanbu yanjiu* [The vassal management during the Qing dynasty] (Harbin: Heilongjiang jiaoyu chubanshe, 2001), 27–28, 293; and Chen Fengjun and Wang Chuanzhao, *Yatai daguo yu chaoxian bandao* [Asian-Pacific major powers and the Korean peninsula] (Beijing: Beijing daxue chubanshe, 2002), 279.

16. The former is quoted from *Sonjo sujong sillok* [Court records of the Sonjo reign] while the latter is from *Ming shenzong shilu* [The Ming imperial court records of the Shenzong reign]. Both are cited in Choi Soja, *Myung-chong sidae jung-han gwangyesa yongu* [Study of China-Korea relations during the Ming and Qing dynasties] (Seoul: Ewha Woman's University Press, 1997), 26, 28.

17. See the interesting comparison between early Chosun's Chung Dojon and late Chosun's Yi I on their views of China in Peter Yun, "Confucian Ideology and the

Tribute System in Chosun-Ming Relations," 72–79. On the importance of Japan's invasion of Korea in 1592 to Korea-China relations, see Han Myung-ki, *Yimjin woelan gwa hanjung gwangye* [The Yimjin invasion by Japan and Korea-China relations] (Seoul: Yoksa bipyongsa, 1999).

18. Choi, *Myung-chong sidae jung-han gwangyesa yongu*, 59, 116; and Zhang, *Qingdai fanbu yanjiu*, 36–38.

19. See Swaine and Tellis, *Interpreting China's Grand Strategy*, 25, 66; and Mark Mancall, *China at the Center: Three Hundred Years of Foreign Policy* (New York: Free Press, 1984), 16–33.

20. Andre Schmid, *Korea Between Empires, 1895–1919* (New York: Columbia University Press, 2002), chap. 2.

21. On this point, see Yang and He, *Zhongguo chaoxian hanguo guanxi*, 2:792–935; and Shi Yuanhua, *Hanguo duli yundong yu zhongguo* [Korea's independence movements and China] (Shanghai: Shanghai renmin chubanshe, 1995).

22. See *Chosunjok yaksa* [A short history of the Korean nationality in China] (Seoul: Baeksan sodang, 1989), 29.

23. See, for instance, Zhang Liangui, *1945nian yiqian guojizhengzhi zhong de chaoxian he zhongguo* [Korea and China in international politics before 1945] (Harbin: Heilongjiang jiaoyu chubanshe, 1996), 250–272.

24. It can be speculated that Mao's plan to "liberate" Taiwan was spoiled by Kim Il Sung's own war plan. For such a view, see Qing Shi, "Jin Richeng zhuzhile Mao Zedong jingong Taiwan de jihua [Kim Il Sung blocked Mao Zedong's plan to attack Taiwan]," *Mingbao yuekan* [Ming Pao Monthly], July 1994.

25. For the dire conditions that China was facing at the time, see Maurice Meisner, *Mao's China: A History of the People's Republic* (New York: Free Press, 1977), 77–79; and Zhihua Shen, "China Sends Troops to Korea: Beijing's Policy-Making Process," in *China and the United States: A New Cold War History*, ed. Xiaobing Li and Hongshan Li (Lanham, Md.: University Press of America, 1999), 13–47. For the lasting economic impact of the Korean War, see Carl Riskin, *China's Political Economy* (New York: Oxford University Press, 1987), 43–49, 74–76.

26. See Chae-Jin Lee, *China and Korea: Dynamic Relations* (Stanford, Calif.: The Hoover Press, 1996), 10–21; "Zhongguo xuezhe yanzhong de kangmei yuanchao [The "Resist America and aid North Korea" war in the eyes of Chinese scholars]," *Banyuetan neibuban* [Semimonthly Talks], no. 10 (2000): 33–34; and Xiaobing Li, Allan R. Millet, and Bin Yu, eds., *Mao's Generals Remember Korea* (Lawrence: University Press of Kansas, 2001).

27. These two expressions were first used in the late nineteenth century by Li Hungzhang, who saw the ultimate strategic importance of Korea to the security of Northeast Provinces (*dongsansheng*) in Manchuria. See Li Hungzhang, "Lun riben paishi ru chaoxian [On Japan's entry to Chosun by dispatching emissaries]," and "Sanda xiangguo Li Yuwon shu [Three replies to former imperial councillor Li Yuwon]," in *Li Hungzhang quanji* [Complete collections of Li Hungzhang] (Haikou: Hainan chubanshe, 1997), 6:3013, 9:4785.

28. For these expressions (*tifa*), see Liu Jinzhi, Zhang Minqiu, and Zhang Xiaoming, *Dangdai zhonghan guanxi* [Contemporary China-Korea relations] (Beijing: Zhongguo shehuikexue chubanshe, 1998), 2, 30.

29. See Jae Ho Chung, "Korea and China in Northeast Asia: From Reactive Bifurcation to Complicated Interdependence," in *Korea at the Center: Dynamics of Regionalism in Northeast Asia*, ed. Charles K. Armstron, Gilbert Rozman, Samuel S. Kim, and Stephen Kotkin (Armonk, N.Y.: M. E. Sharpe, 2006), 203–205. For Pyongyang's use of anticronyistic slogans, see Liu et al., *Dangdai zhonghan guanxi*, 42.

30. Except for 1967 through 1969, when the radicalization of ideology reached its zenith, North Korea generally maintained a more amicable relationship with China than with the Soviet Union. See Liu et al., *Dangdai zhonghan guanxi*, 41–44.

31. Qian Qichen's memoir, for instance, provides details on the special effort Beijing made in this regard. Detailed discussions on this will be provided in chapter 6.

32. For such indications, see Andrew Scobell, "China and North Korea: The Limits of Influence," *Current History* (September 2003): 274–278; and Jae Ho Chung, "China's Ascendancy and the Korean Peninsula: From Interest Re-evaluation to Strategic Re-alignment?" in *Power Shift: China and Asia's New Dynamics*, ed. David Shambaugh (Berkeley: University of California Press, 2005), 155–156.

33. As early as 1973, South Korea's foreign ministry issued internal guidelines for conducting "active contact" with the diplomats from the People's Republic of China. See the Republic of Korea Foreign Policy Archive, File no. 722.2CP, microfiche C-0061-17.

34. These three perspectives are discussed in more detail in chapter 3.

35. See, for instance, Michael C. Desch, "Culture Clash: Assessing the Importance of Ideas in Security Studies," *International Security* 23, no. 1 (Summer 1998): 150–153.

36. See *Chosun Ilbo* [Chosun Daily], January 5, 2003; and *Dong-A Ilbo* [Dong-A Daily], February 7, 2005. As of May 2005, the number of South Korea–China flights per week was 380, while the total number of South Korea–U.S. flights per week was 257.

37. See Jae Ho Chung, *The Korean-American Alliance and the "Rise of China": A Preliminary Assessment of Perceptual Changes and Strategic Choices* (Stanford, Calif.: Institute for International Studies, February 1999), available at http://ldml.stanford.edu/aparcpubsearch.

38. See *Chosun Ilbo*, April 29 and 30, 2004; and *Dong-A Ilbo*, May 4, 2004.

39. Some argue that this is mutual from the Chinese viewpoint as well. See Zheng Chenghong, "Hanju keyi dadong Zhongguo [Korean dramas are moving China]," *Shijie zhishi* [World Knowledge], no. 4 (2005): 17–19.

40. Some signs of this are already in sight, as China made unprecedented efforts to incorporate part of Korea's ancient history into its "local history" (*difangshi*), with its pronounced "Northeast Project" (*Dongbei gongcheng*). See *Dong-A Ilbo*, August 6 and 7, 2004. For the "Northeast Project," see Ma Dazheng, ed., *Zhongguo dongbei bianjiang yanjiu* [Study of China's northeast border areas] (Beijing: Zhongguo shehuikexue chubanshe, 2003), 14–19, 149–150.

41. For the inherent artificiality of many seemingly obvious watershed periodizations, see Paul A. Cohen, *China Unbound: Evolving Perspectives on the Chinese Past* (London: Routledge Curzon, 2003), 136–141.

## 3. Perspectives on the Origins of the South Korea–China Rapprochement

1. "Stable marriage" refers to a relationship of amity between two of the players (China and North Korea) and a relationship of enmity between each and the third player (South Korea); "romantic triangle" denotes a relationship of amity between one pivotal player (China) and two "wing" players, with enmity between each of the latter two; and "ménage à trois" means symmetrical amity among all three. See Lowell Dittmer, "The Strategic Triangle: An Elementary Game-Theoretical Analysis," *World Politics* 33, no. 4 (July 1981): 489. Also see Hong Yung Lee, "The Emerging Triangle Among China and Two Koreas," in *Korea and the World: Beyond the Cold War*, ed. Young Whan Kihl (Boulder, Colo.: Westview, 1994), 97–110; and Jae Ho Chung, "Korea and China in Northeast Asia: From Reactive Bifurcation to Complex Interdependence," in *Korea at the Center: Dynamics of Regionalism in Northeast Asia*, ed. Charles Armstrong, Samuel S. Kim, Stephen Kotkin, and Gilbert Rozman (Armonk, N.Y.: M. E. Sharpe, 2006), chap. 12.

2. As noted in the literature review in chapter 1, most of the studies on this theme are temporally short-term, fragmented in coverage, and mostly descriptive policy overviews, and are devoid of comprehensive and analytical perspectives.

3. For a comprehensive and persuasive coverage of these themes, see Arthur A. Stein, *Why Nations Cooperate: Circumstance and Choice in International Relations* (Ithaca, N.Y.: Cornell University Press, 1990), chap. 7; and Benjamin Miller, *When Opponents Cooperate: Great Power Conflict and Collaboration in World Politics* (Ann Arbor: University of Michigan Press, 1995).

4. For the realist paradigm, see Kenneth N. Waltz, *Theory of International Politics* (New York: Random House, 1979), chaps. 6 and 8; and David A. Baldwin, "Neoliberalism, Neorealism, and World Politics," in *Neorealism and Neoliberalism: The Contemporary Debate*, ed. David A. Baldwin (New York: Columbia University Press, 1993), 3–25.

5. Debates persist as to whether such perceptions of national humiliations are real or myths. However, the bottom line is that Chinese policy makers have acted on what is called "siege mentality." See Fei-Ling Wang, "Self-Image and Strategic Intentions: National Confidence and Political Insecurity," in *In the Eyes of the Dragon: China Views the World*, ed. Yong Deng and Fei-Ling Wang (Lanham, Md.: Rowman and Littlefield, 1999), 21–46. On not forgetting "past humiliations," see Paul A. Cohen, *China Unbound: Evolving Perspectives on the Chinese Past* (London: Routledge Curzon, 2003), 166–169.

6. See Joseph Camilleri, *Chinese Foreign Policy: The Maoist Era and Its Aftermath* (Oxford: Martin Robertson, 1980), 6, 19, 83. For China's hypersensitivity to sovereignty, see Peter Van Ness, "China and the Third World," in *China and the World: Chinese Foreign Policy Faces the New Millennium*, ed. Samuel S. Kim (Boulder, Colo.: Westview, 1998), 158–159; and Hongying Wang, "Multilateralism in Chinese Foreign Policy: The Limits of Socialization," *Asian Survey* 40, no. 3 (May/June 2000): 486.

7.  Carol Lee Hamrin, "China Reassesses the Superpowers," *Pacific Affairs* 56, no. 2 (Summer 1983): 210–212. Also see Michel C. Oksenberg, "China's Confident Nationalism," *Foreign Affairs* 65, no. 3 (May–June 1987): 501–523.

8.  There is no doubt that China's new confidence was based on its gaining a minimum nuclear deterrence capability by the mid-1980s. See General Armament Department of the People's Liberation Army, ed., *Liangdan yixing* [Two bombs and one satellite] (Beijing: Jiuzhou chubanshe, 2001).

9.  For Chinese interpretation of this crucial change, see Wang Xuhe and Ren Xiangqun, *Guo zhi zun—xin zhongguo waijiao jishi* [The prestige of China: chronicles of new China's diplomacy] (Hangzhou: Zhejiang renmin chubanshe, 1999), chap. 5; and Wang Taiping, *Xinzhongguo waijiao wushinian* [On the fifty years of new China's diplomacy] (Beijing: Beijing renmin chubanshe, 1999), 1:33–37.

10. On this line of argument, see Samuel S. Kim, "China and the Third World: In Search of a Neorealist World Policy," in *China and the World: Chinese Foreign Policy in the Post-Mao Era*, ed. Samuel S. Kim (Boulder, Colo.: Westview, 1984), 189–205; and Zhu Hongqian, "China and the Triangular Relationship," in *The Chinese View of the World*, ed. Hao Yufan and Huan Guocang (New York: Pantheon Books, 1989), 42–43.

11. Gu Weiqun, "Security in the Asian-Pacific Region," in *The Chinese View of the World*, 25–26. Also see Jianwei Wang and Xinbo Wu, *Against Us or With Us: The Chinese Perspective of America's Alliances with Japan and Korea* (Discussion Papers, the Asia/Pacific Research Center, Stanford University, May 1998), 34–35.

12. In efforts to enlist China in preventing North Korea's aggression against the South, Seoul was willing to initiate and expand contact with Beijing as early as 1971. See the Foreign Policy Archive of the Republic of Korea, File 721.1CP, microfiche C-0044-02 (1971); File 721.1CP, microfiche C-0051-03 (1972); and File 727.1CP, microfiche E-0009-02 (1971–1972). For a brief overview of Seoul's overtures toward Beijing in the early 1970s, see Ilpyong J. Kim, "Policies Toward China and the Soviet Union," in *The Foreign Policy of the Republic of Korea*, ed. Youngnok Koo and Sung-joo Han (New York: Columbia University Press, 1985), 202–203, 209–210.

13. This is what Stein terms a "force of circumstance." See Stein, *Why Nations Cooperate*, 195.

14. Richard Rosecrance, *The Rise of the Trading State: Commerce and Conquest in the Modern World* (New York: Basic Books, 1986), ix, 223.

15. See, for instance, Seweryn Bialer, *The Soviet Paradox: External Expansion, Internal Decline* (New York: Basic Books, 1986). Also see Lawrence C. Reardon, *The Reluctant Dragon: Crisis Cycles in Chinese Foreign Economic Policy* (Hong Kong: Hong Kong University Press, 2002), chap. 7.

16. Robert Keohane, *After Hegemony: Cooperation and Discord in the World Political Economy* (Princeton, N.J.: Princeton University Press, 1984), 51.

17. Charles Lipson, "International Cooperation in Economic and Security Affairs," *World Politics* 37, no. 1 (October 1984): 1–23.

18. For South Korea's economic motives, see Eul Yong Park, "Foreign Economic Policies and Economic Development," in *The Foreign Policy of the Republic of Korea*,

125–127. For China's motives, see Jonathan Woetzel, *China's Economic Opening to the Outside World: The Politics of Empowerment* (New York: Praeger, 1989).

19. For such confidence, see Hao Yufan, "China and the Korean Peninsula," in *The Chinese View of the World*, 198.

20. See Jae Ho Chung, "South Korea–China Economic Cooperation: The Current Situation and Its Implications," *Asian Survey* 28, no. 10 (October 1988): 1047.

21. For this logic, see Robert Axelrod and Robert O. Keohane, "Achieving Cooperation Under Anarchy: Strategies and Institutions," in *Neorealism and Neoliberalism*, 108–110.

22. For discussions along this line, see James N. Rosenau, ed., *Linkage Politics: Essays on the Convergence of National and International Systems* (New York: The Free Press, 1969); and Bruce Russett, "International Interactions and Processes: The Internal vs. External Debate Revisited," in *Political Science: The State of the Discipline*, ed. Ada W. Finifter (Washington D.C.: American Political Science Association, 1983), 541–568. For China-specific studies, see Kenneth Lieberthal, "Domestic Politics and Foreign Policy," in *China's Foreign Relations in the 1980s*, ed. Harry Harding (New Haven, Conn.: Yale University Press, 1984), 43–70; and David Bachman, "Domestic Sources of Chinese Foreign Policy," in *China and the World: New Directions in Chinese Foreign Relations*, ed. Samuel S. Kim (Boulder, Colo.: Westview, 1989), 31–54.

23. Detailed discussions of the key actors and their complex interactions in the process of normalization are provided in chapter 6.

24. See Richard Fagen, Carmen Diana Deere, and Jose Luis Coraggio, *Transition and Development: Problems of Third World Socialism* (New York: Monthly Review, 1986), 9–27.

25. David J. Carroll, Jerel A. Rosati, and Roger A. Coate, "Human Needs Realism: A Critical Assessment of the Power of Human Needs in World Society," in *The Power of Human Needs in World Society*, ed. Roger A. Coate and Jerel A. Rosati (Boulder, Colo.: Lynne Rienner Publishers, 1988), 261.

26. Ferenc Feher, Agnes Heller, and György Markus, *Dictatorship Over Needs: An Analysis of Soviet Societies* (New York: Basil Blackwell, 1983).

27. See Carl Riskin, "Neither Plan Nor Market: Mao's Political Economy," in *New Perspectives on the Cultural Revolution*, ed. William A. Joseph, Christine P. W. Wong, and David Zweig (Cambridge, Mass.: Harvard University Press, 1991), 133–152; and Wang Shaoguang, *Lixing yu fengkuang* [Reason and madness] (Wuhan: Hubei renmin chubanshe, 1995).

28. For the option of international trade for socialist states, see Alec Nove, *The Economics of Feasible Socialism* (London: Allen and Unwin, 1983), 108.

29. While there was an interregnum of Hua Guofeng's rule during 1977 through 1978, the period was too brief to have any serious effect on the post-Mao era as a whole.

30. See Harry Harding, *China's Second Revolution: Reform After Mao* (Washington D.C.: Brookings Institution, 1987); Barry Naughton, *Growing out of the Plan: Chinese Economic Reform, 1978–1993* (Cambridge: Cambridge University Press, 1995);

and Chien-min Chao and Bruce J. Dickson, eds., *Remaking the Chinese State: Strategies, Society, and Security* (London: Routledge, 2001).

31.  For details of these developments, see Robert Kleinberg, *China's "Opening" to the Outside World: The Experiment with Foreign Capitalism* (Boulder, Colo.: Westview, 1990); Elizabeth Economy and Michel Oksenberg, eds., *China Joins the World: Progress and Prospects* (New York: Council on Foreign Relations, 1999); and David Zweig, *Internationalizing China: Domestic Interests and Globla Linkages* (Ithaca, N.Y.: Cornell University Press, 2002).

32.  See, for instance, Ma Licheng and Ling Zhijun, *Jiaofeng—dangdai zhongguo sanci sixiang jiefang shilu* [Sword-crossing: chronicles of three "thought liberations" in Contemporary China] (Beijing: Jinre zhongguo chubanshe, 1998); and Yang Jisheng, *Deng Xiaoping shidai—zhongguo gaige kaifang ershinian jishe* [The era of Deng Xiaoping: chronicles of twenty years of reform and opening] (Beijing: Zhongyang bianyi chubanshe, 1998), vol. 1, chap. 3.

33.  Jia Qingguo, "China's Foreign Economic Policy," in *The Chinese View of the World*, 67.

34.  The quotation is from the second edition of Bruce Russett and Harvey Starr, *World Politics: The Menu for Choice* (New York: W.H. Freeman and Company, 1985), 45. For an excellent and comprehensive discussion of nationalism, see Anthony D. Smith, *Nationalism* (Cambridge: Polity Press, 2001), chap. 2.

35.  Lloyd Jensen, *Explaining Foreign Policy* (Englewood Cliffs, N.J.: Prentice-Hall, 1982), 28, 53–59.

36.  See, for instance, Mark Mancall, *China at the Center: Three Hundred Years of Foreign Policy* (New York: The Free Press, 1984).

37.  See Michael H. Hunt, "Chinese Foreign Relations in Historical Perspective," in *China's Foreign Relations in the 1980s*, 1–42; Chih-yu Shih, *The Spirit of Chinese Foreign Policy: A Psychocultural View* (London: Palgrave McMillan, 1990); and Michael H. Hunt, *The Genesis of Chinese Communist Foreign Policy* (New York: Columbia University Press, 1996), chap. 1. To a considerable extent, the nationalism of this sort differs from the popular nationalistic sentiments targeted at the United States and Japan and discussed in Peter H. Gries, *China's New Nationalism: Pride, Politics, and Diplomacy* (Berkeley: University of California Press, 2004).

38.  See Yongnian Zheng, *Discovering Chinese Nationalism in China: Modernization, Identity, and International Relations* (Cambridge: Cambridge University Press, 1999), chap. 1; and Lin Shangli, "Xiandaihua yu wenhua rentong—zhongguo de luoji [Modernization and cultural identity: the logic of China]," in *Zhongguo shehui bianqian* [Social transformation in China], ed. Zhu Guohong, Lin Shangli, and Zhang Jun (Shanghai: Fudan daxue chubanshe, 2001), 36–57.

39.  Between 1979 and 2001, China normalized relations with sixty-three countries, making for a total of 162. See *Zhongguo waijiao cidian* [Encyclopedia of Chinese diplomacy] (Beijing: Shijie zhishi chubanshe, 2000), 814–821; and *Zhongguo waijiao 2001* [China's diplomacy 2001] (Beijing: Shijie zhishi chubanshe, 2001), 714.

40.  For the definition, see Charles A. Lave and James G. March, *An Introduction to Models in the Social Sciences* (New York: Harper and Row, 1975), 5, 341–405.

41. See Glenn D. Paige, "North Korea and the Emulation of Russian and Chinese Behavior," in *Communist Strategies in Asia*, ed. A. Doak Barnett (New York: Praeger, 1963), 228–262; "Beihan de zhongguohua qushi [The trend of North Korea's emulation of China]," *Jiushi niandai* [The Nineties] (December 1984): 38–42; Selig Harrison, "Kim Il Sung Promotes a Chinese Style Open-Door Policy," *Far Eastern Economic Review* (December 3, 1987): 37–38; and Yang Ho-min, "Mao Zedong's Ideological Influence on Pyongyang and Hanoi: Some Historical Roots Reconsidered," in *Asian Communism: Continuity and Transition*, ed. Robert A. Scalapino and Dalchoong Kim (Berkeley: Institute of East Asian Studies, University of California, 1988), 37–66.

42. Dwight H. Perkins, *China: Asia's Next Economic Giant?* (Seattle: University of Washington Press, 1986), 5–6.

43. For a similar line of argument, see Hajime Izumi and Susumu Kohari, "Sino–South Korean Relations Under the Roh Administration," *China Newsletter*, no. 91 (1991): 17.

44. Author's interview with a Chinese scholar from the CASS, November 14, 1987. A Korean source also suggests that Liu Guoguang, an influential economist with political clout, paid a visit to Seoul in 1980, although this could not be independently substantiated. See Lee Ho, *Han jung so gan eui bukbang woegyo silche* [The real story of Korea's diplomacy with China and the Soviet Union] (Seoul: Cheil Media, 1997), 193–194.

45. See Chung Yong-seok, "Junggong eui daehan insik [Communist China's perception of Korea]," *Bukhan* [North Korea] (April 1984): 79; and Shin Myung-soon, "Hangukgwa junggong eui gwangye gaeson e gwanhan yongu [Study on how to improve Korea's relations with communist China]," *Hanguk gwa gukje jongchi* [Korea and World Politics] 1 (January 1985): 59.

46. See Wu Linggeng, "Yazhou sixiaolong jingji qiji puoxi [Analyzing the economic miracle by Asia's four little dragons]," *Hongqi* [Red Flag] (April 1987): 29–32; Pu Zhengluo, Wang Rui, and Cong Ronglian, *Yazhou sixiao yu waixiangxing jingji* [Asia's four small dragons and their outward-oriented economies] (Beijing: Zhongguo duiwai jingji maoyi chubanshe, 1990); and Yim Gey-soon, *Junggukin yi barabon hanguk* [Korea in the eyes of the Chinese] (Seoul: Samsung Economic Research Institute, 2002), chap. 5.

47. See Bruce Cummings, "The Political Economy of China's Turn Outward," in *China and the World: Chinese Foreign Policy in the Post-Mao Era*, 246–247. China also allegedly collected all the information on South Korea's Five-Year Plans for Economic Development. See Li Ki-taek, "Hanjunggong daehwa-ui kilun yollyonunga? [Has the communication channel been opened between Korea and communist China?]" *Shindong-a* [New East Asia] (June 1983): 84.

48. Hwang Byung-Tae, "Hanjung gyungje sumeun juyok eun deungsopyong adeul [Deng Xiaoping's son is the hidden hand behind South Korea–China economic cooperation]," *Shindong-a* (March 1996): 471.

49. While there were rumors that South Korea–China indirect trade began in 1976, there is no hard data available to confirm them. It may well be that the size of the bilateral indirect trade in 1976 through 1978, if any, was almost negligible.

## 4. South Korea–China Relations Before 1988

1. The 1988 watershed was crucial in several respects, as will be noted later, most notably in terms of making the burgeoning bilateralism more public, if not yet governmental.

2. See, for instance, Robert Jervis, "The Impact of the Korean War on the Cold War," *Journal of Conflict Resolution* 24, no. 4 (December 1980): 563–592.

3. At one point in 1963, even a military alliance between Seoul and Taipei was floated as a possibility. See *Chosun Ilbo* [Chosun Daily], February 22, 1963.

4. See Jae Ho Chung, "Korea and China in Northeast Asia: From Stable Bifurcation to Complicated Interdependence," in *Korea at the Center: Dynamics of Regionalism in Northeast Asia*, ed. Charles K. Armstron, Gilbert Rozman, Samuel S. Kim, and Stephen Kotkin (Armonk, N.Y.: M. E. Sharpe, 2006), 202–203.

5. *Chosun Ilbo*, September 19, September 30, and October 18, 1961.

6. On a few occasions, these fishermen were released with the mediating help of the British Embassy in Beijing. See *Chosun Ilbo*, May 18 and 23, 1965; and *Dong-A Ilbo* [Dong-A Daily], April 20, 1967.

7. There were two additional factors on the part of South Korea: (1) Plans were being considered by Washington to reduce its forces in Korea by an amount equivalent to an infantry division; and (2) China's accession to the United Nations in 1971 generated an urgent need for Seoul to rethink its overall strategic posture in Northeast Asia.

8. See Chae-Jin Lee, *China and Korea: Dynamic Relations* (Stanford, Calif.: The Hoover Press, 1996), 105.

9. Foreign Policy Archive of the Republic of Korea, File 721.1CH/CP, Microfiche C-0044-021.

10. See *Chosun Ilbo*, February 17, March 16, April 11, and July 24, 1971.

11. The main beneficiary of the amendment was the Soviet Union. In 1974, the volume of indirect trade between South Korea and the Soviet Union already amounted to US$4 million. See Lee Beom-chan, "Hanso kyoryu hyonhwanggwa hwakdae bang-an [The current situation of South Korea–Soviet exchanges and the measures for expansion]," *Kongsangwon yongu* [Studies of Communist Area] (May 1987): 15.

12. According to a survey in early 1972, as many as 38 percent of the National Assembly members were in support of diplomatic normalization with communist China. *Chosun Ilbo*, March 30, 1972. For the media's self-criticism of its excessive anticommunist tone in reporting on the mainland China, see *Chosun Ilbo*, March 4, 1973. According to Ambassador Zhang Ruijie, an experienced Chinese diplomat, after the Nixon visit in 1972, North Korea also asked China to work as a go-between for improving relations with the United States. Interview with Zhang in Seoul in June 2005.

13. See the Foreign Policy Archive of the Republic of Korea, File 721.1CP, Microfiche C-0051-03; and File 722.2CP, Microfiche C-0072-10.

14. *Chosun Ilbo*, March 17, 1973.

15. *Chosun Ilbo*, March 20 and April 23, 1974.

16. *Chosun Ilbo*, November 27, 1974.

17. Shin Myung-soon, "Hangukgwa junggong-ui gwangye gaeson-e gwanhan yongu [On how to improve South Korea's relations with China]," *Hangukgwa gukje jongch'i* [Korea and World Politics] 1, no. 1 (January 1985): 55–56; and Chi-jeong Park, "Han-junggong min'gan gyoryu hwakdae bang'an [Measures to expand nongovernmental exchanges between South Korea and China]," *Jungguk yongu* [China Studies] 5 (1986): 44.

18. Parris H. Chang, "Beijing's Policy Toward Korea and PRC-ROK Normalization of Relations," in *The Changing Order in Northeast Asia and the Korean Peninsula* (Seoul: Institute for Far Eastern Studies, 1993), 163. Cited in Lee, *China and Korea*, 68.

19. The rumor was cited in Shin, "Hangukgwa junggong-ui gwangye gaeson-e gwanhan yongu," 59. Another rumor circulating during this period stated that South Korean officials visited China several times to buy cereals. See Li Ki-taek, "Hanjunggong daehwa-ui kilun yollyonunga? [Has the communication channel been opened between Korea and communist China?]" *Shindong-a* (June 1983): 84. No detailed information or statistics are yet available on Sino–South Korean trade prior to 1979.

20. Lee, "Hanso kyoryu hyonhwanggwa hwakdae bang'an," 15.

21. See Kim Young-moon, "Choegun jungso-ui daehan jongchaek [Recent policies of China and the Soviet Union toward Korea]," *Tongil munje yongu* [Journal of Unifications Studies] 11 (April 1984): 36. Originally quoted in *Nepszabadsag*, December 29, 1978. Also see *Chosun Ilbo*, December 19, 1978; and *Washington Post*, January 1, 1979.

22. Yong-Seok Chung, "Junggong eui daehan insik [Communist China's perceptions of South Korea]," *Bukhan* [North Korea] (April 1984): 79.

23. The most crucial location was, of course, Hong Kong, due to its geographical proximity, its intelligence-friendly environment, and its role as entrepot. Regarding the importance of Hong Kong with regard to Israel's rapprochement with China, see Reuven Merhav and Yitzhak Shichor, "The Hong Kong Connection in Sino-Israeli Relations," in *China and Israel 1948–1998: A Fifty-Year Perspective*, ed. Jonathan Goldstein (Westport, Conn.: Praeger, 1999), 95–106.

24. Author's interviews in Hong Kong in August 1987.

25. For this incident, see Qi Xin, "Cong jieji shijian kan zhonghan guanxi [China–South Korea Relations Seen in Light of the Hijacking Incident]," *Qishi niandai* [The Seventies] (June 1983): 55.

26. Kim, "Choegun jungso-ui daehan jongchaek," 37–39.

27. *Los Angeles Times*, January 20, 1988. Cited in Liu Jinzhi, Zhang Minqiu, and Zhang Xiaoming, *Dangdai zhonghan guanxi* [Contemporary China-Korea relations] (Beijing: Zhongguo shehuikexue chubanshe, 1998), 104.

28. Korean Overseas Information Office, *Forging a New Era: The Fifth Republic of Korea* (Seoul: KOIO, 1981), 78.

29. See Lee, *China and Korea*, 106–108. For a Chinese take on the event, see Shen Tu, "Pal'yi jjalbaso aksuleul halsu opso [My Hands Are Too Short to Shake Hands with You]," *Shindong-a* [New East Asia] (August 1988): 520.

30. Shin, "Hangukgwa junggong-ui gwangye gaeson-e gwanhan yongu," 63. These channels were temporary in nature, and only for the sake of resolving the case at hand.

31. *Dong-A Ilbo*, May 11, 1983.

32. *Joong-ang Ilbo*, September 27 and October 2, 1983; and *Dong-A Ilbo*, October 3, 1983.

33. Shin, "Hangukgwa junggong-ui gwangye gaeson-e gwanhan yongu," 64, 66.

34. In the torpedo boat incident, Seoul was much more forthcoming and accommodating, as the two soldiers who had led the mutiny were extradited to China despite the certainty that they would be executed upon returning. During the process of resolving this incident, however, an official channel of communication was set up between South Korea's Consulate General and the New China News Agency's branch in Hong Kong, although it was intended more for special occasions of dispute settlement than for permanent communication. Interview with a knowledgeable South Korean official in January 2003. Also see Lee Sang-Ok (former foreign minister), *Jonhwan'gi eui han'guk woegyo* [Korea's diplomacy in an era of transition] (Seoul: Life and Dream, 2003), 119.

35. In economic terms, North Korea was no match for South Korea, since by the 1980s, Pyongyang's debt to China was already reported to have amounted to US$3.2 billion. See "Pyongyang Warns of Capitalist Contamination While Seeking Trade with West," *Vantage Point* 7, no. 10 (1984): 13.

36. On the other hand, the Rangoon bombing might have influenced the Chinese leadership's view of North Korea, which in turn worked well for the improvement of Sino–South Korean relations thereafter.

37. Details of this project are provided later.

38. *Dong-A Ilbo*, January 19, 1989.

39. Chung, "Junggong eui daehan insik," 78; and Shin, "Hangukgwa junggong-ui gwangye gaeson-e gwanhan yongu," 69. Also see Xing Fuquan, "Hanguo yu zhongguo de tiyu waijiao ji weilai fazhan [The Sino–South Korean sports diplomacy and its future prospects]," *Dongfang zazhi* [The Eastern Magazine] 17, no. 12 (December 1984): 58–59.

40. *Foreign Broadcast Information Service--China* (hereafter FBIS-China) (June 5, 1987): D3. It was also in 1987 that China referred to Seoul as South Korea at various sporting events held in China. On other occasions—like the Sino–South Korean electronics technological exchanges—such designations as "Korea, Seoul" and "China, Beijing" were used. See *Chosun Ilbo*, June 6, 1987; and *Joong-ang Ilbo*, June 11, 1988.

41. The data on South Korea's imports from China were compiled by the Customs Administration. Since January 1980, KOTRA had the official mandate to monitor Seoul's exports to the countries with which South Korea did not have normal diplomatic relations. See Lee Byung-gook, *Hanjung gyungje gyoryu hyonjangron* [A field report on South Korea–China economic exchanges] (Seoul: Nanam, 1997), 144.

42. Information from an interview in Hong Kong in August 1987.

43. Concerning this period, the IMF data in *Direction of Trade* were grossly incorrect, while Nicholas Lardy's estimates—in his *China's Entry Into the World Economy: Implications for Northeast Asia and the United States* (New York: The Asia Society, 1987), 7—matched a more precise trend. For details, see Jae Ho Chung, "South Korea–China Economic Relations: The Current Situation and Its Implications," *Asian Survey* 28, no. 10 (October 1988): 1035–1036.

44. The official data, however, have problems with regard to the 1982–1983 period, during which the trade volume via Hong Kong appears to be larger than the total trade between South Korea and China.

45. Due to North Korea's complaint, China detained fourteen merchant vessels carrying South Korean goods in April 1982. It also announced a ban on trade with South Korea, along with South Africa and Israel, thus indirectly acknowledging its trade with the country. See Qi, "Cong jieji shijian kan zhonghan guanxi," 55.

46. See Paul Ensor, "Grains of a Secret," *Far Eastern Economic Review* (April 4, 1985): 54, 56.

47. Interview in Seoul in August 1987.

48. Ibid.

49. Martin Weil, "China's Troubled Coal Sector," *The China Business Review* (March–April 1982): 30.

50. Thomas Stern, "Korean Economic and Political Priorities in the Management of Energy Liabilities," in *Energy, Security, and Economic Development in East Asia*, ed. Ronald C. Keith (London: Croom Helm, 1986), 154.

51. Interviews in Seoul and Pusan in August 1987.

52. This section is indebted to the information obtained from the Korean Consulate General in Hong Kong; Korean Traders Association (KTA) in Hong Kong; and Thomas M. H. Chan, "What to Sell to China and to Buy from China," paper presented at a bimonthly conference on the China market organized by the Korean Traders Association, Hong Kong branch (May 28, 1987), 5.

53. See "Trade Precedes the Flag," *The Economist*, November 2, 1985; and "Trade Flows Where No Diplomat Goes," *The Economist*, March 22, 1986. Also see Han S. Park and Kyung A. Park, "China and Inter-Korean Relations," *The Korean Journal of International Studies* 17, no. 3 (Summer 1986): 33–34.

54. See "Fuzhou Refrigerator Co.," *Business Korea*, August 1989, 78–79.

55. According to a knowledgeable interviewee in Hong Kong, after the trip, one of the executives went to the Blue House—South Korea's presidential mansion—to brief President Chun Doo Hwan on the project.

56. These cases involving KSCC are based on extensive interviews in Hong Kong in August 1987 with a former executive of the firm.

57. Interview in Seoul in June 1987.

58. See Zhu Songbo, "Zhonghan guanxi de huigu yu zhanwang [Retrospect and prospect for China-Korea Relations]," *Wenti yu yanjiu* [Issues and Studies] (August 1987): 12–21, esp. 13; "Trade Precedes the Flag," 77; "Trade Flows Where No Diplomat Goes," 77; and for a list of South Korean companies involved in joint-venture negotiations in this period, see Hong Kwon-hee, "Junggong barame sollenun jae-

gyepunghyang [Korea's business community holding high hopes for communist China]," *Shindong-a* (March 1988): 368–377.

59. Analogies can be made with the interconnection between the developments in the Middle East Peace Process and the momentum in the China-Israeli rapprochement. See E. Zev Sufott, "The Crucial Year 1991," in Goldstein, ed., *China and Israel 1948–1998*, 111–118.

60. *Chosun Ilbo*, November 10, 1987.

61. See *Joong-ang Ilbo*, May 26, 1987. For Hwang Chang Yop's revelation of Pyongyang's willingness to go along with cross-recognition, see *New York Times*, November 22, 1987.

62. This was suggested in Chae-jin Lee, "China's Policy Toward North Korea: Changing Relations in the 1980s," in *North Korea in a Regional and Global Context*, ed. Robert A. Scalapino and Hongkoo Lee (Berkeley: University of California Press, 1986), 180–225, esp. 205.

## 5. The Political Economy of Rapprochement, 1988–1992

1. For the first time, *Zhongguo waijiao gailan 1987* [Overview of China's foreign affairs in 1987], published by China's Ministry of Foreign Affairs, made a reference to the fact that both China and South Korea were "entitled" to attend sporting events hosted by each other. See *Hangook Ilbo* [Korea Daily], January 8, 1988.

2. See *China Daily*, January 27, 1988; and "Nanhan yu zhonggong jianjiao zhi hou [After South Korea and communist China normalize relations]," *Shibao zhoukan* [China Times Weekly], March 5, 1988. China also began to note South Korea's "China fever" in its internal publications. For the coverage on South Korea's Western Coastal Development and booming Chinese-language lessons, see Zou Weidong, "Trends in South Korea's Preparations for Developing Trade with China," *Jingji cankao* [Economic References], September 1, 1988, in *Foreign Broadcast Information Service—China* (hereafter *FBIS-China*) (September 15, 1988): 7–8. Also see Sang-Seek Park, "Northern Diplomacy and Inter-Korean Relations," *Korea and World Affairs* 12, no. 4 (Winter 1988); and Tae Dong Chung, "Korea's Nordpolitik: Achievements and Prospects," *Asian Perspectives* 15, no. 2 (Fall/Winter 1991).

3. See *Joong-ang Ilbo* [Joong-ang Daily], February 5, February 9, and March 15, 1988.

4. *New York Times*, March 14, 1988. A more detailed discussion will be provided in chapter 6, concerning Tian Jiyun, one of the most important players from the Chinese side in the normalizing of Sino–South Korean relations.

5. See *FBIS-China* (February 28, 1989): 15.

6. During this period, several envoys from Seoul paid secret visits to Beijing. This will be discussed in detail in chapter 6.

7. The total trade volume for 1989 marked a mere 1.8 percent increase over the previous year, while the comparable rate for 1987 and 1988 was 26 and 84 percent, respectively. This rate of 1.8 percent was extremely low compared to Taiwan's 46 percent and Singapore's 28 percent increases in 1989. For the impact of the Ti-

ananmen incident on South Korea–China trade, see Jae Ho Chung, "Sino–South Korean Economic Cooperation: An Analysis of Domestic and Foreign Entanglements," *Journal of Northeast Asian Studies* 9, no. 2 (Summer 1990): 73–74.

8.  *Joong-ang Ilbo*, November 24, 1989, and June 20, 1990.

9.  See *China Daily*, August 1, 1989.

10. Due to the application of differential duties, the price of South Korean goods was on the average 10 to 20 percent higher than those of other countries—most notably, Taiwan and Singapore—on which preferential duties were levied. Interview in Seoul in July 1990. South Korea was not alone in this, however, as differential duties were levied on goods from Israel and South Africa as well. See *Hanguk gyungje sinmun* [Korea Economic Daily], July 19, 1990.

11. *Segye Ilbo* [World Daily], August 3, 1989.

12. The number of business delegations from the United States and Japan was reduced by more than 50 percent. See Thomas E. Jones, "Gaining Visibility: Sino–South Korean Commerce Is Becoming Too Big to Hide," *The China Business Review* (November-December 1990): 46.

13. See *China Trade Report*, July 1990, 5.

14. See David Johns, "Sino-Korean Trade: Moving Out of the Shadow," *Business Korea* (August 1989): 68; and *Hanguk gyungje sinmun*, July 11, 1990.

15. South Korea was among the very few countries (others being the Philippines and the Soviet Union), which marked an increase in the number of visitors to China after the Tiananmen incident. In contrast, Japan and the United States scored a decrease of 40 and 29 percent, respectively. See *China Trade Report*, February 1991, 15. Also see Peter Polomka, "The Two Koreas," in *China's Crisis: The International Implications*, ed. Gary Klintworth (Canberra: RSPS, Australian National University, 1989), 57–59.

16. For South Korean corporations' activism toward China in the wake of the Tiananmen tragedy, see Byung-gook Lee, *Hanjung gyungje gyoryu hyonjangron* [A field report on South Korea–China economic exchanges] (Seoul: Nanam, 1997), 42–44.

17. It should also be noted that South Korea had dispatched to China two intermediate-level diplomats in April 1990, who were to carry out temporary consular duties for South Korean visitors to China during the Beijing Asian Games. See *Joong-ang Ilbo*, February 12, 1990.

18. *Hanguk gyungje sinmun*, June 13, 1991.

19. According to the memoir of Lee Sang-Ok, South Korea's foreign minister in 1991 and 1992, the Seoul government had contemplated in 1985 the possibility of exchanging trade missions with China. The proposal was allegedly rejected by Beijing. See Lee Sang-Ok, *Jonhwan'gi eui han'guk woegyo* [Korea's diplomacy in an era of transition] (Seoul: Life and Dream, 2003), 119.

20. The establishment of trade offices was widely rumored to materialize in late 1988 after the Seoul Olympic Games. See, for instance, *Far Eastern Economic Review*, December 24, 1987.

21. *Hanguk gyungje sinmun*, June 13, 1990. Yet even these three firms used their Hong Kong subsidiaries in registering with the Chinese government. The first South

Korean firm to use its Korean entity for branch registration was Sunkyung Corporation. See *Hanguk gyungje sinmun*, October 13, 1990.

22. For the agreements, see *Gongsangwon gyungje* [Economic Survey of Socialist Countries] 2, no. 1 (March 1989): 11–12.

23. *Hangook Ilbo*, November 27, 1989; and *Joong-ang Ilbo*, December 29, 1989.

24. *Chosun Ilbo* [Chosun Daily], June 22, 1990.

25. Interview in Seoul in July 1990; *Joong-ang Ilbo*, September 27, 1990; and Lee Ho, *Han jung so gan eui bukbang woegyo silche* [The real story of Korea's diplomacy with China and the Soviet Union] (Seoul: Cheil Media, 1997), 214–215. While the South Korean signatory was semigovernmental KOTRA, China's counterpart was changed, though nominally, from semigovernmental CCPIT to the nongovernmental China Chamber of International Commerce (*Zhongguo guoji shanghui* or CCOIC). See Lee, *Jonhwangi eui hanguk woegyo*, 121.

26. See *Joong-ang Ilbo*, September 27 and October 15, 1990; and Lee, *Han jung so gan eui bukbang woegyo silche*, 199.

27. *Chosun Ilbo*, October 21, 1990, and January 30, 1991, and a list of the staff dated June 1, 1991. Among the eleven members, nine were formal staff and seven of them had Chinese-language proficiency. Of the eight staff members of China's trade office in Seoul, headed by a deputy bureau chief of the Ministry of Foreign Trade and Economic Cooperation, seven had Korean-language proficiency and four came from Shandong. Interview in Seoul in June 2000.

28. Initially, the trade-office staff were not permitted to contact China's Foreign Ministry officials. It was only in February 1991 that the South Korean officials in the Beijing Trade Office were able to meet with Chinese officials in the Bureau of International Organization of the Foreign Ministry. See Lee, *Jonhwangi eui hanguk woegyo*, 127.

29. It is perhaps highly illustrative of this rationale on the part of the Seoul government that South Korea, which had granted a special favorable tariff on goods from China in June 1982, waited nine years to acquire most-favored-nation status from China. See Beom-chan Lee, "Hanso kyoryu hyonhwang gwa hwakdae bangan," *Kongsankwon yongu* [Studies of Communist Area] (May 1987): 15.

30. Vice Premier Tian Jiyun and Deputy Minister of Foreign Economic Relations and Trade Shen Jueren commented on this possibility in March 1988. See *Joong-ang Ilbo*, March 14, 1988; and *New York Times*, March 14, 1988.

31. *Hanguk gyungje sinmun*, March 3 and July 13, 1992. A Hong Kong report suggested that China had allegedly secured Kim Il Sung's tacit consent to China's opening direct trade with South Korea during his visit to China in May 1987. See *Jiushi niandai* [The Nineties], January 1988. Cited in *Hangook Ilbo*, December 30, 1987.

32. Chinese studies often cite different trade statistics based on varied estimates of indirect trade and customs figures. Yet the overall trend extrapolated for the bilateral trade is quite similar. See, for instance, Liu Jinzhi, Zhang Minqiu, and Zhang Xiaoming, *Dangdai zhonghan guanxi* [Contemporary China's relations with Korea] (Beijing: Zhongguo shehuikexue chubanshe, 1998), 146–147.

33. The ranks were calculated on the basis of the data in *China Newsletter* 89 (1990): 6; *China Newsletter* 99 (1992): 14; *China Trade Report* (June 1991): 14–15; and *China Trade Report* (June 1992): 14–15.

34. This reflected a significant level of continuity in terms of the mutually complementary nature of the trade. Contrast this with the section on the sectoral composition of the period from 1984 to 1986, in the previous chapter. Also see Doo-Hyun Kim, "Hanjung gyoryu eui silje wa daechaek [The current situation in South Korea's exchanges with China]," *Bukbang gyongje* [Economies of the Northern Area] (September 1991): 98.

35. For the vertical nature of the intraindustry trade, see Kwang-Soo Han, "Hanjung gyongje gyongjaenginga bowaninga [Korea-China economic relations: competing or complementing?]," *Shindong-a* [New East Asia] (June 1992): 387; and *Hanguk gyungje sinmun*, July 9, 1992.

36. It was also in early 1988 that China for the first time convened an investment roadshow in Hong Kong for prospective South Korean investors. See *Hangook Ilbo*, February 3, 1988. China's local governments also became increasingly aggressive in attracting South Korean investment. For such interests expressed by Li Quanwen, mayor of Weihai, see the New China News Agency dispatch on April 3, 1988, reported in *Hangook Ilbo*, April 5, 1988.

37. Beijing Xinhua, November 4, 1988, in *FBIS-China* (November 4, 1988): 15–16.

38. *Shijie jingji daobao*, November 14, 1988.

39. Compared to Taiwan, whose cumulative investment in China exceeded US$3.4 billion as of 1991, South Korean investment in China was fairly marginal. The Taiwan figure is from Noriyoshi Ehara, "China's Foreign Trade in 1991," *China Newsletter* 99 (1992): 17. An interview with a Chinese official at the Seoul Trade Office indicated that Beijing had been very much dissatisfied with the small scale of South Korean investment. Interview in July 1992.

40. By 1989, the average monthly wage in South Korea ($732) was seventeen times higher than China's ($43). See *Chosun Ilbo*, September 3, 1992.

41. In 1990, Japan's average per project investment in China was US$2.1 million. See Kozue Hiraiwa, "Foreign Investment in the PRC, 1990–1991," *China Newsletter* 96 (1992): 14.

42. The postnormalization phase of South Korean investment in China is discussed in chapter 7.

43. The Hong Kong Branch of the New China News Agency had broader responsibilities than simply being a media organization. In fact, it acted as China's diplomatic arm in the territory and played a similar role in China's clandestine dealings with Israel during the 1980s. See Reuven Merhav and Yitzhak Shichor, "The Hong Kong Connection in Sino-Israeli Relations," in *China and Israel 1948–1998: A Fifty-Year Perspective*, ed. Jonathan Goldstein (Westport, Conn.: Praeger, 1999), 99.

44. This measure was at the time deemed indispensable for the contingency of Seoul not being able to normalize relations with China prior to Hong Kong's handover in 1997. China had earlier hinted that in such a contingency the Consulate General would be downgraded to an economic mission. See *South China Morning*

*Post*, December 4, 1991; and Lee, *Hanjung gyungje gyoryu hyonjangron*, 185. For a similar concern in the case of South Africa, see Chris Alden, "Solving South Africa's Chinese Puzzle: Democratic Foreign Policy-Making and the 'Two Chinas' Question," in *South Africa's Foreign Policy: Dilemmas of a New Democracy*, ed. Jim Broderick, Gary Burford, and Gordon Freer (Basingstoke: Palgrave, 2001), 132.

45. Detailed discussions on these high-level informal channels are provided in chapter 6.

46. *Joong-ang Ilbo*, January 11, 1990.

47. *Chosun Ilbo*, February 1 and June 30, 1990.

48. See "Golden Bridge Bridges the Yellow Sea," *Business Korea* (October 1990): 59.

49. Kwang-soo Han, "Hanjung gyongje gyongjaenginga bowaninga," 385.

50. *South China Morning Post*, September 29, 1988.

51. *Chosun Ilbo*, June 9, 1990; *Hanguk gyungje sinmun*, September 27, 1990; *Joong-ang Ilbo*, March 4, 1992; and *Hangook Ilbo*, July 2, 1992.

52. For the Chinese government's authorization for the China Travel Service (CTS) to arrange group tours for South Koreans, see *FBIS-China* (September 22, 1988): 14. For the changes to China's tourism policy at large in this period, see Linda Richter, *The Politics of Tourism in Asia* (Honolulu: The University of Hawaii Press, 1989), chap. 2.

53. Author's interview in Hong Kong in July 1989. Also see *Joong-ang Ilbo*, July 25, 1988.

54. It was on June 9, 1991, that China's trade office in Seoul began to issue entry visas. *Joong-ang Ilbo*, June 10, 1991.

55. *The Korea Times*, January 6, 1989; and *Chosun Ilbo*, April 1 and July 4, 1992.

56. *Business Korea* (March 1989): 64.

57. All of China's branch offices were located in Seoul, while South Korea had fourteen in Beijing, two in Dalian, two in Shanghai, and one in Qingdao. See *Joong-ang Ilbo*, June 22, 1992. Compared to the number of branch offices established by Japanese and American firms, 677 and 307, respectively, South Korea's fourteen was still too small for its increasing business stake in China. For the figures, see *Hanguk gyungje sinmun*, July 13, 1992. For the establishment of branch offices of banks, see *Chosun Ilbo*, August 23, 1992.

58. For more details on the trade-office issue, see Chung, "Sino–South Korean Economic Cooperation," 63–64.

59. *Hanguk gyungje sinmun*, January 1 and May 3, 1992.

60. Between March 1989 and December 1990, Hungary, Poland, Yugoslavia, Czechoslovakia, Bulgaria, Rumania, and the Soviet Union normalized diplomatic relations with South Korea. While East Germany proposed the establishment of trade offices, South Korea declined due to the fluid situation between the two Germanys at the time. From 1988 to 1990, a total of sixteen countries normalized relations with South Korea.

61. Even in the prenormalization phase, the nature of Soviet contacts with South Korea had been much more explicit than those contacts with China. While the volume of South Korea–Soviet trade was far smaller than that of South Korea–

China trade, a much larger scale of investment was decided by Seoul for Siberian development. Given the tacit nature of trade compared to more visible joint ventures and trade offices, Beijing clearly maintained a more cautious stance toward Seoul than Moscow did. See *Wolgan Chosun* [Chosun Monthly] (April 1990): 385–387; and *Hangook gyungje sinmun*, June 1, 1990.

62. For a Chinese account that defines China–North Korean relations as "special," see Liu Jinzhi et al., *Dangdai zhonghan guanxi*, 103.

63. An important analogy can be made regarding North Korea's propensity to emulate China's policy despite the fact that the Soviet Union had provided more material support.

64. This is the rationale for the "lip-to-teeth" (*chun wang chi han*) relationship between Beijing and Pyongyang. Various historical records also support such perceptions. The Official Chronicle of the Yi Dynasty's King Sonjo writes that "Liaodong is like Beijing's Arm and Chosun is the fence protecting Liaodong." The Ming Chronicle also stipulated that "the protection of Chosun is tantamount to the security of China." Both are cited in Choi Soja, *Myung-chong sidae jung-han gwangyesa yongu* [Study of China-Korea relations during the Ming and Qing dynasties] (Seoul: Ewha Woman's University Press, 1997), 26, 28.

65. An official publication published in 1990 by China's Ministry of Foreign Affairs acknowledged Beijing's will to expand exchanges with South Korea on all nonpolitical fronts. See *Zhongguo waijiao gailan 1990* [Overview of China's diplomacy 1990] (Beijing: Shijie zhishi chubanshe, 1990), 40.

66. The lack of consensus on how to deal with South and North Korea was manifested in the writings of two Chinese scholars at the time. Compare Gu Weiqun's "Security in the Asia-Pacific Region" with Hao Yufan's "China and the Korean Peninsula" in *The Chinese View of the World*, ed. Hao Yufan and Huan Guocang (New York: Pantheon Books, 1989), 26, 190, and 199.

67. Washington did not explicitly oppose South Korea's effort for rapprochement with China. Yet evidence abounds of its concern with the pace, which was seen as overly fast. See the view of Ambassador James Lilley in Park Chul-un, *Bareun yoksa reul wihan jeungun* [Testimonies for correct history] (Seoul: Random House Joong-ang, 2005), 1:355, 2:148. For a slightly different take, see James Lilley, *China Hands: Nine Decades of Adventure, Espionage, and Diplomacy in Asia* (New York: Public Affairs, 2004), 292–294.

68. For Taiwan's resentment and concern, see *FBIS-Korea* (July 18, 1988): 69; *FBIS-Korea* (March 28, 1989): 85; and *FBIS-Korea* (February 21, 1990): 51.

69. On Taiwan's dispatch of military units to South Korea during the Korean War, see Hong Dukhwa, "Daeman teuksubudae bimil chamjonhada" [On the secret involvement of Taiwanese forces]," *Wolgan Chosun* (February 1995): 278–288.

70. See, for instance, Robert E. Bedeski, "Sino-Korean Relations: Some Implications for Taiwan," *Asian Perspective* 13, no. 1 (Spring–Summer 1989): 112–113.

71. *Chosun Ilbo*, April 14, 1992.

72. See Shim Jae Hoon, "Backyard Rivalries: South Korea and Taiwan Compete for China Trade," *Far Eastern Economic Review*, March 30, 1989.

73.   For Taiwan's approach to North Korea, see Shim, "Backyard Rivalries," 48. Taipei's overture was rejected by Pyongyang, which might have been pressured by Beijing. See *Joong-ang Ilbo*, January 29, 1990.

74.   For Taiwan's economic sanction against South Korea, see Shim, "Backyard Rivalries," 48; and Bedeski, "Sino-Korean Relations," 113–114. For South Korea–Taiwan trade, see *Korea Economic Daily*, May 27, 1990.

75.   *Chosun Ilbo*, March 8, 1991. An interview with a knowledgeable South Korean official suggested that most of Taiwan's offers at the time had been exaggerated and involved relatively little substance. Interview in January 2003.

## 6. The Politics of Normalization

1.   Three major studies on Sino–South Korean relations—Chae-Jin Lee, *China and Korea: Dynamic Relations* (Stanford, Calif.: The Hoover Press, 1996); Song Chengyou et al., *Zhonghan guanxishi* [History of China-Korea relations] (Beijing: Shehuikexue wenxuan chubanshe, 1997); and Liu Jinzhi et al., *Dangdai zhonghan guanxi* [Contemporary China-Korea relations] (Beijing: Zhongguo shehuikexue chubanshe, 2001)—do not delve into the politics and the policy process of diplomatic normalization in 1992.

2.   When the foreign policy archive for the year 1992 is declassified in 2022, we will be able to have a more complete picture of the entire process and dynamics of Sino–South Korean normalization.

3.   See Kenneth Lieberthal and David M. Lampton, eds., *Bureaucracy, Politics, and Decision Making in Post-Mao China* (Berkeley: University of California Press, 1992); and Kenneth Lieberthal and Michel Oksenberg, *Policy Making in China: Leaders, Structures, and Processes* (Princeton, N.J.: Princeton University Press, 1988).

4.   All Chinese interviewees, without a single exception, concurred on this point.

5.   See Lee, *China and Korea*, 106.

6.   Their views have been described in detail in chapter 3.

7.   Hong Duckhwa, *Dugae eui jungguk gwa silli oegyo* [This China, that China] (Seoul: Jajak Academy, 1998), 86. According to a Chinese interviewee, since 1981, fifteen to twenty young Chinese students were selected every year from the provinces on the coast and sent to Pyongyang to study Korean language and culture. This makes one suspect that China had been preparing early on for the eventual rapprochement with South Korea. Interview in Shandong in July 1994.

8.   See his *Waijiao shiji* [Ten stories of China's diplomacy] (Beijing: Shijie zhishi chubanshe, 2003), 151.

9.   See Yan Jing (penname of Zhang Tingyan, China's first ambassador to South Korea, and his wife, Tan Jing), *Chushi hanguo* [Being the ambassador to Korea] (Jinan: Shandong daxue chubanshe, 2004), 17.

10.   This process is called "advice seeking" (*zhengxun*) and was first disclosed by Jiang Zemin, who confirmed in an interview that the central party leadership had main-

tained a principle of soliciting policy advice from Deng. See *Ta Kung Pao*, May 19, 1990. This norm is also described in Zhang Liang, ed., *Zhongguo liusi zhenxiang* [The Tiananmen papers] (Hong Kong: Mingjing chubanshe, 2001), 1:343–348, 1:364–369, 1:440–447, 2:753–759.

11. See Lee Ho, *Han jung so gan eui bukbang woegyo silche* [The real story of Korea's diplomacy with China and the Soviet Union] (Seoul: Cheil Media, 1997), 252.

12. Author's interviews in Beijing and Shandong in April 1992 and June 1994.

13. Li Peng had been the chairman of the Central Foreign Affairs Leadership Small Group from 1988 to 1997, after which Jiang Zemin took over the responsibility. For the role of the Central Foreign Affairs Leadership Small Group, see Carol Lee Hamrin, "The Party Leadership System," in *Bureaucracy, Politics, and Decision Making in Post-Mao China*, 95–124; and Lu Ning, "The Central Leadership, Supraministry Coordinating Bodies, State Council Ministries, and Party Departments," in *The Making of Chinese Foreign and Security Policy in the Era of Reform*, ed. David M. Lampton (Berkeley: University of California Press, 2001), 45–49.

14. Of course, other members of the Central Foreign Affairs Leadership Small Group—Wu Xueqian (Ministry of Foreign Affairs), Qin Jiwei (People's Liberation Army), Zheng Tuobin (Ministry of Foreign Economic Relations and Trade), and Zhu Liang (Department of International Liaison)—must have also played a role, but the absence of pertinent information renders detailed discussions very difficult.

15. See Yan Jing, *Chushi hanguo*, 16–17.

16. Roh Jae Won, South Korea's first ambassador to China, confirmed this point in an interview. See Lee, *Han jung so gan eui bukbang woegyo silche*, 248. Also see Qian, *Waijiao shiji*, 148.

17. On Tian's positive position on the rapprochement with South Korea, see Lee, *Han jung so gan eui bukbang woegyo silche*, 251.

18. Tian's role in this was hinted earlier, though not publicized at the time, in *Hanguk gyungje sinmun* [Korea Economic Daily], June 12, 1990. South Korean interviewees suggest that few were aware of this unit at the time. Detailed discussions on this are provided in "Bukbang woegyo pail" [Secret files on northern diplomacy], *Hangook Ilbo* [Korea Daily], August 26, 1996.

19. See *China Directory 1997* (Tokyo: Radiopress, 1996), 201. Yue was (as of 2003) a standing committee member of the Chinese People's Political Consultative Conference. See *China Directory 2003* (Tokyo: Radiopress, 2002), 170.

20. For "princelings," see Jae Ho Chung, "The Politics of Prerogatives in Socialism: The Case of *Taizidang* in China," *Studies in Comparative Communism* 24, no. 1 (March 1991): 58–76. Liu is currently (as of 2003) a major-general in the air force and political commissar for the Chengdu military region. See *China Directory 2003*, 227.

21. See "Bukbang woegyo pail," *Hangook Ilbo*, August 26, 1996. Also see Lee, *Han jung so gan eui bukbang woegyo silche*, 252; and Park Chul-un, *Bareun yoksa reul wihan jeungun* [Testimonies for correct history] (Seoul: Random House Joong-ang, 2005), 2:195, 2:208–209.

22. Author's interview in Hong Kong in August 1987.

23. President Park's efforts to buy garlic and red pepper directly from China during 1977 to 1979 are described in Lee, *Han jung so gan eui bukbang woegyo silche*, 188–190. Also see Byung-gook Lee, *Hanjung gyungje gyoryu hyonjangron* [A field report on South Korea–China economic exchanges] (Seoul: Nanam, 1997), 183. For South Korea's relations with China during President Park's tenure, see Ilpyong J. Kim, "Policies Toward China and the Soviet Union," in *The Foreign Policy of the Republic of Korea*, ed. Youngnok Koo and Sung-joo Han (New York: Columbia University Press, 1985), 202–203, 209–210.

24. According to an interviewee, President Chun was personally briefed about the visits to China by several corporate executives, including that of the Korean Shipbuilding and Construction Corportation described in chapter 4.

25. Young-Soo Shin, "Han junggong gyoryu odiggaji wanna [The current situation of South Korea–China exchanges]," *Bukhan* [North Korea] (April 1984): 86.

26. See Lee, *Hanjung gyungje gyoryu hyonjangron*, 209.

27. The Commission was made up of bureau chiefs from relevant ministries and headed by Second Assistant Minister of Foreign Affairs Soon-young Hong, who later became foreign minister and ambassador to China. Interview in Washington in January 2003.

28. On this point, see Byung Chul Koh, *The Foreign Policy Systems of North and South Korea* (Berkeley: University of California Press, 1984), 16.

29. To a considerable extent, Roh can be compared to Indonesia's Suharto and South Africa's Mandela in making the normalization of relations with China a sort of personal mandate. See Rizal Sukma, *Indonesia and China: The Politics of a Troubled Relationship* (London: Routledge, 1999), chap. 7; and Chris Alden, "Solving South Africa's China Puzzle: Democratic Foreign Policy-Making and the 'Two-China' Question," in *South Africa's Foreign Policy: Dilemmas of a New Democracy*, ed. Jim Broderick, Gary Burford, and Gordon Freer (Basingstoke: Palgrave, 2001), 132–134.

30. For President Roh's remarks, see *Joong-ang Ilbo* [Joong-ang Daily], June 11, 1988; and *Roh Tae Woo daetongryung yonsolmunjip* [Selected speeches of President Roh Tae Woo] (Seoul: Office of the Presidential Secretariat, 1989), 176–179. According to a report, Roh sent a secret envoy, former foreign minister Dong-Jin Park, to Hong Kong, to relay his wish to pay a visit to China even before the presidential inauguration. See *Hangook Ilbo*, October 28, 1996. Park Chul-un, Roh's protégé, reveals in his memoir that he had worked in vain to facilitate a meeting between Roh and Deng Xiaoping before the former's inauguration. See *Bareun yoksa reul wihan jeungun*, 1:280.

31. Author's interviews in Hong Kong in July 1991. On December 7, 1988, President Roh provided support for Park by remarking that under the current circumstances, the Foreign Ministry would not be able to be in charge of the northern diplomacy. See Park, *Bareun yoksa reul wihan jeungun*, 2:50.

32. This was in fact the secret to Seoul's diplomatic normalization with Budapest and Moscow in 1989 and 1990, respectively. See, for instance, Huh Eui-Do, "Kim Bok-

Dong Park Chul-Un eui hangunjuyi wa heogong e geoaek bburin milsa eogyo [On the hasty and secret diplomacy that squandered huge sums of money]," *Wolgan Joong-ang* [Joong-ang Monthly] (March 1993): 559–560.

33.  Lee, *Hanjung gyungje gyoryu hyonjangron*, 194.

34.  For Park's waning influence over the northern policies in 1990 and after, see *Chosun Ilbo* [Chosun Daily], September 28, 1990. See Park's self-description of the years during the Sixth Republic (1988 to 1993), *Wolgan Chosun* [Chosun Monthly] (1997): 114. For Park's failed efforts to "buy off" the normalization with China in 1990, see *Hangook Ilbo*, October 7 and 14, 1996.

35.  For Qian Qichen's discussion of Park's last-ditch effort along this line, see *Waijiao shiji*, 148.

36.  For other cases, see Park, *Bareun yoksa reul wihan jeungun*, 1:290, 1:427, 2:192.

37.  This story is from the front-page article "Zhonghan jianjiao miwenlu [A secret file on China–South Korea normalization]," *Nanfang zhoumo* [Southern Weekend], October 27, 1995. Han's visit to Shandong was earlier anonymously hinted at in *Ta Kung Pao*, May 24, 1988.

38.  For details, see *Hangook Ilbo*, September 9, 1996.

39.  The discussion of this particular channel relies heavily on a series of fortnightly special reports on Seoul's northern diplomacy in "Bukbang woegyo pail," *Hangook Ilbo*, August 26, September 2, 9, 16, 23, and 30, October 7, 14, 21, and 28, November 4, 11, 18, and 25, December 2, 9, and 16, 1996.

40.  The existence of this clandestine channel was tacitly hinted at in "Zhonghan jianjiao neiqing [Inside stories on Sino–South Korean normalization]," *Dongxiang* [Trends] (September 1992): 20.

41.  In his memoirs, Park Chul-un reveals that his main contact was not Tian Jiyun and that his scheduled meeting with Tian in July 1991 was even cancelled for political reasons. It is not clear why Park did not command this particular channel, but a speculation can be made that President Roh wished to maintain his own line of communication, at the exclusion of Park and others. See Park, *Bareun yoksa reul wihan jeungun*, 2:188, 2:193, 2:208–209.

42.  For instance, the SGSK used this channel to hint on the timing of China's agreement to the establishment of the trade offices in October 1990. See *Hangook Ilbo*, September 30, 1996. Reportedly, the SGSK often offered key information on high-level politics, including that Zhao Ziyang would stand no chance of rehabilitation after the Tiananmen incident. See *Hangook Ilbo*, October 28, 1996.

43.  See Jae Ho Chung, *Central Control and Local Discretion in China* (Oxford: Oxford University Press, 2000), chap. 2.

44.  For MOFERT's organizational mission and ethos, see Lieberthal and Oksenberg, *Policy Making in China*, 114–116.

45.  The desirability of South Korea–China trade was first hinted in December 1978 by the minister of foreign trade, Li Qiang. The Ministry of Foreign Trade was MOFERT's predecessor.

46.  For the role of CCPIT in communicating with South Korea, see *Foreign Broadcast Information Service—China* (hereafter *FBIS-China*) (October 21, 1988): 9–10. For

MOFERT's general sponsorship in CCPIT, see James P. Horsley, "The Regulation of China's Foreign Trade," in *Trade, Investment, and the Law in the People's Republic of China*, ed. Michael J. Moser (Oxford: Oxford University Press, 1984), 13.

47. For the organizational mission and ethos of MOFA, see Lu Ning, *The Dynamics of Foreign-Policy Decisionmaking in China* (Boulder, Colo.: Westview, 1997), 20–32, 108–111.

48. Pyongyang filed complaints at least on two occasions: once in 1982, which resulted in the aforementioned detainment of cargo vessels carrying South Korean goods in Qingdao; and again in 1986, over the much publicized joint-venture deal between Daewoo and Fujian Province. For the impact of Pyongyang's complaint on the delay of the materialization of the deal, see "Trade Flows Where No Diplomat Goes," *The Economist*, March 22, 1986.

49. See Shaun Breslin, "The Foreign Policy Bureaucracy," in *Chinese Politics and Foreign Policy Reform*, ed. Gerald Segal (London: The Royal Institute of International Affairs, 1990), 125–127. David M. Lampton calls this "corporate pluralization." See "China's Foreign and National Security Policy-Making Process: Is It Changing and Does It Matter?" in *The Making of Chinese Foreign and Security Policy in the Era of Reform*, 12–19.

50. *Joong-ang Ilbo*, March 14, 1988.

51. The fact that the Chinese party in charge of the negotiations for the investment-guarantee agreement in late 1991 was upgraded from the China Chamber of Industry and Commerce (CCOIC) to MOFERT also points to its enhanced role in expanding ties with South Korea. See "Chronology," in *Bukbang gyongje* [Northern Economies] (March 1992): 92. The relatively reduced role of MOFA and the elevated status of MOFERT are also noted in Breslin, "The Foreign Policy Bureaucracy," 128; and Xu Zhijia, *Zhonggong waijiao juece moshi yanjiu* [Study of foreign policy-making models in communist China] (Taipei: Shuiniu chubanshe, 2000), 156.

52. See *Hanguk gyungje sinmun*, June 12, 1990.

53. The role of the Central Committee's Department of International Liaison (*duiwai lianluobu*) is understood to have declined over the years. See Xu, *Zhonggong waijiao juece moshi yanjiu*, 194n39.

54. For such an observation, see Jae Ho Chung, "Sino–South Korean Economic Cooperation: An Analysis of Domestic and Foreign Entanglements," *Journal of Northeast Asian Studies* 9, no. 2 (1990): 65–66. And for the "comrades-in-arms" relationship between the Chinese and North Korean militaries, see Chae-Jin Lee, "China's Policy Toward North Korea: Changing Relations in the 1980s," in *North Korea in a Regional and Global Context*, ed. Robert A. Scalapino and Hongkoo Lee (Berkeley: Center for Korean Studies, University of California, 1987), 196.

55. The South Korean military establishment also initially opposed President Roh Tae Woo's *nordpolitik*. See Sanghyun Yoon, *South Korea's "Nordpolitik" with Special Reference to Its Relationship with China* (Ph.D. dissertation, Department of Political Science, George Washington University, 1994), 235–239.

56. On China's think tanks during the 1980s, see Wang Jisi, "International Relations Theory and the Study of Chinese Foreign Policy," in *Chinese Foreign Policy: Theory*

*and Practice*, ed. Thomas Robinson and David Shambaugh (Oxford: Clarendon Press, 1994), 496–497. For their increasing influence during the 1990s, see Phillip C. Saunders, "China's America Watchers: Changing Attitudes Towards the United States," *The China Quarterly* 161 (March 2000): 44; and Bonnie S. Glaser and Phillip C. Saunders, "Chinese Civilian Foreign Policy Research Institutes: Evolving Roles and Increasing Influence," *The China Quarterly* 171 (September 2002): 597–616.

57. Jae Ho Chung, "Reappraising Central-Local Relations in Deng's China: Decentralization, Dilemmas of Control, and Diluted Effects of Reform," in *Remaking the Chinese State: Strategies, Society, and Security*, ed. Chien-min Chao and Bruce J. Dickson (London: Routledge, 2001), 46–75.

58. This was noted earlier by Susan Shirk, "The Domestic Political Dimensions of China's Foreign Economic Relations," in *China and the World: Chinese Foreign Policy in the Post-Mao Era*, ed. Samuel S. Kim (Boulder, Colo.: Westview, 1984), 60–64; and Jonathan R. Woetzel, *China's Opening to the Outside World: The Politics of Empowerment* (New York: Praeger, 1989), 142–143.

59. Peter Ferdinand, "Regionalism," in *Chinese Politics and Foreign Policy Reform*, 141–142, 153.

60. See, for instance, Jae Ho Chung, "Study of Provincial Politics and Development in Post-Mao China: Issues, Approaches, and Sources" in *Provincial Strategies of Economic Reform in Post-Mao China: Leadership, Politics, and Implementation*, ed. Peter T. Y. Cheung, Jae Ho Chung, and Lin Zhimin (Armonk, N.Y.: M. E. Sharpe, 1998), 429–456; and Peter T. Y. Cheung and James T. H. Tang, "The External Relations of China's Provinces," in *The Making of Chinese Foreign and Security Policy in the Era of Reform*, 91–120.

61. Liu Jinzhi et al., *Dangdai zhonghan guanxi*, 78.

62. In June 1988, Qian Qichen, China's foreign minister, was reported to have said that "the central government cannot be informed of everything that happened in localities." See *Joong-ang Ilbo*, July 22, 1988.

63. Two anecdotes illustrate Beijing's security-related wariness at the time. One concerns an incident where a Korean Chinese from Liaoning Province was arrested in 1987 for allegedly working for the Korean Central Intelligence Agency. Second, a South Korean businessman based in Hong Kong was denied an entry visa for two years simply because he had allegedly briefed the Blue House about a joint-venture deal he had pursued with China. The information on the former is from *FBIS-China* (July 28, 1987): S2. The information on the latter is from the author's interview in Hong Kong in February 1992.

64. For China's policy of regional designation, see Shi Min, "Zhongguo yanhai diqu fazhan zhanlue yu dongbeiya jingji hezuo [The economic development strategy of coastal China and Northeast Asian economic cooperation]," *Dongbeiya luntan* [Northeast Asia Forum] 1, no. 1 (1992): 19–20.

65. For the official designation of Shandong, see *South China Morning Post*, October 25, 1988. The designation was made sometime in December 1987. See Shi, "Zhongguo yanhai diqu jingji fazhan zhanlue yu dongbeiya jingji hezuo," 17, 19. This was confirmed by the author's interviews with several knowledgeable Chinese.

66. For the establishment of the Liaoning liaison office in Seoul, see *Chosun Ilbo*, August 9, 1988. And for the designation of Liaoning as another key-point province, see *New York Times*, November 25, 1988; and *FBIS-China* (March 6, 1989): 7–8. Li Changchun, governor of Liaoning, however, backpedaled in 1990, saying that "the establishment of a Liaoning Office in Seoul would require Beijing's approval." See *Ming Pao*, April 1, 1990.

67. *Business Korea* (March 1989): 64.

68. This was also the turning point in China's foreign relations, as China began to stress "good neighborly relations" (*mulin youhao guanxi*) in the Asian region. See Zhu Tingchang, "Lun zhongguo mulin zhengce de lilun yu shijian [Theory and practice of China's 'good neighbor policy']," *Guoji zhengzhi yanjiu* [Study of International Politics] 2 (2001): 43–47. Also see Chen Xiangyang, *Zhongguo mulin waijiao* [China's good neighborly foreign policy] (Beijing: Shishi chubanshe, 2004), chap. 5.

69. For the January 1991 reform, see "Learning the Rules of Foreign Trade," *China News Analysis* 1464 (July 15, 1992): 1–9. And for the new regional concept, see Xiao Xiangqian, "Woguo dongbei geshengshi zai dongbeiya diqu de diwei," *Dongbeiya luntan* 1, no. 1 (1992): 13–15.

70. See Koh, *The Foreign Policy Systems of North and South Korea*, 8–10.

71. A discussion on the role of Kim Bok-Dong, retired general and elder brother of President Roh's wife, is provided below.

72. While the Customs Administration and the Bank of Korea were also involved in the areas of import supervision and investment approval, KOTRA had a much broader mission concerning economic cooperation with the socialist bloc.

73. *Hangook Ilbo*, October 7 and 14, 1996.

74. See *Naewoe gyungje sinmun* [Naeway Economic Daily], May 31, 1990.

75. For Liaoning's contact with IPECK, see *Shindong-a* [New East Asia] (November 1989): 138.

76. See *Joong-ang Ilbo*, August 4, 1989.

77. *Joong-ang Ilbo*, September 27, 1990.

78. *Joong-ang Ilbo*, November 16, 1990, and August 24, 1991. On KOTRA's victory over IPECK, also see Lee, *Han jung so gan eui bukbang woegyo silche*, 198.

79. See *Hangook Ilbo*, October 14, 1996.

80. Whereas US$600 million and US$3 billion were used to attain diplomatic recognition of Hungary and the Soviet Union, respectively, no such conditionality was attached to Seoul's normalization with Beijing. Yet the option of providing economic aid in exchange for diplomatic normalization with China had been seriously considered at least twice in 1988 and 1990. On the first occasion, Kim Bok-Dong had negotiated with Hua Di of the CITIC Research Institute and, on the second occasion, Park Chul-Un reportedly offered a US$2.7 billion package. The first proposal was nullified due to the Tiananmen incident, after which Hua fled to the United States. The second offer was considered unrealistic not only because South Korea had already provided a US$3 billion aid package for Moscow but also because the presidential economic advisor, Kim Jong-In, did not endorse such a

proposal. See Lee, *Han jung so gan eui bukbang woegyo silche*, 150, 157, 172–173, 219; *Hangook Ilbo*, October 7 and 14, 1996; and interviews in Beijing in January 1999.

81. In a commentary, *Chosun Ilbo* characterized this problem as follows: "President Roh's greed for the first South Korea–China summit totally messed up Seoul's negotiations for the normalization." See the issue of February 12, 1994. Qian Qichen and Zhang Tingyan, in their memoirs, also referred to Chinese knowledge of President Roh's "haste" (*zhaoji*) in pushing for the normalization. See *Waijiao shiji*, 145, 154; and Yan Jing, *Chushi hanguo*, 16–17.

82. According to a Hong Kong report, there were some secret negotiations between Beijing and Pyongyang on the terms of China's normalization of relations with South Korea. According to this report, Deng Xiaoping personally invited Kim Il Sung and Kim Jong Il to China and pledged support of RMB 3.6 billion as well as a rollover on Pyongyang's debt, worth RMB 19 billion. See Tao Yi, "Zhonghan jianjiao neiqing [Inside stories on China's normalization with South Korea]," *Dongxiang* (September 1992): 20–21.

83. For this line of interpretation, see *Sankei Shimbun*, April 1, 1990. Of course, an alternative interpretation would be that Beijing had intentionally let Moscow test the waters with Pyongyang before itself venturing into normalizing relations with Seoul. See *Korea Times*, June 7, 1990.

84. For a characterization of the Korean issue as an "internal affair and international problem" (*neibu shiwu youshi guoji wenti*), see Li Xiangwen, "Chaoxian heping tongyi de qianjing [Prospects for Korea's peaceful reunification]," *Yatai yanjiu* [Asia-Pacific Studies] 1, no. 1 (January 1992): 53. Also see Tao Bingwei, "Chaoxian bandao xingshi de lishixing zhuanzhe [The historical transformation of the situation on the Korean Peninsula]," *Guoji wenti yanjiu* [Journal of International Studies] 2 (1992): 2; and *Hangook Ilbo*, September 30, 1996.

85. *Joong-ang Ilbo*, March 30, 1990. For the importance of the two Koreas' joining the United Nations as a key catalyst for China's normalization decision, see Qian, *Waijiao shiji*, 153–154.

86. Such a breakthrough also occurred in Beijing's relations with Tel Aviv, when Israel decided to participate in the international peace conference framework in 1991. See E. Zev Sufott, "The Crucial Year 1991," in *China and Israel 1948–1998: A Fifty-Year Perspective*, ed. Jonathan Goldstein (Westport, Conn.: Praeger, 1999), 118.

87. See *Hangook Ilbo*, November 11, 1996. It was around this time that China's Foreign Ministry instructed the Chinese media organizations that the official designation of the Republic of Korea could be used instead of South Korea. See Lee Sang-Ok, *Jonhwan'gi eui han'guk woegyo* [Korea's diplomacy in an era of transition] (Seoul: Life and Dream, 2003), 118.

88. For the information on China's "intensive research" (*shenru yanjiu*), see Yan Jing, *Chushi hanguo*, 16–17.

89. Li Peng, in his report to the National People's Congress in March 1992, referred to Seoul as the Republic of Korea (*hanguo*). Qian was also reported to have used the same designation in his report. See *Joong-ang Ilbo*, March 13, 1992; and *Chosun Ilbo*, March 24, 1992.

90.   In March 1992, China's deputy foreign minister, Liu Huaqiu, reportedly hinted on the cross-recognition option (pursuing Beijing-Seoul and Washington-Pyongyang normalization simultaneously), which was rejected by the United States. See Lee, *Jonhwan'gi eui han'guk woegyo*, 151.

91.   See *Hangook Ilbo*, November 18, 1996. During Minister Lee's stay in Beijing in April, Yang Shangkun was visiting Pyongyang, informing Kim Il Sung of China's intention to normalize its relations with South Korea. See *Hsin Wan Pao* [New Evening Post], April 19, 1992. This was supposedly China's response to North Korea's high-level envoy sent in March to dissuade China from normalizing relations with South Korea. See *Ching Pao* [The Mirror], May 1992. According to Hwang Chang-yop, Kim Il Sung asked Yang to delay the normalization for one year, but Yang replied in the negative. Interview with Hwang in Seoul in January 2005.

92.   Given that Chinese Foreign Minister Qian Qichen first suggested normalization talks on April 13, 1992, Beijing's initiative might have been closely related to Deng's efforts to provide a crucial boost for the reform, which had stagnated since the Tiananmen incident. In retrospect, it could have been expected that President Roh's postnormalization state visit to China was to be utilized by the Reformers to obtain crucial external support, as the summit meeting just preceded the Fourteenth Party Congress. At the Fourteenth Party Congress, Li Lanqing, the minister of foreign economic relations and trade, was made a member of the Politburo for the first time. In addition, the party secretaries of Shandong and Guangdong, two front-runners in foreign trade and investment, joined their counterparts from Shanghai and Tianjin on the Politburo.

93.   Secrecy prevailed over everything. Even the airline tickets for the South Korean negotiators were individually purchased, with their destinations being Tokyo, Hong Kong, and Beijing. On the South Korean side, allegedly, roughly only ten people were aware at the time of the secret negotiations underway. See *Hangook Ilbo*, November 18, 1996; and *Chosun Ilbo*, August 24, 1997. According to an interviewee, most of the expenses of the trips to China and negotiations were borne by the National Agency for Security Planning and not by the Foreign Ministry. Interviews in Seoul in February 2004.

94.   See *Hangook Ilbo*, November 25, 1996.

95.   In early 1992, South Korea's Foreign Ministry designated 1992 as the year of "wrapping up the northern diplomacy." See Lee, *Hanjung gyungje gyoryu hyonjangron*, 196. For the Chinese keen awareness of South Korea's haste, see Yan Jing, *Chushi hanguo*, 16.

96.   See *Chosun Ilbo*, February 12, 1994; and *Hangook Ilbo*, December 2, 1996.

97.   While South Korea did propose initially that it wished to maintain "semiofficial relations" (*banguan guanxi*) with Taiwan after normalization, the time constraint did not allow Seoul to hold on to its demand. See Yan Jing, *Chushi hanguo*, 18.

98.   Lee, *Jonhwan'gi eui han'guk woegyo*, 214–216, 254, 277–279.

99.   Not only out of consideration for North Korea but, more importantly, also out of its concern with ethnic stability in the northeast, where nearly two million Korean Chinese resided and most of South Korea's investment was concentrated,

China staunchly opposed the establishment of South Korea's Consulate General in Shenyang. For China's ethnic concern with this region, see Sun Yunlai and Sha Yunzhong, eds., *Jilinsheng bianjiang minzudiqu wending he fazhan de zhuyao wenti yu duice* [Major problems and solutions for stability and development in the minority regions in Jilin] (Beijing: Zhongyang minzu daxue chubanshe, 1994), 223–252.

100. One South Korean diplomat regretted that South Korea had not been able to utilize its unique position as a divided nation to gain more concessions from China, by pushing a "two China" formula more strategically. Interview in January 2003.

101. For resentments voiced by Taiwan's high-ranking officials, including its ambassador to South Korea, see *FBIS-China* (July 18, 1988): 69; *FBIS-China* (March 28, 1989): 85; and *FBIS-China* (February 21, 1990): 51.

102. For these reports, see *Joong-ang Ilbo*, March 18 and June 16, 1991, and April 5 and 14, 1992; and *Chosun Ilbo*, April 14, 1992. It was also reported that Kim Il Sung asked Beijing to defer the normalization for a year in vain. See *Munhwa Ilbo* [Culture Daily], July 4, 2003.

103. In 1991, South Korea had a surplus of US$460 million in trade with Taiwan, as opposed a to US$1.1 billion deficit with China. See *Joong-ang Ilbo*, August 22, 1992.

104. For Taipei's lobbying efforts, see *Wolgan Chosun*, November 1992, 408–409.

105. See Park Jong-moon, "Hanjung sugyo gyosop makjon makhu [South Korea–China negotiations over diplomatic normalization: an inside story]," *Shindong-a* (October 1992): 718–721.

106. For such a contrast, see *Far Eastern Economic Review* (September 3, 1992): 10.

107. Interview in Beijing in January 2002. For Beijing's efforts along this line, see Qian, *Waijiao shiji*, 156–160; and Yan Jing, *Chushi hanguo*, 2, 6–7.

108. For an excellent account of South Korea's poor handling of relations vis-à-vis Taiwan in this period, see Hong Duckhwa, *Dugae eui jungguk gwa silli oegyo* [This China, that China] (Seoul: Jajak Academy, 1998), 31, 140.

109. On Chiang's visit, see *Chosun Ilbo*, May 9, 1992. For President Roh's alleged remark, see Hong Duckhwa, *Dugae eui jungguk gwa silli oegyo*, 41. A South Korean diplomat, then deeply involved in the policy process, denied that President Roh had ever made such a remark. Interview in Seoul in July 2002.

110. A knowledgeable South Korean official suggested that, in retrospect, Seoul's decision not to give Taiwan early notice had been correct, since Taipei would have done everything it could have done to interrupt the normalization. Interview in Seoul in July 2002.

111. See Hong Duckhwa, *Dugae eui jungguk gwa silli oegyo*, 143–144; and *Hangook Ilbo*, December 9 and 16, 1996. According to an interviewee, the classified memorandum of understanding attached to the South Korea–China agreements on normalization stipulated that all of Taiwan's official properties be handed over to the People's Republic effective of August 24, 1992. Interview in Seoul in February 2004.

112. In his memoirs, former foreign minister Lee Sang-Ok sheds some light on this issue. He points out both the pressure from China and the strong disagreements

within the Chinese community in Seoul regarding Taiwan's sale of the embassy buildings. Yet Lee does acknowledge that Taiwan's Consulate General's buildings in Pusan, which Taipei had purchased in 1976—rather than inheriting from the Qing—should have been given to Taiwan. See Lee, *Jonhwan'gi eui han'guk woegyo*, 196–197, 242, 259.

113. Interviews in July 2002 and January 2003. One interviewee revealed that Ambassador Chin had even thought of taking a month-long vacation to the United States in August 1992 but had been tacitly discouraged by the South Korean government.

114. See *Hangook Ilbo*, July 28, 1993; and *Chosun Ilbo*, November 17, 1993. Also see Lee, *Jonhwan'gi eui han'guk woegyo*, 210.

## 7. Beyond Normalization

1. The quotation is from Robert W. Tucker, "1989 and All That: Reconsiderations," in *Sea-Changes: American Foreign Policy in a World Transformed*, ed. Nicholas X. Rizopoulos (New York: Council on Foreign Relations, 1990), 217.

2. See, for instance, Aaron L. Friedberg, "Ripe for Rivalry: Prospects for Peace in a Multipolar Asia," *International Security* 18, no. 3 (Winter 1993/94): 27–31.

3. The significant reduction of tension in the Sino-Soviet border regions and the elimination of intermediate- and short-range nuclear missiles in the United States and the Soviet Union were examples of the amicable relationships among the three powers. See Charles E. Ziegler, *Foreign Policy and East Asia: Learning and Adaptation in the Gorbachev Era* (Cambridge: Cambridge University Press, 1993), 143–152.

4. See Lowell Dittmer, *Sino-Soviet Normalization and Its International Implications, 1945–1990* (Seattle: University of Washington Press, 1992), 249, 253–254.

5. For this fragility of amity, see Mohan Malik, *Dragon on Terrorism: Assessing China's Tactical Gains and Strategic Losses Post-September 11* (Carlisle, Penn.: U.S. Army War College, 2003); and Peter Gries, "The Future of U.S.-China Relations: System, State, and Individual-Level Drivers," in *Charting China's Future: Political, Social, and International Dimensions*, ed. Jae Ho Chung (Lanham, Md.: Rowman & Littlefield, 2006), chap. 7.

6. William T. Tow, "Post–Cold War Security in East Asia," *The Pacific Review* 4, no. 2 (1991): 101. Also see Victor D. Cha, "Defining Security in East Asia: History, Hotspots, and Horizon-Gazing," in *The Four Asian Tigers: Economic Development and the Global Political Economy*, ed. Eun Mee Kim (San Diego, Calif.: Academic Press, 1998), 55–56. Skeptics would argue, "Japan has no vital interests that would be served by a large-scale rearmament.... Why should Japan be tempted to follow the old days, or even to appear to do so, given the advantages of its present situation?" See Tucker, "1989 and All That," 226. Also see Gary Klintworth, "Asia-Pacific: More Security, Less Uncertainty, New Opportunities," *The Pacific Review* 5, no. 3 (1992): 223.

7.  See, for instance, David M. Lampton, ed., *Major Power Relations in Northeast Asia: Win-Win or Zero-Sum Game* (New York and Tokyo: Japan Center for International Exchange, 2001).

8.  While there were a few multilateral arrangements—such as the trilateral oversight and coordination group (TCOG) among the United States, South Korea, and Japan; the Korean Energy Development Organization (KEDO); and the three-, four-, and six-party talks on North Korean affairs—they all fell short of becoming formal security arrangements.

9.  Jae Ho Chung, "China and Northeast Asian Cooperation: Building an Unbuildable?" in *China Into the Hu-Wen Era: Policy Initiatives and Challenges*, ed. John Wong and Lai Hongyi (Singapore: World Scientific, 2006).

10. For the multilateral framework of "Greater China," see the special issue in *The China Quarterly*, no. 136 (December 1993).

11. See Seizaburo Sato, "The Interrelationship Between Global and Regional Security Issues for the Pacific-Asian Region," in *Asian Security Issues: Regional and Global*, ed. Robert A. Scalapino et al. (Berkeley, Calif.: Institute of East Asian Studies, 1988), 12; Gu Weiqun, "Security in the Asian-Pacific Region," in *The Chinese View of the World*, ed. Hao Yufan and Huan Guocang (New York: Paragon, 1989), 7–8; and Peter Katzenstein and Takashi Shiraishi, eds., *Network Power: Japan and Asia* (Ithaca, N.Y.: Cornell University Press, 1997).

12. For the potential benefits of regional cooperation in East Asia, see Norman D. Palmer, *The New Regionalism in Asia and the Pacific* (Lanham, Md.: Lexington Books, 1991), chaps. 3 and 10; and John Ravenhill, "A Three-Bloc World: The New East Asian Regionalism," *International Relations of the Asia-Pacific* 2 (2002): 176–195.

13. For the return of bilateralism in the region, see John Ravenhill, "The New Bilateralism in the Asia-Pacific," in *Asian Regional Governance*, ed. Kanishka Jayasuriya (London: Routledge, 2004), 61–81.For the importance of interstate distrust in the region as the major hurdle, see Gilbert Rozman, *Northeat Asia's Stunted Regionalism: Bilateral Distrust in the Shadow of Globalization* (Cambridge: Cambridge University Press, 2004).

14. See Charles Lipson, "International Cooperation in Economic and Security Affairs," *World Politics* 37, no. 1 (October 1984): 1–23.

15. Richard Rosecrance, *The Rise of the Trading State: Commerce and Conquest in the Modern World* (New York: Basic Books, 1986); and Donald M. Snow, *The Shape of the Future: The Post–Cold War World* (Armonk, N.Y.: M. E. Sharpe, 1991).

16. Harry Harding, *A Fragile Relationship: The United States and China Since 1972* (Washington D.C.: The Brookings Institution, 1992), 13–16.

17. See Zhao Suisheng, "Changing Leadership Perceptions: The Adoption of a Coercive Strategy," in *Across the Taiwan Strait: Mainland China, Taiwan, and the 1995–1996 Crisis*, ed. Zhao Suisheng (London: Routledge, 1999), 99–125. Also see Taiwan Affairs Office of the State Council, *Taiwan yu yige zhongguo de yuanze* [Taiwan and the one-China principle] (Beijing: Taiwan Affairs Office, 2000), 13–14.

18. For South Korea's "nordpolitik," see Jae Ho Chung, "The Political Economy of South Korea–China Bilateralism," in *Korea and China in a New World: Beyond Normalization*, ed. Ilpyong Kim and Hong Pyo Lee (Seoul: The Sejong Institute, 1993), 257–309; Robert Bedeski, *The Transformation of South Korea: Reform and Reconstruction in the Six Republic under Roh Tae Woo, 1987–1992* (London: Routledge, 1994), 148–165; and Yong-Chool Ha et al., *Bukbang jongchaek: giwon jongae yonghyang* [Northern diplomacy: origins, developments, and impact] (Seoul: Seoul National University Press, 2004).

19. For details, see Jae Ho Chung, "From a Special Relationship to Normal Partnership: Interpreting the 'Garlic Battle' in Sino–South Korean Relations," *Pacific Affairs* 76, no. 4 (Winter 2003–2004): 549–568.

20. *Chosun Ilbo* [Chosun Daily], February 21, 1997; *Dong-A Ilbo* [Dong-A Daily], February 13, 2001; and the data from the Korean Institute for International Economic Policy (KIEP).

21. China's rapidly increasing trade deficits with South Korea constitutes a thorny issue. In 2001 alone, South Korea's surplus with China amounted to US$4.9 billion, which soared to US$13.2 billion in 2003, accounting for 88 percent of South Korea's total trade surplus. If we take the Chinese official statistics that include the trade via Hong Kong, as well as the values added in Hong Kong, the deficit figures are far larger. For the differences caused by Beijing's procedures for compiling trade statistics, see Robert C. Feenstra et al., "Discrepancies in International Data: An Application to China–Hong Kong Entrepot Trade," *American Economic Review* 89, no. 2 (May 1999): 338–343.

22. See *Hanjung sugyo sipjunyon eui gyungje songgwa wa munjejom*, 16–17.

23. *Hanguk gyungje sinmun* [Korea Economic Daily], August 7, 1992.

24. *Chosun Ilbo*, August 25, 2003.

25. See *Chosun Ilbo*, October 4, 2003.

26. *Joong-ang Ilbo* [Joong-ang Daily], September 29, 2004.

27. During 1998 to 2003, 71 percent of South Korean firms that were relocated overseas chose to move to China. See *Chosun Ilbo*, October 24, 2003.

28. *Joong-ang Ilbo*, May 10, 1993.

29. *Munhwa Ilbo* [Munhwa Daily], February 20, 1997.

30. For the adverse impact, see Song Longhao, "Jinrong weiji yihou de hanguo duihua zhijie touzi [Korea's direct investment in China after the financial crisis]," *Dongbeiya luntan* [Northeast Asia Forum] 4 (2001): 41–45.

31. In 2001, South Korean wages in the manufacturing sector were 13.4 times as high than they were in China. See *Chosun Ilbo*, December 7, 2001. In the textile industry, wages were eight times higher in South Korea. See *Dong-A Ilbo*, August 11, 2003.

32. *Hanjung sugyo sipjunyon eui gyungje songgwa wa munjejom*, 11; and Liu et al., *Dangdai zhonghan guanxi*, 166, 168. The size of South Korean investment in Shandong was much larger, at US$1.7 million. See "Hanguo zaihua touzi qiye tedian yanjiu [Study of South Korean–invested firms in China]," *Shandong duiwai jingmao* [Shandong foreign economic relations and trade] 10 (1999): 38.

33. Mansoo Jee, *Hanguk giupeui daejungguk gwonyokbyol jinchul gwa jonlyak* [The regional distribution and strategy of Korean enterprises in China] (Seoul: KIEP, December 2002), 81.

34. For South Koreans' preference for Shandong, see Jae Ho Chung, "Shandong's Strategies of Reform in Foreign Economic Relations: Preferential Policies, Entrepreneurial Leadership, and External Linkages," in *Provincial Strategies of Economic Reform in Post-Mao China: Leadership, Politics, and Implementation*, ed. Peter T. Y. Cheung, Jae Ho Chung, and Lin Zhimin (Armonk, N.Y.: M. E. Sharpe, 1998), 282–284; and Liu Yajing, "Hanguo weishenmo xihuan zai Shandong touzi [On why South Korea prefers to invest in Shandong]," *Shandong duiwai jingmao* 4 (1999): 12. For the figures, see Ma Yonghuan and Fan Shengyue, "Shandongsheng liyong hanshang touzi de xianzhuang yu duice [The current situation of South Korea's investment in Shandong Province]," *Dongbeiya luntan* 1 (2002): 69; and data from the Korea Export and Import Bank at http://www.koreaexim.go.kr/kr/ oeis/mo3/so1–0401.jsp (last accessed on January 23, 2006).

35. See *Chosun Ilbo*, August 24, 1997; *Hanjung sugyo sipjunyon eui gyungje songgwa wa munjejom*, 11; and data from the Korea Export and Import Bank at http://www. koreaexim.go.kr/kr/oeis/mo3/so1–0401.jsp (last accessed on January 23, 2006).

36. On China's overseas investment, see Kevin G. Cai, "Outward Foreign Direct Investment: A Novel Dimension of China's Integration Into the Regional and Global Economy," *The China Quarterly* 160 (December 1999): 856–880.

37. *Hanguk gyungje sinmun*, September 30, 1992; *Chosun Ilbo*, February 25, 1995; and *Munhwa Ilbo*, February 20, 1997.

38. See "Gyoyok tuja tonggye [Statistics on trade and investment]" compiled by the Department of Trade in the Asia-Pacific Region, November 2002, at http://www. mofat.go.kr, last accessed on February 17, 2003.

39. *Chosun Ilbo*, April 15, 1994; and *Dong-A Ilbo*, January 29, 1999. Regarding the establishment of a South Korean consular unit in the northeast, China had consistently maintained a negative position, due to its concern with the two million Korean Chinese (*chaoxianzu*) there. When Beijing finally agreed to its establishment in 1999, however, it was not opened as a consulate general but as a consular office (*lingshi banshichu*), with limited functions and powers. For China's sensitivity to the issue of Korean Chinese in the northeast, see Sun Yunlai and Sha Yunzhong, eds., *Jilinsheng bianjiang minzudiqu wending he fazhan de zhuyao wenti yu duice* [Key questions and measures concerning the stability and development in the minority regions in Jilin Province] (Beijing: Zhongyang minzu daxue chubanshe, 1994), 223–252.

40. See *Chosun Ilbo*, June 16, 1994, and January 16, 1997; and interview in December 2005.

41. *Chosun Ilbo*, August 24, 1997, and April 15, 2004; and interview in December 2005.

42. *Chosun Ilbo*, June 3, 1998.

43. Niu Aimin, "Beijing you ge Hanguocun [A Korean town in Beijing]," *Banyuetan neibuban* [Semi-Monthly Talks] 3 (2003): 46–49; and *Maeil gyungje sinmun* [Maeil Economic Daily], January 28, 2006.

44. *Chosun Ilbo*, May 16, 1995, May 28, 1997, and November 1, 2000. In 1997, Chinese residents in South Korea outnumbered their American counterparts.

45. *Joong-ang Ilbo*, April 22, 2000.

46. It should be noted that the United States—particularly under the Bush administration—increasingly appears to be a variable instead of a constant. This will be discussed in detail in chapter 9.

47. For an exemplary projection of "Pax Nipponica," see Steve Chan, *East Asian Dynamism: Growth, Order, and Security in the Pacific Region*, 2nd ed. (Boulder, Colo.: Westview, 1993), 134–137. For a special report on the formidable strength of Japan's Self-Defense Forces (SDF), see Evan Thomas and Hideko Takayama, "Japan's Unknown Soldiers," *Newsweek*, July 19, 2004, 29–31.

48. *Hanguk, Jungguk, Ilbon gungmin uisik josa baekso* [White paper on the National Consciousness Surveys in Korea, China, and Japan] (Seoul: Korea Broadcasting System and Yonsei University, December 1996), 431, 436. Also see George Hicks, *Japan's War Memories: Amnesia or Concealment?* (Aldershot: Ashgate, 1998), chap. 8.

49. For American views of South Korea as a peripheral security interest at best, see Ted G. Carpenter, "South Korea: A Vital or Peripheral U.S. Security Interest?" and Doug Bandow, "America's Korean Protectorate in a Changed World: Time to Disengage," in *The U.S.-South Korean Alliance: Time for a Change*, ed. Doug Bandow and Ted G. Carpenter (New Brunswick, N.J.: Transactions Publishers, 1992), 1–15, 75–93. For a more cautious perspective, see Robert W. Sennewald, "The United States: A Continuing Commitment," in *Korea 1991: The Road to Peace*, ed. Michael J. Mazarr et al. (Boulder, Colo.: Westview, 1991), 41–51. Also see Sun Cheng, "Meiguo yao tisheng riben [America promoting Japan to an enhanced status]," *Shijie zhishi* [World Knowledge] 8 (2001): 14–15.

50. See *1995 Sejong Survey* (Seoul: The Sejong Institute, 1995), 78; and *1997 Sejong Survey* (Seoul: Dongseo Research, 1997), 11.

51. See, for instance, Seymour Martin Lipset, *American Exceptionalism: A Double-Edged Sword* (New York: W. W. Norton, 1996), chap. 7.

52. See William Watts, *Americans Look at Asia* (Washington, D.C.: Asia Society Washington Center, 1999), 42.

53. See *1997 Sejong Survey* (Seoul: Dongseo Research 1997), 12; and *Dong-A Ilbo*, December 5, 2000.

54. See Victor D. Cha, *Alignment Despite Antagonism: The U.S.-Korea-Japan Security Triangle* (Stanford, Calif.: Stanford University Press, 1999), chap. 1; and Ralph A. Cossa, ed., *U.S.-Korea-Japan Relations: Building Toward a "Virtual Alliance"* (Washington, D.C.: CSIS, 1999).

55. For China's expressed concern with Japan's potential military ambitions, see Li Luye, "The Current Situation in Northeast Asia: A Chinese View," *Journal of Northeast Asian Studies* 10, no. 1 (Spring 1991): 79–80. For the idea of a South Korea–China alliance against a Japanese threat, see Gerald Segal, "Northeast Asia: Common Security or *a la Carte*?" *International Affairs* 67, no. 4 (1991): 765. In fact, one reason for Beijing's decision to normalize relations with Seoul was allegedly to

create an anti-Japanese coalition. See Yan Jing, *Chushi Hanguo* [Being ambassador to Korea] (Jinan: Shandong daxue chubanshe 2004), 17.

56. On South Korea's efforts to acquire a partner status vis-à-vis the United States, see Joo-Hong Nam, *America's Commitment to South Korea* (Cambridge: Cambridge University Press, 1986), 97–106, 147–159. For China's view of the South Korea–U.S. alliance as constraining Japan, see Gao Ao, "Zhonghan liangguo zai guoji lingyu de waijiao hezuo [Sino–South Korean diplomatic cooperation in the international arena]," in *Zhonghan luntan disici huiyi lunwenji* [Collection of essays from the fourth China-Korea forum], ed. The Center for Korean Studies of CASS (Beijing: Shehuikexue wenxuan chubanshe, 1996), 43; and Wang Fan, "Meihan tongmeng ji weilai zouxiang [The U.S.-Korean alliance and its future prospects]," *Waijiao xueyuan xuebao* [Journal of the Foreign Affairs University], no. 2 (2001): 65.

57. See Wu Xinbo, "The End of the Silver Lining: A Chinese View of the U.S.-Japanese Alliance," *The Washington Quarterly* 29, no. 1 (Winter 2005–2006).

58. While the joint chiefs of staff visited China twice in 1992 and 1994, it was as an accompaniment to the South Korean presidents' state visits.

59. The section on military cooperation is based on two documents from the Ministry of National Defense dated 1996 and 1997, as well as on interviews in Seoul in June 2002 and July 2005.

60. See Samuel S. Kim, "China as a Regional Power," *Current History* (September 1992): 247–252; and Harold C. Hinton, "China as an Asian Power," in *Chinese Foreign Policy: Theory and Practice*, ed. Thomas W. Robinson and David Shambaugh (Oxford: Oxford University Press, 1994), 371–372. Also see Chen Xiangyang, *Zhongguo mulin waijiao—sixiang shijian qianjing* [China's good neighborly diplomacy—ideas, practice, and prospects] (Beijing: Shishi chubanshe, 2004).

61. Since the NPT did not prevent signatory states from converting spent reactor wastes into plutonium, signing the NPT and seeking nuclear weapons capability were not totally incompatible. Besides, there are non-NPT states with nuclear weapons programs, most notably India, Israel, and Pakistan. See Andrew Mack, "The Nuclear Crisis on the Korean Peninsula," *Asian Survey* 33, no. 4 (April 1993): 341–355.

62. Of the 262 retired South Korean generals surveyed, 83 percent believed Japan would become a nuclear power and 77 percent recommended that South Korea follow suit in such a contingency. See Korean Institute of Military Studies, *Yebiyok gogeup janggyodeul eui gukbang hyon'an e daehan insik yongu* [Study of defense-related perceptions of retired high-ranking military officers] (Seoul: Korean Institute of Military Studies, December 1995), 16. For Japan's "nuke option," see Benjamin L. Self and Jeffrey W. Thompson, eds., *Japan's Nuclear Option: Security Politics and Policy in the Twenty-First Century* (Washington, D.C.: The Henry Stimpson Center, December 2003).

63. According to a Hong Kong report, China's Shenyang military region carried out a large-scale military drill in late August 1994, allegedly designed to show its willingness to engage in the case of a U.S.–South Korea joint military action against North Korea. See *Jing Bao* [Mirror] (October 1994): 34–36. For the problematic

nature of the military option, see William Taylor, Jr., and Michael J. Mazarr, "North Korea and the Nuclear Issue: U.S. Perspectives," *Journal of East Asian Affairs* 7, no. 2 (Summer/Fall 1993): 366–368.

64. A detailed documentation of war planning at the time suggests a lack of meaningful coordination beween the United States and South Korea. See Ashton B. Carter and William J. Perry, *Preventive Defense: A New Security Strategy for America* (Washington, D.C.: The Brookings Institution, 1999), 125–132. Author's interviews with two high-level South Korean officials during the period concerned also confirmed that the Kim Young-Sam administration had not been properly consulted or informed during this process. Interviews in Seoul and Stanford in July 1997.

65. For North Korea's dependence on China for trade and other arrangements, see *Chosun Ilbo*, March 23 and April 28, 1994. China's opposition to economic sanctions was clearly stipulated by Foreign Minister Qian Qichen, as well as by Jiang Zemin. See, respectively, *Joong-ang Ilbo*, May 28, 1993; and *Chosun Ilbo*, March 29, 1994.

66. See, for instance, The General Armament Department of the People's Liberation Army, ed., *Liangdan yixing* [Two bombs and one satellite] (Beijing: Jiuzhou chubanshe, 2001).

67. See Zhang Xiaochuan, "Chinese Nuclear Strategy," in *The Chinese View of the World*, ed. Hao Yufan and Huan Guocang (New York: Paragon, 1989), 92; Ilpyong J. Kim, "The Korean Question in Sino-American Relations," *In Depth* 3, no. 3 (Fall 1993): 58–60; and Samuel S. Kim, "China's Korea Policy in a Changing Regional and Global Order," *China Information* 8, no. 1/2 (Summer/Autumn 1993): 87–88.

68. For reports on the role of China, see *Hong Kong Standard*, November 9, 1993; *Chosun Ilbo*, November 16, 1993; and *New York Times*, April 3, 1994.

69. Carter and Perry, for instance, leave China's precise position on the issue undefined. See *Preventive Defense*, 219–220. Charles Kartman, U.S. representative to the Korean Energy Development Organization (KEDO), in a remark made in a seminar at the Brookings Institution in January 2003, was quite doubtful of China's role in the resolution of the crisis in 1994. Chinese sources, however, stress the positive role Beijing played in defusing the crisis situation. See, for instance, Chen Fengjun and Wang Chuanjian, *Yatai daguo yu chaoxian bandao* [Asia-Pacific major powers and the Korean peninsula] (Beijing: Beijing daxue chubanshe, 2002), 349–351.

70. For a good summary of this earlier episode, see Don Oberdorfer, *The Two Koreas: A Contemporary History* (Reading, Mass.: Addison-Wesley, 1997), 320–321.

71. See *North Korea's Decline and China's Strategic Dilemmas*, United States Institute for Peace Special Report (Washington, D.C.: USIP, October 1997), 6.

72. See "Hanguo wending zhong qiu gaige [Korea seeks change in the midst of stability]," *Renmin ribao* [Peoples' Daily], January 8, 2003.

73. John Pompret and Glenn Kessler, "China's Reluctance Irks U.S.: Beijing Shows No Inclination to Intervene in North Korea Crisis," *Washington Post*, February 4, 2003.

74. A *People's Daily* piece reported the following in January 2003: "Within a dozen days, five delegations came to seek China's cooperation.... The world is watching us." See *Renmin ribao*, January 20, 2003, at http://www.peopledaily.com.cn/GB/junshi/20030120/910932.html.

75. Elisabeth Rosenthal, "China Asserts It Has Worked to End Nuclear Crisis," *New York Times*, February 13, 2003; interviews in Washington in 2003; *Renmin ribao*, February 8, 2003; and Joseph Kahn, "Turnaround by China: Center Stage as a Diplomatic Power," *New York Times*, August 28, 2003.

76. See *Renmin ribao*, February 20, March 11, and March 13, 2003.

77. Gady A. Epstein, "China Seen Toughening Stance Against North Korea Nuclear Developments," *Baltimore Sun*, March 28, 2003; and David M. Lampton, "China: Fed Up with North Korea," *Washington Post*, June 4, 2003.

78. Charles Hutzler and Gordon Fairclough, "The Koreas: China Breaks with Its Wartime Past," *Far Eastern Economic Review*, August 7, 2003.

79. See "China Seen Toughening Stance Against North Korea Nuclear Developments," *Baltimore Sun*, March 28, 2003. The author's interviews in China in January 2004 suggest that Chinese analysts were well aware of the incident and were convinced that it had really occurred.

80. When Hu Jintao met with General Cho Myung-rok in April—the highest-ranking military figure, second only to Kim Jong Il—their "stylized language" was starkly different. Whereas Cho emphasized the "blood and bullets" North Korea and China had endured together in the past, Hu soberly stressed the "traditional friendship" (*chuantong youyi*) between the two. See *Renmin ribao*, April 23, 2003.

81. For Beijing's self-praise about its "shuttle diplomacy" (*chuanjun waijiao*), see *Renmin ribao*, August 7, 2003. Also see Jae Ho Chung, "China's Ascendancy and the Korean Peninsula: From Interest Reevaluation to Strategic Realignment?" in *Power Shift: China's and Asia's New Dynamics*, ed. David Shambaugh (Berkeley: University of California Press, 2005), 155–156.

82. See You Ji, "China and North Korea: A Fragile Relationship of Strategic Convenience," *Journal of Contemporary China*, no. 28 (2001): 34–57; and Jae Ho Chung, "China's Korea Policy Under the New Leadership: Stealth Changes in the Making?" *Journal of East Asian Affairs* 18, no. 1 (Spring/Summer 2004): 1–18.

83. Many interviewees—particularly those from the Foreign Ministry—confirmed that much of Seoul's northern diplomacy had been conducted independently of Washington. Ambassador Donald Gregg, in a conversation with this author in August 2004, on the other hand, argues that Washington was well informed of Seoul's northern initiatives. For America's concern with the pace of rapprochement with Beijing, see Park Chul-Un, *Bareun yoksa reul wihan jeungun* [Testimonies for correct history] (Seoul: Random House Joong-ang, 2005). 1:355, 2:148.

84. One key goal of South Korea's *nordpolitik* was to "expand the horizons of Seoul's foreign policy, which were hitherto limited to the countries like the U.S. and Japan." See Ministry of Information, "Great Strides Made During the First Four Years of the Roh Tae Woo presidency," *Backgrounder* 94 (February 8, 1992): 10.

85. See Nam, *America's Commitment to South Korea*, 153, 158.

86. These sentiments were to come to the surface within a decade, particularly after the election of Roh Moo-hyun to the presidency, in 2002. See chapter 9 for details.

87. Edward A. Olsen, "Korean Security: Is Japan's Comprehensive Security Model a Viable Alternative?" in *The U.S.-Korean Alliance*, 146–148.

88. For an hour-by-hour description of the event, see *Chosun Ilbo*, March 31, 1994.

89. For a strong endorsement of Ambassador Hwang's view, see *Sisa Journal* (April 14, 1994): 112. Author's interviews with some South Korean diplomats at the time were also indicative of their sympathy with Ambassador Hwang's remark. For a similar appraisal at a later point in time, which characterized the event as a "meaningful incident," see *Dong-A Ilbo*, September 8, 1998.

90. I have noted this trend in *The Rise of China and the Korean-American Alliance* (Stanford, Calif.: Institute of International Studies, February 1999); and "South Korea Between Eagle and Dragon: Perceptual Ambivalence and Strategic Dilemma," *Asian Survey* 41, no. 5 (September–October 2001).

## 8. The Rise of China and the U.S.–South Korean Alliance Under Strain

1. *East Asia Strategic Report, Quadrennial Defense Review, Joint Vision 2020*, and *Asia 2025* well demonstrate America's sustained commitment to the East Asian region.

2. On the Boao Asian Forum, see Chen Boxian, "Zhonggong zhudao yazhou shiwu kuachu yidabu [A big step made in communist China's Asian affairs]," *Zhonggong yanjiu* [Studies of Communist China] 35, no. 3 (March 2001): 23–25; and on the Shanghai Cooperation Organization (SCO), see the China Institute for Contemporary International Relations (CICIR), ed., *Shanghai hezuo zuzhi—xin anquanguan yu xinjizhi* [Shanghai Cooperation Organization: The new security perspective and the new institution] (Beijing: Shishi chubanshe, 2002), chaps. 4–5.

3. America's war against terrorism has somewhat mitigated but not changed these resentments on the part of Russia and China. Their similarly reserved position concerning America's use of force against Iraq in 2003 is a key example in point.

4. The choice of contrasting terms for China—"a strategic competitor" in the *Quadrennial Defense Review* (2001) versus "a cooperative partner" in the *National Security Strategy*—is also noteworthy, although the change seems more tactical than strategic in nature.

5. For such a process in the German case, see Philip Zelikow and Condoleezza Rice, *Germany Unified and Europe Transformed: A Study in Statecraft* (Cambridge, Mass.: Harvard University Press, 1995). On the implications inferable from the German case, see Gary L. Geipel, "The Diplomacy of German Unification: Lessons for Northeast Asia," in *The Future of Korea-Japan Relations*, ed. Robert Dujarric (Washington, D.C.: The Hudson Institute, 2001), 151–152.

6. Americans believe that China generally prefers the status quo on the Korean Peninsula. Chinese, on the othe hand, consider Americans as the ones that least want the unification. See Chen Fengjun, "Ershiyi shiji chaoxian bandao dui zhongguo de zhanlue yiyi [The strategic meaning of the Korean Peninsula to China for the twenty-first century]," *Guoji zhengzhi yanjiu* [Study of International Politics], no. 4 (2001): 8–9.

7. Until 2003, America was still South Korea's number-one trading partner and largest investor in South Korea. *Chosun Ilbo* [Chosun Daily], June 12, 2004.

8. For the former scenario, see Steven Mosher, *The Hegemon: China's Plan to Dominate Asia and the World* (San Francisco: Encounter, 2000); and, for the latter,

see Michael D. Barr, *Cultural Politics and Asian Values: The Tepid War* (London: Routledge, 2002), 46–63.

9.  South Korea is one of the few countries with which the United States still maintains a formal bilateral security alliance. South Korea was America's seventh-largest trading partner in 2003.

10. For the role of cultural proximity as a key factor in Sino–South Korean relations, see Xu Derong and Xiang Dongmei, "Zhonghan jianli mianxiang 21shiji hezuo huoban guanxi de beijing fenxi [Analyzing the background of China and South Korea establishing a cooperative partnership for the twenty-first century]," *Dangdai Hanguo* [Contemporary Korea] 22 (1999): 34.

11. See *Chosun Ilbo*, May 1, 2004.

12. *Chosun Ilbo*, January 12, 2004.

13. See *Maekyung Economy* (December 10, 2003): 29; and "Korea's China Play," *Business Week*, March 29, 2004.

14. For an argument that Korea's efforts to develop military-to-military ties with China is related to Seoul's desire to prevent the South Korea–U.S. alliance from taking up the role of constraining China, see Liu Ming, "Hanguo de diyuan weizhi yu qi waijiao he anquan zhengce [Korea's geographical location and its diplomatic and security policy]," *Yatai luntan* [Asia-Pacific Forum] 3/4 (1999): 37.

15. See Eric A. McVadon, "Chinese Military Strategy for the Korean Peninsula," in *China's Military Faces the Future*, ed. James R. Lilley and David Shambaugh (Armonk, N.Y.: M. E. Sharpe, 1999), 271–294.

16. See, for instance, Harold Brown et al., eds., *Chinese Military Power* (New York: Council on Foreign Relations, 2003).

17. *The Defense White Paper*, published annually by South Korea's Ministry of National Defense, generally devotes two to three pages to briefly outlining China's military modernization and another two to three pages to summarizing intermilitary exchanges. No trace of security concern is evident.

18. For a disclosure of China's intention to enhance China's influence over the region by participating in the four-party talks, see Li Qiang, "Chaoxian bandao wenti sifang huitan de xianzhuang yu qianjing [The current situation of and prospects for the four-party talks over the Korean problem]," *Dangdai yatai* [Contemporary Asia and the Pacific] 3 (1999): 33–37.

19. China's provision of food and energy as grants or at "friendly prices" has been central to the survival of the North Korean regime. To what extent such aid can be directly translated into Beijing's explicit influence over Pyongyang is hard to gauge, however. There is no doubt that, so far, China has been potentially more influential than any other major country. Kim Jong Il's surprise visits to China in May 2000, January 2001, May 2004, and January 2006 should be interpreted in the context of Pyongyang soliciting Beijing's support for its new policy framework.

20. See Chul Koo Woo and Jinwoo Choi, eds., *Korea and China in the Global System* (Seoul: KAIS, 2002); and Zheng Chenghong, "Hanju dadong Zhongguo [Korean dramas are moving China]," *Shijie zhishi* [World Knowledge] 4 (2005): 17–19.

21. The five exceptions are *Dong-A Ilbo–Asahi Shimbun* surveys reported in *Dong-A Ilbo* [Dong-A Daily], October 25, 1999, and December 5, 2000; Chicago Council

on Foreign Relations, *Global Views 2004*; *Chosun Ilbo*, January 1, 2005; and *Dong-A Ilbo*, November 7, 2005.

22. One survey conducted in 1990 found that only 28 percent of the respondents wished to see the Seoul-Washington relationship further strengthened. Gi-Wook Shin, "South Korean Anti-Americanism: A Comparative Perspective," *Asian Survey* 36, no. 8 (August 1996): 795. According to a survey conducted by *Hankyoreh Sinmun* in 1995, 33.6 percent called for the strengthening of South Korea–U.S. relations, while 71.4 percent called for the consolidation of South Korea–China relations. See *Hankyoreh Sinmun*, August 15, 1995.

23. For Washington's assessment as such, see the Office of Research (Department of State), "For South Koreans, China's Draw Is Mainly Economic," *Opinion Analysis*, M-127-03 (September 30, 2003). A survey by *Dong-A Ilbo* in early 2004 asked the respondents which country need be regarded most important in diplomatic and security affairs. China was chosen by 48 percent, while 38 percent selected the United States. *Dong-A Ilbo*, May 4, 2004.

24. See The Pew Research Center, *What the World Thinks in 2002: How Global Public View Their Lives, Their Countries, The World, America* (December 4, 2002): 53–55, available at http://people-press.org (last accessed on December 9, 2002); and *Worldviews 2002: American and European Public Opinion and Foreign Policy*, by the Chicago Council on Foreign Relations, available at http://www.worldviews.org/detailedreports/compreports/index.htm (last accessed on December 9, 2002).

25. According to a China-focused survey conducted by the Korean Broadcasting System (KBS) in September 2004, right after the Kokuryo history controversy erupted, 58 percent of the respondents did not like China. See http://find.joins.com/joinsdb_content_f.asp?id = DY01200409140126 (last accessed on September 29, 2004).

26. For a perceptual divide between the elite and public in Japan and the United States regarding the rise of China, see Hideo Sato, *Japan's China Perceptions and Its Policies in the Alliance with the United States* (Stanford, Calif.: Institute for International Studies, September 1998), 10; and William Watts, *Americans Look at Asia* (Washington, D.C.: Asia Society Washington Center, October 1999), 36.

27. For generally conservative foreign-policy orientations of the South Korean elite, see Sam Sung Lee, "The Korean Society and Foreign Policy," in *Korea in the Age of Globalization and Information*, ed. Yong Soon Yim and Ki-Jung Kim (Seoul: KAIS, 1997), 110–122. Also, refer to chapter 7 on the 1994 incident involving Ambassador Hwang and the numerous media reports warning against the "progressive" (*jinbo*) foreign-policy orientation of the new President Roh Moo-Hyun and his advisors in 2003 and 2004.

28. Detailing elite perceptions is always a daunting task. While the interviews with twenty experts do not offer a solid base for generalization, it may nevertheless provide a rough sketch. The interviewees included seven government officials and military officers, five researchers at government-affiliated think tanks, four journalists, and four university professors. For more details, see Jae Ho Chung, *The*

*Korean-American Alliance and the "Rise of China": A Preliminary Assessment of Perceptual Changes* (Stanford, Calif.: Institute for International Studies, February 1999), appendix 1.

29. 1995 Sejong survey, 78; and 1997 Sejong survey, 11. A survey conducted in 2002 with thirty-two National Assembly members below the age of fifty also found that 66 percent (twenty-one members) considered Japan the most serious threat to the stability of Northeast Asia. See *Chosun Ilbo*, February 24, 2002.

30. See the outcomes reported in *Dong-A Ilbo*, October 25, 1999, and December 5, 2000.

31. According to the survey jointly conducted in 2000 by *Asahi Shimbun* and *Dong-A Ilbo*, the respective negative response rates toward the consolidation of the U.S.-Japan alliance was 15 percent in Japan, 20 percent in the United States, 44 percent in South Korea, and 55 percent in China. See *Dong-A Ilbo*, December 5, 2000.

32. A Chinese official offered an interesting rebuttal to this characterization as follows: "As far as the separation of politics from economics is concerned, Seoul has done quite the same—following the U.S. very closely in military-security issues while engaging actively with China in economic realms."

33. For Pyongyang's initial perception of China's participation, see McVadon, "Chinese Military Strategy for the Korean Peninsula," 289.

34. See Andrew Scobell, "China and North Korea: The Limits of Influence," *Current History* (September 2003): 274–278.

35. See "Special Report," *Weekly Hankook* (December 16, 1999): 48–58.

36. According to a 1998 study, 66 percent of South Korea's airborne intake of sulfur dioxide (SO2) originated from China, and a quarter of nitrogen oxide (NOx) and up to a third of the acid rain affecting South Korea were also attributed to China. *Chosun Ilbo*, October 23, 1997; and *Wolgan Chosun* [Chosun Monthly] (June 2000): 583–589. For China's own evaluation that environmental cooperation between Seoul and Beijing has not been on a par with that with Japan, Europe, and the United States, see Xu Songling, "Zhongguo-dongbeiya guojia zhi jian de huanjing hezuo: zhuangkuang fenxi yu pingjia [Analysis and evaluation of China's current environmental cooperation with Northeast Asian countries]," *Dongbeiya luntan* [Northeast Asia Forum] 1 (2002): 51.

37. See *Dong-A Ilbo*, October 13 and 18, 1999; *Chosun Ilbo*, January 27, 2000; *Wolgan Chosun* (June 2000): 458–472; and *New York Times*, May 31, 2000.

38. Seoul has generally remained silent on most human-rights controversies related to China, including the Tiananmen tragedy in 1989, since it had its own dark past of Kwangju. Seoul's *modus operandi* on these issues was often sarcastically dubbed "quiet diplomacy." Overall, South Korea appears to have decided to deal with the "refugee" problem quietly rather than actively seeking multilateral support.

39. *Dong-A Ilbo*, May 30 and June 29, 2000.

40. See *Chosun Ilbo*, June 2, 2004; and *Dong-A Ilbo*, June 2, 2004.

41. For such concerns, see *Dong-A Ilbo*, December 3, 2003; *Joong-ang Ilbo*, December 4, 2003; and Nan Liming, "Hanguo dui Zhongguo de wenhua kangyi [Korea's cultural opposition to China]," *Yazhou zhoukan* [Asia Weekly] (July 25, 2004):

16–21. For the goals of the Northeast Project, see Ma Dazheng, ed., *Zhongguo dongbei bianjiang yanjiu* [Study of China's northeastern border areas] (Beijing: Zhongguo shehuikexue chubanshe, 2003), 14, 15, 19. Also see "Rewriting National History: The 'Zeng Guofan' Phenomenon," in Yingjie Guo, *Cultural Nationalism in Contemporary China* (London: Routledge Curzon, 2004), chap. 3.

42.  As of April 2004, over two-thirds (68 percent) of the National Assembly members in the incumbent Open Party and nearly a half (43 percent) of those in the Grand National Party are younger newcomers.

43.  See William Watts, *Next Generation Leaders in the Republic of Korea: Opinion Survey Reports and Analysis* (Washington, D.C.: Potomac Associates, April 2002), 12.

44.  See *Dong-A Ilbo*, April 19, 2004.

45.  *Dong-A Ilbo*, April 13, 2005.

46.  One discernible change is that Chinese international-relations experts have recently become much less concerned about a South Korea–dominant mode of reunification, which they had staunchly opposed in the past out of the fear that it would boost America's influence on the peninsula at China's expense.

47.  During 1953 through 1973, America's aid to South Korea amounted to nearly US$10 billion, accounting for 8 percent of its total overseas assistance. See Young-nok Koo and Dae-sook Suh, *Korea and the United States: A Century of Cooperation* (Honolulu: University of Hawaii Press, 1984), 145.

48.  For the trade-offs between these two options, see James D. Morrow, "Arms Versus Allies: Trade-Offs in the Search for Security," *International Organization* 47, no. 2 (Spring 1993): 207–233.

49.  For President Park Chung Hee's "arms-for-allies" bargaining with the United States, see Don Oberdorfer, *The Two Koreas: A Contemporary History* (Reading, Mass.: Addison-Wesley, 1997), 85–94, 101–108.

50.  For the entanglements of political, economic, and military ties as a derivative of the great power's military assistance to smaller powers, see Marshall R. Singer, *Weak States in a World of Powers: The Dynamics of International Relationships* (New York: The Free Press, 1972), 279.

51.  See, for instance, Bruce Cumings, *Korea's Place in the Sun: A Modern History* (New York: Norton, 1998), chaps. 4–5.

52.  On "omnibalancing," see Steven R. David, "Explaining Third-World Alignment," *World Politics* 43, no. 2 (January 1991): 233–256.

53.  Edward A. Olsen, "Korean Security: Is Japan's Comprehensive Security Model a Viable Alternative?" in *The U.S.-Korean Alliance: Time for a Change*, ed. Doug Bandow and Ted Galen Carpenter (New Brunswick, N.J.: Transactions Publishers, 1992), 146–148. Also see Dan Reiter, "Learning, Realism, and Alliances: The Weight of the Shadow of the Past," *World Politics* 46, no. 4 (July 1994): 494, 503.

54.  This trend was also confirmed by two independent surveys by *Dong-A Ilbo* in 1990 and *Chosun Ilbo* in 1995. While the former survey found that 65.2 percent of the respondents preferred the withdrawal, the comparable figure from the latter survey was only 46.2 percent. See *Dong-A Ilbo*, January 1, 1990; and *Chosun Ilbo*, August 15, 1995.

55. 1997 Sejong survey, 12.

56. *Dong-A Ilbo*, December 5, 2000.

57. For a similar concern in Europe regarding the "German question," see Joyce Marie Mushaben, "A Search for Identity: The 'German Question' in Atlantic Alliance Relations," *World Politics* 40, no. 3 (April 1988): 395–417. For an East Asian context, see Aaron Friedberg, "Ripe for Rivalry: Prospects for Peace in a Multipolar Asia," *International Security* 18, no. 3 (1993–94): 5–34. For U.S. insensitivity to such perceptual undercurrents, see Nicholas D. Kristof, "The Problem of Memory," *Foreign Affairs*, (November/December 1998), 37–49.

58. The inter-Korean summit communiqué, for instance, confirmed Beijing's long-held position of "*independent* and peaceful unification" (*zizhu he heping tongyi*) as opposed to Washington's "peaceful unification." Compare *Washington Post*, June 21, 2000, with *Renmin ribao* [Peoples' Daily], June 16, 2000.

59. While Seoul has been more interested in the inter-Korean summit, family reunions, confidence building, economic cooperation, and overall tension reduction with Pyongyang, Washington has paid specific attention to such issues as nuclear nonproliferation, missile control, weapons of mass destruction, and so on. These different policy horizons are noted in Catharin Dalpino and Bates Gill, eds., *Brookings Northeast Asia Survey 2000–01* (Washington, D.C.: The Brookings Institution, 2001), 31.

60. *Joong-ang Ilbo*, February 12, 2003.

61. See Mustafa Chaudhary, "Dynamics of Superpower–Small Power Relationship," in *Security for the Weak Nations: A Multiple Perspective*, ed. Syed Farooq Hasnat and Anton Pelinka (Lahore, Pakistan: Izharsons, 1986), 33–35.

62. See, for instance, Joo-Hong Nam, *America's Commitment to South Korea* (Cambridge: Cambridge University Press, 1986), 153, 158.

63. The concept stresses both sustaining the alliance with the United States and cultivating the ability for independent defense. See National Security Council, *Pyonghwa bonyong gwa gukga anbo* [Peace, prosperity, and national security] (Seoul: NSC, 2004), 15, 24–28.

64. This is perhaps something that has to be accepted by all countries other than the United States, according to Robert Kagan. See his *Of Paradise and Power: America and Europe in the New World Order* (New York: Basic, 2002).

65. This was in line with the findings of the survey conducted on 262 South Korean retired generals, according to which 85 percent of the respondents viewed SOFA to be unequal. See Korea Institute of Military Studies, *Yebiyok gogeup changgyodul eui gukbang hyon'an e daehan insik yonku* [Study of defense-related perceptions of retired high-ranking military officers] (Seoul: Korea Institute of Military Studies, December 1995), 38. According to a survey by *Joong-ang Ilbo* in 2003, 77 percent of the respondents replied that SOFA need be amended even if that meant an adverse impact on U.S.-Korea relations. *Joong-ang Ilbo*, January 17, 2003.

66. This is not applicable only to Americans' perception of South Korea. For the overall ignorance of the American public about international affairs, see Mark Hertsgaard, *The Eagle's Shadow: Why America Fascinates and Infuriates the World* (New York: FSG, 2002), chap. 1. As for their indifference to South Korea, see Philip

J. Powlick, "U.S. Public Opinion of the Two Koreas," in *The U.S. and the Two Koreas: A New Triangle*, ed. Tong Whan Park (Boulder, Colo.: Lynne Rienner, 1998), 197–228.

67. See *Chosun Ilbo*, July 23, 1995.

68. Harris Poll #8, January 31, 2001. At http://www.harrisinteractive.com (last accessed on June 30, 2004).

69. See Harris Poll #8, January 31, 2001, table 2.

70. See Harris Poll #8, January 31, 2001, table 3.

71. In March 2005, when the Roh Administration introduced the now defunct concept of "strategic balancer in Northeast Asia," Washington was very critical of it. In stark contrast, Beijing was highly supportive of the concept. See Li Dunqiu, "Lu Wuxuan—zuo junhengzhe [Roh Moo-Hyun to perform as Northeast Asia's balancer]," *Shijie zhishi* 11 (2005): 30–33.

## 9. Between Dragon and Eagle

1. See Song Byung-ki, *Geundae hanjung gwangyesa yongu* [Historical study of modern Korea-China relations] (Seoul: Dankook University Press, 1985), 59–69.

2. Although, theoretically, U.S.-China dynamics over the Korean peninsula do not have to be a zero-sum game, many seem to think otherwise. See, for instance, Eric A. McVadon, "China's Goals and Strategies for the Korean Peninsula," in *Planning for a Peaceful Korea*, ed. Henry D. Sokolski (Carlisle, Penn.: Strategic Studies Institute, 2001), 149, 169; and Chen Fengjun, "Ershiyi shiji chaoxianbandao dui zhongguo de zhanlue yiyi [The strategic meaning of the Korean peninsula to China in the twenty-first century]," *Guoji zhengzhi yanjiu* [Study of International Politics] 4 (2001): 7–9.

3. See, for instance, David I. Steinberg, ed., *Korean Attitudes Toward the United States: Changing Dynamics* (Armonk, N.Y.: M. E. Sharpe, 2005).

4. South Korea's growing concern with China's "imposing" diplomacy—ignited by the recent "historical whitewashing" controversy—will have some lasting impact on the views of South Koreans, elites in particular, concerning the long-term implications of a stronger China. See, for instance, Robert J. Myers, *Korea in the Cross Currents: A Century of Struggle and the Crisis of Reunification* (New York: Palgrave, 2001), chap. 2.

5. This is not to suggest that the future of America's role is not important. Rather, the key premise here is that America's commitment to Asia will remain largely unchanged in the foreseeable future.

6. Maria Hsia Chang, "China's Future: Regionalism, Federation, or Disintegration," *Studies in Comparative Communism* 25, no. 3 (September 1992): 211–227; and Gerald Segal, *China Changes Shape: Regionalism and Foreign Policy* (London: IISS, 1994).

7. While China has consistently denied any inspiration to become a hegemon, it has nevertheless been willing to assign itself a great-power (*daguo*) status. See

Tao Wenzhao, ed., *Jujue baquan—yu 2049nian zhongguo duihua* [Rejecting hegemony—communicating with China in 2049] (Beijing: Zhongguo jingji chubanshe, 1998); and Ye Zicheng, "Zhongguo shixing daguo waijiao zhanlue shi zai bixing [It is inevtable that China perform great-power diplomacy]," *Shijie jingji yu zhengzhi* [World Economy and Politics] 1 (2000). For China's self-conscious effort to distinguish itself from other great powers in the past, see Zhang Wenmu, "Daguo jueqi de lishi jingyan yu zhongguo de xuanze [The historical precedents of the rise of great powers and China's choice]," *Zhanlue yu guanli* [Strategy and Management] 2 (2004): 70–84.

8.  At least seventeen different concepts have been employed by academia to characterize the current Chinese system. See Richard Baum and Alexei Shevchenko, "The 'State of the State,'" in *The Paradox of China's Post-Mao Reform*, ed. Merle Goldman and Roderick MacFarquhar (Cambridge, Mass.: Harvard University Press, 1999), 333–334.

9.  For the former position, see Gordon Chang, *The Coming Collapse of China* (New York: Random House, 2001), chap. 6. For the latter, see Bruce J. Dickson, "Cooptation and Corporatism in China: The Logic of Party Adaptation," *Political Science Quarterly* 115, no. 4 (2000–2001): 517–540.

10. See Alastair Finlan, *The Collapse of Yugoslavia, 1991–99* (London: Osprey, 2004). The "China collapse" literature has over the years amounted to a genre of its own. See David S. G. Goodman and Gerald Segal, eds., *China Deconstructs: Politics, Trade, and Regionalism* (London: Routledge, 1994); Jack Goldstein, "The Coming Chinese Collapse," *Foreign Policy* 99 (Summer 1995): 35–52; and Chang, *The Coming Collapse of China*. Chinese publications include Wu Guoguang and Wang Zhaojun, *Deng Xiaoping zhihou de zhongguo* [China after Deng Xiaoping] (Taipei: Shijie shuju, 1994), 181–282; Xin Xiangyang, *Daguo zhuhou* [Feudal empire] (Beijing: Zhongguo shehui chubanshe, 1996); and Tong Zhongxin, *Shiheng de diguo* [The empire off balance] (Guiyang: Guizhou renmin chubanshe, 2001), chap. 3.

11. For views critical of this scenario, see John Fitzgerald, "Reports of My Death Have Been Greatly Exaggerated: The History of the Death of China," in *China Deconstructs*, 21–58; Yasheng Huang, "Why China Will Not Collapse," *Foreign Policy* 99 (Summer 1995): 54–68; Barry J. Naughton and Dali L. Yang, eds., *Holding China Together: Diversity and National Integration in the Post-Deng Era* (Cambridge: Cambridge University Press, 2004); and Jae Ho Chung, "Forecasting China's Future: Scenarios, Uncertainties, and Determinants," in *Charting China's Future: Political, Social, and International Dimensions*, ed. Jae Ho Chung (Lanham, Md.: Rowman & Littlefield, 2006), chap. 1.

12. See, for instance, Benshu nianxie zu [Book-writing team], *Xingshuai zhi lu—waiguo butong leixing zhengdang jianshe de jingyan yu jianxun* [The road to flourishing and perishing: the experiences and lessons from different types of party building] (Beijing: Zhonggong zhongyang dangxiao chubanshe, 2002), 127–158; Guan Haiting, *Zhonge tizhi zhuanxing moshi de bijiao* [Comparison of system transition models of China and Russia] (Beijing: Beijing daxue chubanshe, 2003), chaps. 5, 6, 9; and Lu Nanquan et al., eds., *Sulian xingwang shilun* [Historical analyses of

the rise and fall of the Soviet Union], 2nd ed. (Beijing: Renmin chubanshe, 2004), part 5, especially chaps. 26–29.

13. During the summer of 2004, however, Indonesia held its first-ever direct presidential election, although to what extent that should constitute a sufficient indicator of democratic transition remains to be specified. See Jacques Bertrand and John Ravenhill, eds., *Nationalism and Ethnic Conflict in Indonesia* (Cambridge: Cambridge University Press, 2003).

14. The dangers of a frail China are well noted in Bruce Cumings, "The More Things Change, the More They Remain the Same: The World, the United States, and the People's Republic of China, 1949–1999," in *China Briefing 2000: The Continuing Transformation*, ed. Tyrene White (Armonk, N.Y.: M.E. Sharpe, 2000), 298.

15. Jonathan Watts, "China Admits First Rise in Poverty Since 1978," *The Guardian*, July 20, 2004; *Wenhuibao*, February 19, 2005; George J. Gilboy and Eric Heginbotham, "The Latin-Americanization of China," *Current History* 674 (September 2004): 256–261; and Zheng Bingwen, "Dui 'zhongguo lameihua' de jidian kanfa [Some views on China's 'Latin Americanization']," *Lingdao canyue* [Leadership References] 2 (2005): 17–19.

16. See Thomas M. Kane and Lawrence W. Serewicz, "China's Hunger: The Consequences of a Rising Demand for Food and Energy," *Parameters* (Autumn 2001), at http://carlisle-www.army.mil/usawe/Parameters/01autumn/Kane.htm (last accessed January 14, 2005); and Vaclav Smil, *China's Past, China's Future: Energy, Food, Environment* (London: Routledge Curzon, 2004).

17. The juxtaposition of democracy and discontent is borrowed from Atul Kohli, *Democracy and Discontent: India's Growing Crisis of Governability* (Cambridge: Cambridge University Press, 1990).

18. See UBS Wealth Management, *China and India (Research Focus)* (August 2004): 1–28.

19. See, for instance, David Zweig, "Undemocratic Capitalism: China and the Limits of Economism," *The National Interest* 56 (Summer 1999): 63–72; and Harvey Nelson, "The Future of the Chinese State," in *The Modern Chinese State*, ed. David Shambaugh (Cambridge: Cambridge University Press, 2000), 230–236. Also see Yingjie Guo, *Cultural Nationalism in Contemporary China: The Search for National Identity Under Reform* (London: Routledge Curzon, 2004).

20. See, for instance, Ye Zicheng, *Zhongguo dazhanlue* [China's grand strategy] (Beijing: Zhongguo shehuikexue chubanshe, 2003), 116–126 for "socialist democracy with Chinese characteristics." Also see Wei Pan, "Toward a Consultative Rule of Law Regime in China," *Journal of Contemporary China* 34 (2003): 32–43.

21. See, for instance, Pang Zhongying, "Ruguo riben chengwei yazhou de deguo [If Japan should become Asia's Germany]," *Shijie zhishi* [World Knowledge] 9 (2001): 17.

22. An interim analysis as of 2003 viewed China as not possessing manifest zeal for revisionism. See Alastair I. Johnston, "Is China a Status Quo Power?" *International Security* 27, no. 4 (Spring 2003): 12–34. Some signs are, however, suggestive of China's growing interest in soft power. See, for instance, Zhang Xiaoming,

"Zhongshi ruan quanli yinsu [Prioritizing soft-power elements]," *Xiandai guoji guanxi* [Contemporary International Relations], 3 (2004): 21–22; and Zhu Majie, "Jiaqiang ruan guoli jianshe shi zhongguo heping fazhan de zhanlue xuanze [The strategic choice for China's peaceful development is to strengthen its soft power]," in *Xinshiji jiyuqi yu zhongguo guoji zhanlue* [Strategic opportunities of the new century and China's international strategy], ed. Chen Peixiao and Xia Liping (Beijing: Shishi chubanshe, 2004), 25–42.

23. See Richard Bernstein and Ross H. Munro, *The Coming Conflict with China* (New York: Knopf, 1997); Gerald Segal "East Asia and the 'Constrainment' of China," *International Security* 20, no. 4 (Spring 1996): 107–135; Bill Gertz, *The China Threat: How the People's Republic of China Targets America* (Washington, D.C.: Regnery, 2000); and Steven W. Mosher, *Hegemon: China's Plan to Dominate Asia and the World* (San Francisco: Encounter Books, 2000). Also see the debate between Zbigniew Brzezinski and John Mearsheimer on China's rising and the inevitability of conflict between Beijing and Washington: "Clash of the Titans," *Foreign Policy* (January–February 2005).

24. A. F. K. Organski and Jacek Kugler, *The War Ledger* (Chicago: University of Chicago Press, 1980), chap. 2.

25. See Alastair Iain Johnston and Robert S. Ross, eds., *Engaging China: The Management of an Emerging Power* (London: Routledge, 1999); Herbert Yee and Ian Storey, eds., *China Threat: Perceptions, Myth, and Reality* (London: Routledge Curzon, 2002); Barry Buzan, "How and to Whom Does China Matter?" in *Does China Matter? A Reassessment*, ed. Barry Buzan and Rosemary Foot (London: Routledge, 2004), chap. 10; and David Shambaugh, ed., *Power Shifts: China and Asia's New Dynamics* (Berkeley: University of California Press, 2005).

26. See, for instance, Alastair I. Johnston, "China's Militarized Interstate Dispute Behavior, 1949–1992: A First Cut at the Data," *China Quarterly* 153 (March 1998): 1–30.

27. The expected annual growth rate for 2006 to 2010 announced at the Fifth Plenum in October 2005 is 8.5 percent, compared to 7 percent for 2001 through 2005. See *Renmin ribao* [People's Daily], October 11, 2005.

28. See John Mearsheimer, *The Tragedy of Great Power Politics* (New York: Norton, 2001), 373–377; Franz Schurmann, "China Replaces Russia as America's Global Partner," at http://news.pacificnews.org (November 4, 2002); and Peter Gries, "The Future of U.S.-China Relations: System, State, and Individual-Level Drivers," in *Charting China's Future*, chap. 7.

29. Several of these options are adapted from Randall L. Schwaller, "Managing the Rise of Great Powers: History and Theory" and Alastair Iain Johnston and Robert S. Ross, "Conclusion," in *Engaging China*, 7–17, 273–278; Mearsheimer, *The Tragedy of Great Power Politics*, chap. 5; and Jae Ho Chung, "South Korea Between Eagle and Dragon: Perceptual Ambivalence and Strategic Dilemma," *Asian Survey* 41, no. 5 (September–October 2001): 788–793.

30. For the logic of preventive wars in general, see Jack Levy, "Decling Power and the Preventive Motivation for War," *World Politics* 40, no. 1 (October 1987): 82–107.

31. For a Chinese view well aware of this geopolitical "inseparability," see Liu Ming, "Hanguo de diyuan weizhi yu qi waijiao he anquan zhengce [Korea's geographical location and its diplomatic and security policy]," *Yatai luntan* [Asia-Pacific Forum] 3/4 (1999): 37.

32. For the adverse impact of China's ban in 2000, see Jae Ho Chung, "From a Special Relationship to a Normal Partnership: Interpreting the 'Garlic Battle' in Sino-South Korean Relations," *Pacific Affairs* 76, no. 4 (Winter 2003–2004): 549–568.

33. For the definitions of buffer state and rim-state, see Trygve Mathisen, *The Functions of Small States in the Strategies of the Great Powers* (Oslo: Universitetsforlaget, 1971), 84, 107. For the infeasibility of neutrality for buffer states, see Efraim Karsh, *Neutrality and Small States* (London: Routledge, 1988), 82–83. With regard to the South Korean context, a similar conclusion was drawn by Robert A. Manning and James J. Przystup, "Asia's Transition Diplomacy: Hedging Against Futureshock," *Survival* 41, no. 3 (Autumn 1999): 54.

34. For the concept of "pivotal state," see Robert Chase, Emily Hill, and Paul Kennedy, eds., *Pivotal States: A New Framework for U.S. Policy in the Developing World* (New York: Norton, 1999), 1–14.

35. See National Security Council, *Pyonghwa bonyong gwa gukga anbo* [Peace, prosperity, and national security] (Seoul: NSC, March 2004), 15, 24, 28.

36. See, for instance, Randall L. Schweller, "Bandwagoning for Profit: Bringing the Revisionist State Back In," *International Security* 19, no. 1 (Summer 1994).

37. See Fitzgerald, "The Reports of My Death Have Been Greatly Exaggerated," 19–24. Also see Hongyi Harry Lai, "The Life Span of Unified Regimes in China," *The China Review* 2, no. 2 (Fall 2002): 93–124.

38. Many in China, therefore, took an issue with the term *jueqi*, which denotes a relatively swift process of rising and some even suggested an alternative of *rongqi*. Yet it should be noted that it may take less time for China to establish itself as a regional hegemon in East Asia than establish itself as a global hegemonic competitor.

39. The voice in favor of South Korea joining the Sinocentric order will nevertheless grow over time in tandem with the rapidly expanding influence of Beijing both regionally and globally.

40. China's promotion of "partnership" (*huoban guanxi*) is actually designed in part to substitute for conventional alliance ties.

41. See Yin Guiyun, "Hezuo anquan: Yatai diqu kexing de anquan moshi xuanze [Cooperative security: security arrangement options for Asia and the Pacific]," *Dangdai yatai* [Contemporary Asia and the Pacific] 10 (1999): 33.

42. See Alastair Iain Johnston, "The Myth of the ASEAN Way? Explaining the Evolution of the ASEAN Regional Forum," in *Imperfect Unions: Security Institutions Over Time and Space*, ed. Helga Haftendorn, Robert O. Keohane, and Celeste A. Wallander (Oxford: Oxford University Press, 1999), 287–324.

43. See, for instance, Michael Mastanduno, "The Strategy of Economic Engagement: Theory and Practice," in *Economic Interdependence and International Conflict: New Perspectives on an Enduring Debate*, eds. Edward D. Mansfield and Brian M. Pollins (Ann Arbor: University of Michigan Press, 2003), 175–186.

44. See Victor D. Cha, "Engaging China: The View from Korea," in *Engaging China*, 43–46; Chung, "South Korea Between Eagle and Dragon," 781–785; and Jae Ho Chung, "Korea and China in Northeast Asia: From Stable Bifurcation to Complex Interdependence," in *Korea at the Center: Dynamics of Regionalism in Northeast Asia*, ed. Charles K. Armstrong, Gilbert Rozman, Samuel S. Kin, and Stephen Kotkin (Armonk, N.Y.: M.E. Sharpe, 2006), 206–210.

45. The hollowing out of Korean industries—as noted in chapter 7—has already created the term "China fear" (*gongjungjeung*).

46. See Jianwei Wang and Xinbo Wu, *Against Us or With Us: The Chinese Perspective of America's Alliances with Japan and Korea*, Discussion Papers, the Asia/Pacific Research Center, Stanford University, May 1998; and Wang Fan, "Meihan tongmeng ji weilai zouxiang [The Korea-U.S. alliance and its future direction]," *Waijiao xueyuan xuebao* [Bulletin of the Foreign Affairs College], 2 (2001): 62–63.

47. For the definition of containment, see John Lewis Gaddis, *Strategies of Containment: A Critical Appraisal of Postwar American National Security Policy* (Oxford: Oxford University Press, 1982), chap. 1.

48. According to the Chinese interpretation, "partnership" involves the dimensions of "not antagonizing each other and sharing risks [*hu bu weidi tongdang fengxian*]." See Zhang Jianhua, *Jiejue zhongguo zaidu mianlin de jinyao wenti* [On the resolution of some crucial problems China faces again] (Beijing: Jingji ribao chubanshe, 2000), 503, 517, 523.

49. More discussions on this important contingency are given later.

50. For a view that characterizes Seoul as shying away from hedging, see Johnston and Ross, "Conclusion," 288.

51. See chapter 7 for details of this incident.

52. See *Chosun Ilbo* [Chosun Daily], November 20, 1998.

53. In this row, Seoul initially sided with Moscow by supporting the continuation of the ABM treaty but later stood on Washington's side by stating that it would not oppose the National Missile Defense (NMD) plans pushed by the United States. Consequently, both the United States and Russia became critical of South Korea. See *Dong-A Ilbo* [Dong-A Daily], March 3, 10, and 24, 2001.

54. See Gilbert Rozman, *Northeast Asia's Stunted Regionalism: Bilateral Distrust in the Shadow of Globalization* (Cambridge: Cambridge University Press, 2004), 170–171.

55. South Korea's reservation toward employing sanctions against North Korea does not mean that it is opposed to the U.S. efforts for nonproliferation of weapons of mass destruction.

56. According to a survey done in ten Asian countries in early 1999, South Korea ranked sixth in perceiving a missile threat from North Korea and ninth in approving TMD plans. See *Far Eastern Economic Review* (March 18, 1999): 36.

57. In personal communications with the author, many knowledgeable Chinese diplomats and scholars denote "stability" as the state of affairs where China becomes gradually but increasingly more influential over the Korean peninsula at large, unified or not—a sort of "creeping dominance" per se.

58. No elaboration is needed on the role of opinion leaders and think tanks in the American context. In the Chinese setting, too, the importance of think tanks and policy experts has been on the rise since the late 1990s. For the former, see James A. Smith, *The Idea Brokers: Think Tanks and the Rise of the New Policy Elite* (New York: Free Press, 1991); and Donald E. Abelson, *American Think Tanks and Their Role in U.S. Foreign Policy* (New York: McMillan, 1996). And for the latter, see three essays by Shambaugh, Glaser, and Saunders, and Gill and Mulvenon in *China Quarterly* 171 (September 2002): 575–624.

59. Only 18 percent of the American interviewees chose the military arena as the main realm of competition, whereas not a single Chinese interviewee did so.

60. Joseph S. Nye, "The Decline of America's Soft Power: Why Washington Should Worry," *Foreign Affairs* 83, no. 3 (May/June 2004): 16–20.

61. For China's zeal for its own normative platform, see Rosemary Foot, *The Practice of Power: U.S. Relations with China Since 1949* (Oxford: Oxford University Press, 1995), 264–265. Also see Zhu Majie, "Jiaqiang ruan guoli jianshe shi zhongguo heping fazhan de zhanlue xuanze [Strengthening soft power is China's strategic choice for peaceful development]," in *Xinshiji jiyuqi yu zhongguo guoji zhanlue* [The strategic opportunity of the new century and China's international strategy], ed. Chen Peixiao and Xia Liping (Beijing: Shishi chubanshe, 2004), 25–42.

62. It was only in late 2004 that China emerged as South Korea's top trading partner. These interviews were conducted in 2002 and 2003.

63. This fatal contingency was first noted in Jae Ho Chung, "Jungguk eui busang Miguk eui gyonje Hanguk eui dilemma [The rise of China, America's checking, and South Korea's dilemma]," *Shindong-a* [New East Asia] (October 2000): 255–256. For the exact same dilemma facing Australia, involving the ANZUS security treaty with the U.S., see John Kerin, "Canberra's Catch-22: The U.S. or China," *Weekend Australian*, May 8–9, 2004.

64. For the dilemma of abandonment and entrapment, see Jack Snyder, "The Security Dilemma in Alliance Politics," *World Politics* 36, no. 4 (July 1984): 466–474.

65. The revised U.S.-Japan defense guidelines and a majority of American policy recommendations point to a much-enhanced security role for Japan generally, as well as in Korea-related realms. See, for instance, Morton I. Abramowitz, James T. Laney, and Michael J. Green, *Managing Change on the Korean Peninsula* (New York: Council on Foreign Relations, 1998), 32–33. For China's concern with this trend, see Sun Cheng, "Meiguo yao tisheng riben [America promoting the strategic status of Japan]," *Shijie zhishi* 8 (2001): 14–15.

66. For the "bad" possibilities of entrapment due to tight alliance commitments, see Charles W. Kegley, Jr., and Gregory A. Raymond, "Networks of Intrigue? Realpolitik, Alliances, and International Security," in *Reconstructing Realpolitik*, ed. Frank W. Wayman and Paul F. Diehl (Ann Arbor: University of Michigan Press, 1994), 190–194.

67. See *Chosun Ilbo*, January 21 and February 2, 2006.

68. The United States, due in significant part to security considerations, played a crucial role in helping South Korea recover from the 1997 financial crisis. See

Lawrence B. Krause, *The Economics and Politics of the Asian Financial Crisis of 1997–1998* (New York: Council on Foreign Relations, 1998), 224–225, 228–230. More realistically, according to the 2000 data, out of Seoul's $40 billion exports to the United States, $23 billion were concentrated in semiconductors, automobiles, computers, telecommunications, and textiles, namely South Korea's core industries. See *Dong-A Ilbo*, March 15, 2001.

69. See, for instance, Gerald Segal, "Does China Matter?" *Foreign Affairs* 78, no. 5 (September–October 1999): 24–25.

70. A fundamental question in this vein concerns whether Washington will remain as close to Seoul if a U.S.–North Korea normalization should take place. That is, the United States may find it quite tempting or even useful to play the two Koreas off each other.

71. As of 2005, South Korea has yet to state its specific position as to what needs to be done should North Korea abandon its pledge of denuclearization.

72. For this possibility, see Jae Ho Chung, "China's Korea Policy Under the New Leadership: Stealth Changes in the Making?" *Journal of East Asian Affairs* 18, no. 1 (Spring/Summer 2004): 1–18.

73. For the calls for Seoul's strategic "soul-searching," see Ralph Cossa, *Korea: The Archilles' Heel of the U.S.-Japan Alliance* (Stanford, Calif.: Institute for International Studies, May 1997), 9; and Larry M. Wortzel, "Planning for the Future: The Role of U.S. Forces in Northeast Asian Security," *The Heritage Foundation Backgrounder*, July 26, 2000, available at http://www.heritage.org/library/backgrounder/bg1388html. In 2002, the Ministry of Foreign Affairs and Trade, for the first time since 1948, carried out the task of reevaluating South Korea's long-term strategies toward its four major-power neighbors.

74. Mustafa Chaudhary, "Dynamics of Superpower–Small Power Relationship," in *Security for the Weak Nations: A Multiple Perspective*, ed. Syed Farooq Hasnat and Anton Pelinka (Lahore, Pakistan: Izharsons, 1986), 33.

75. For the difficulties associated with the United States establishing a "benign unipolarity" in East Asia, see Charles A. Kupchan, "After Pax Americana: Benign Power, Regional Integration, and the Sources of a Stable Multipolarity," *International Security* 23, no. 2 (Fall 1998): 63–69.

76. If we subscribe to a realist forecast, the persistence of anarchy in Northeast Asia would lead to a very dangerous possibility. See Richard Betts, "Wealth, Power, and Instability: East Asia and the United States after the Cold War," *International Security* 18, no. 3 (Winter 1993/94): 34–77; Mearsheimer, *The Tragedy of Great Power Politics*, 396–402; and Thomas J. Christensen, "China, the U.S.-Japan Alliance, and the Security Dilemma in East Asia," *International Security* 23, no. 4 (Spring 1999): 49–80.

77. See Nicholas Eberstadt and Richard J. Ellings, "Assessing Interests and Objectives," in *Korea's Future and Great Powers*, ed. Eberstadt and Ellings (Seattle: University of Washington Press, 2001), 320–340.

78. Thomas Hobbes, *Leviathan* (1651), chap. 13, in *Hobbes' Leviathan*, edited by C. B. MacPherson (Harmonsworth: Pelican Books, 1968), 185.

# Index